"This is truly an integration of the old term 'Christian Education' with the current term 'Spiritual Formation.' Habermas challenges the reader to recapture what has been lost by many in the field of Christian education for several decades.... This is a fresh and well thought through approach to the important foundational issues for those serving in areas of educational ministry and spiritual formation. Focusing on the life and ministry of Jesus as the framework, this volume adds significantly to the importance of spiritual formation for all ages and cultures."

—Dennis E. Williams
Distinguished Senior Professor of Leadership and Church Ministry
The Southern Baptist Theological Seminary
Executive Administrator, North American Professors of Christian Education

"Readers will walk with Jesus, discovering his perspective on education, formation, and restoration. They are also challenged to engage the multicultural richness of our world, be formed by it, and participate in God's kingdom work."

—Cathy Stonehouse
Dean, School of Practical Theology
Orlean Bullard Beeson Professor of Christian Discipleship
Asbury Theological Seminary

"... Includes both the best of our twentieth-century heritage and awareness of the emphases emerging in the present century: it is Trinitarian, Christocentric, holistic, and practical. This will be a text of choice for introductory courses in educational ministry as well as an important book for those in ministry to read for vision and orientation in this field."

—Paul Bramer
Professor of Christian Formation and Leadership
Tyndale Seminary, Toronto, Canada

"I used up two yellow highlighters as I read and marked my way through this book. Not your average Christian education resource!"

—Marlene LeFever
Vice President of Educational Development
David C. Cook

INTRODUCTION TO CHRISTIAN EDUCATION AND FORMATION

INTRODUCTION
TO CHRISTIAN EDUCATION
AND
FORMATION

A Lifelong Plan for Christ-Centered Restoration

RONALD T. HABERMAS

ZONDERVAN®

ZONDERVAN.com/
AUTHORTRACKER
follow your favorite authors

Introduction to Christian Education and Formation
Copyright © 2008 Ronald T. Habermas

Requests for information should be addressed to:
Zondervan, Grand Rapids, Michigan 49530

Library of Congress Cataloging-in-Publication Data

Habermas, Ronald T.
    Introduction to Christian Education and formation : a lifelong plan for Christ-centered restoration / Ronald T. Habermas.
        p.   cm.
    Includes indexes.
    ISBN 978-0-310-27426-1
    1. Christian education. 2. Spiritual formation. I. Title.
BV1471.3.H33
2008268--dc22

                                                                        2008021317

Interior design by Sherri L. Hoffman

Printed in the United States of America

08 09 10 11 12 13 14 • 23 22 21 20 19 18 17 16 15 14 13 12 11 10 9 8 7 6 5 4 3 2 1

I dedicate this volume to my faithful mentors,
to whom I am indebted:

Robert and Roberta Habermas

John Vrazo

Adolph Braun

Henry Holloman

James Plueddemann

Ted Ward

CONTENTS

Applications of Global Tasks for Every Church

Applications in Daily Life for Every Believer

CHARTS AND FIGURES

ADDITIONAL RESOURCES

Extensive supplemental resources are available online for instructors. Please visit www.zondervan.com/icef for *free* downloads. These resources contain three kinds of helps:

+ A 50-page "Personal Responses" workbook for students, consisting of interactive questions from each chapter of the book
+ A comprehensive PowerPoint presentation of the book, containing more than 300 slides
+ A wide-ranging collection of appendices (listed below), totaling 250 pages, that can be used for additional readings, Bible study, in-class discussion, extra assignments, and more

Appendices

Appendix A — Full Annotated Website Directory of the Five Global Tasks (Jennifer Jezek)

Appendix B — Full Bibliography

Appendix C — Higher Education as Spiritual Formation: The Creation Mandate (David Brisben)

Appendix 1.1 — Three Keys about God's Signs

Appendix 1.2 — Case Study of Cain

Appendix 2.1 — Five Passages on "Followers of the Way"

Appendix 3.1 — More Biblical Insights on Pleasure

Appendix 3.2 — Godly Pleasure: Superior Sexual Satisfaction

Appendix 4.1 — What Happens as Jesus Suffers?

Appendix 4.2 — Two More Biblical Cases of Acceptable Doubt

Appendix 4.3 — Eleven-Year-Old Atheist or Genuine Questioner?

Appendix 4.4 — The Tribal Wanderer

Appendix 5.1 — Perry's Theory for College-Age Adults

Appendix 6.1 — Key Passages of Jesus as God

ACKNOWLEDGMENTS

"O LORD, our Lord, how majestic is your name in all the earth" (Ps. 8:1)

For the past fifteen years I have been privileged to hold the very first endowed chair at John Brown University. The McGee Chair of Biblical Studies and Christian Formation as provided me, especially in the last half-dozen years, both the necessary release time and the finances to create this *Introduction to Christian Education and Formation*. I have also been blessed with two Shipps' Scholar Grants (2005 – 2006 and 2008 – 2009), along with a Summer Scholars Fellowship (2008). I thank the individuals who played a part in making those significant awards possible.

My work study assistants also played prominent roles in bringing this project together. So I extend my appreciation to Jesse Aughenbaugh's initial research and to the word-processing/proofreading of Jessica Swysgood, Brock Erdman, and especially Jennifer Johnson.

An enormous blessing emerged from the opportunity to work with ten colleagues, designated "The Z Ten." I experienced a taste of heaven's diversity, unity, and comradeship by specifically collaborating with Faye Chechowich, John Dettoni, Cheryl Fawcett, Jennifer Jezek, Steve Kang, Kevin Lawson, Gary Parrett, Robert Pazmiño, Dave Rahn, and Jerry Root. Many thanks, team!

Erin Healy and Bev Browning added their much-needed, excellent advice and editing skills through this challenging project.

Three of Zondervan's personnel, too, contributed through their areas of specialty: Paul Engle, vice president and publisher for Church, Academic and Reference Resources; Jim Ruark, senior editor-at-large; and Jesse Hillman, associate marketing director.

I particularly extend gratitude to Dr. David Brisben, long-time friend and chairman of John Brown University's Biblical Studies Division. His assistance at every turn has been unparalleled, because he championed the significant mission of this publication. This resource could not have been completed without David's steadfast encouragement.

Likewise, I thank my parents and extended family for their many prayers and consistent support from start to finish. I am especially obliged to my three grown daughters and their households, along with my lovely wife, Mary. I praise God for these loved ones, who are, as they say — priceless.

Finally, I give all honor and acclaim to the One who called each of us sinners to be saints and to gain all gracious riches as members of his redeemed family in Christ Jesus.

Ronald T. Habermas
Zechariah 4:6

INTRODUCTION: LAYING THE FOUNDATION

A prominent feature of this book is its Christocentric emphasis. Jesus is shown to be all that he is, which is much more than our glorious Savior. With his many roles, such as that of Great Physician, Jesus provides us with a comprehensive *earthly example* to follow.

Jesus, the Center of Our Life Plan

Of Jesus' many titles, Son of Man is the one he most often chose for himself. Son of Man means simply that Christ was totally human. For thirty-three years he lived a fully human life so that we might literally follow his example. No, we don't need to ride donkeys and wear robes. Yes, we are to emulate him in every major aspect of our lives — how to pray, how to get away for a while, how to relate to difficult individuals, and how to constructively express emotions.

This text is deliberately constructed on this Christ-centered design. All that Jesus *did*, *does*, and *will do* directly shapes our lives as we obey him. And that's why Jesus' life will be studied in great detail. He has been, is now, and will always be the one who desires our total well-being. That's why Jesus was often linked with the Bible, the inspired manual for holistic restoration.

Continuing the Global Tasks of Jesus

In 1988, Robert W. Pazmiño wrote *Foundational Issues in Christian Education.* Seven pages from that resource's "Biblical Foundations" chapter indicate Pazmiño's integrated model "to guide current thought and practice" in Christian education.[1] Pazmiño credits original insights to Edward V. Hill, whose lecture, "A Congregation's Response," given at Gordon-Conwell Theological Seminary on January 21, 1976, uses the illustration of a baseball diamond to convey five global tasks of the church.

First base represents "Education for/of *Evangelism*," which correlates with the Greek concept *kerygma*, or proclamation, and the need for faith (including its intellectual, affective, and volitional dimensions).

Second base symbolizes "Education for/of *Fellowship*." Processes of instruction and nurture — *koinonia* — describe fellowship with God and other believers. Personal and corporate sanctification are valued in this "body life" purpose for all saints, where love is to be particularly expressed.

"Education for/of *Service*" identifies third base in our global objectives. Service includes focus on God, people, and the world, as the Greek term *diakonia* intends. Jesus' complementary call for believers to be both salt and light accents this third task — from home to school, from workplace to community, and from society to the world's global village.

The fourth base, or home plate, figuratively represents "Education for/of *Kingdom Consciousness*." Hope is portrayed in the Greek word *basileia*. Eternal kingdom values are particularly featured here, especially as it pertains to concerns for worldwide justice, peace, and righteousness. As one might expect, this fourth task holds several tensions together, including tensions between subjects related to the future and those pertaining to the past/present; tensions of acculturation (affirming certain aspects of society and the believer's accompanying responsibilities, such as Jesus' support of the Roman government through tax payments) and disenculturation; and proximate versus ultimate values.

The fifth task, *leitourgia*, the "Education for/of *Worship*," is represented by the pitcher's mound. Both figuratively and actually, this final task centers and integrates the previous four universal duties of the church. Emphasis is rightfully directed to the Sovereign Lord, who alone is worthy of honor, glory, and praise.

In Pazmiño's second edition of *Foundational Issues* (1997), three descriptors of the five bases were slightly modified. The five became Proclamation, Community, Service, Advocacy, and Worship. Because both editions offer compelling reasons for their five selections, I use *both* sets of key words to organize chapters 14 – 18.[2] The synthesis of these two editions results in these new pairings:

+ Evangelism – Proclamation
+ Fellowship – Community
+ Service
+ Kingdom – Advocacy
+ Worship

I extend gratitude to Rev. E. V. Hill for his initial presentation of these five universal church tasks. I also thank my good friend and colleague Dr. Pazmiño for his development and application of these significant tasks for Christ-followers.

The Particular Challenge to Readers

Author-theologian Dietrich Bonhoeffer (1906 – 45) pleads for each Christian to be ready "to be interrupted by God."[3] In the 1930s and 40s, Bonhoeffer's own peaceful, scholarly life was interrupted by God's calling him to join a bold resistance against Hitler's unfolding atrocities in Nazi Germany.

Compelled by God's voice, Bonhoeffer had little choice but to become increasingly outspoken and active. He emerged as a leader in the Resistance Movement and as a staunch advocate for persecuted Jews. His noble efforts led to his arrest and imprisonment in 1943 because he helped a group of Jews escape to Switzerland. When he was only 39, he was hanged, along with four family members, in the concentration camp at Flossenbürg on April 9, 1945 — just a few days before the Allies liberated that camp. Bonhoeffer left behind an enduring legacy of courage and obedience to God.

Although most interruptions are disturbing, I nevertheless want to echo this Lutheran pastor-teacher: faithful disciples of Jesus Christ must always prepare for God's interruptions, which *are* going to happen.

Indeed, this book itself may serve as a divine interruption in your life in two ways: by *what* it says or by *how* it says it.

My colleagues and I want to make sure your pathway is clear to the possibility that you are about to be interrupted by God as you read further. So we have done our best to see that the content is free from any possible hindrances, such as a particular denominational slant or a simplistic "program" approach to the subjects of Christian education and formation. Here's what you *will* find in this book:

- A helpful game plan for your life — for personal and professional use
- A Christ-centered emphasis that has theological substance and applications
- A global outlook expansive enough to include the world and you
- Scriptural answers to questions as old as time, like *Who are we?* and *What are we here to do?*
- Social science input for determining what all people have in common regarding human perspectives, needs, and developmental patterns.

Dietrich Bonhoeffer further described what our otherworldly interruptions entail: "God will be constantly crossing our paths and canceling our plans." You may presently find yourself divinely interrupted. Or your sovereignly scheduled time may come tomorrow. Will you be teachable at those times? Will you hear the still, small whisper of God within those unexpected interruptions?

Are You Ready to Be Interrupted?

If God chooses this book to interrupt your life, it will be useful to understand its particular components:

- The book combines the work of one author blended with many other voices into a hybrid resource that reflects both a breadth of coverage and a depth of expertise in the field of Christian education-formation.

- You will be invited into interactions that will strengthen you by integrating practical living with pertinent theology and theories about people.
- We provide you with an array of helps, giving you the tools to navigate through your divine interruptions as a person more knowledgeable, more prepared, and more passionate about engaging your own spiritual journey.

This chart provides an organizational overview of *Introduction to Christian Education and Formation*.

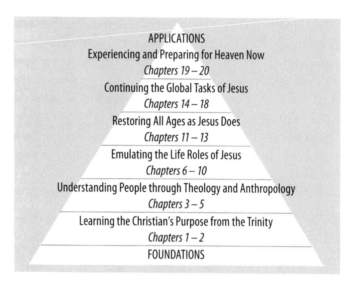

APPLICATIONS
Experiencing and Preparing for Heaven Now
Chapters 19 – 20
Continuing the Global Tasks of Jesus
Chapters 14 – 18
Restoring All Ages as Jesus Does
Chapters 11 – 13
Emulating the Life Roles of Jesus
Chapters 6 – 10
Understanding People through Theology and Anthropology
Chapters 3 – 5
Learning the Christian's Purpose from the Trinity
Chapters 1 – 2
FOUNDATIONS

Are You Ready for a Change?

For the past couple of decades or more, "spiritual formation" has become the term of choice for many evangelicals when discussing Christian maturity. From local churches to seminaries, and from publishing houses to other parachurch organizations, many saints — though not all — have made this switch, frequently dropping long-standing terms such as Christian education, discipleship, and the like. Why the change?

Alterations that are as universal as these never offer one or even a handful of common reasons. On the upside, this change has partially occurred because of the renewed interest, more than a quarter-century ago, in spiritual disciplines like prayer, solitude, and service. Also interfaith issues — including conversations between some evangelical and Roman Catholic leaders over common beliefs — have encouraged diverse voices among various faiths to be heard. One consequence is a preference for the term "spiritual" over "Christian" formation in some theological camps. On the downside, it is much easier to change the wrapping — the labels — than to deal with the complexities and frustrations within that wrapped box (Christian education). Old labels can be quickly discarded; soon many old programs and methods follow. But the unresolved challenges of the box's contents remain.

When new titles appear, as in this case, a contrast between the old and new is inevitable. Unfortunately, the old often assumes a stereotype (if not scapegoat) role. I believe this is what has largely happened in the scenario between Christian education and spiritual formation. For example, if this pair were compared by people promoting "spiritual formation," one could expect the following kind of contrast — assuming that the second column is better:

	Christian Education	vs.	Spiritual Formation
Primary setting	Formal schooling		Informal teaching and learning
Domain target	Mostly cognitive		Holistic maturity
Focus of change	Mainly behaviors		Character then relationships
Best leader title	Teacher		Mentor
Prominent metaphor	Classroom		Pilgrimage
Larger organizational structure	Denominational		Interdenominational

Hearing this same assessment from a proponent of Christian education, several traditional values would be asserted. Again, expect a bias, because these statements are *perceptions*. Christian education, it would be stated, especially provides:

+ Greater accountability to the local church
+ Emphasis on all ages, not just adults
+ Focus on accompanying topics like lifelong strategies for growth, age-appropriateness, and sensitivity to the individual learner
+ A more orderly, comprehensive, and systematic plan for teaching and learning of Scripture, age-related issues, etc.
+ Faithful use of time-honored biblical methods like Scripture memorization and prominent tasks like evangelism
+ More consistent instruction of foundational doctrines like sin, redemption, etc.

This book attempts to synthesize the best of Christian education tradition with godly spiritual formation concepts. We use the term *Christian education-formation* to express this approach.

Final Thoughts

According to Bonhoeffer, one major reason that God interrupts our lives is so that we will "not assume that our schedule is our own to manage, but will allow it to be arranged by God." In Christian education-formation, this statement implies the need for humility and teachability.

My sincere prayer is that each Christian brother and sister welcomes God's interruptions — even embraces them — as privileged opportunities to personally mature and to invest in the kingdom.

Perhaps your time is now. Perhaps this book is here to help you.

— Ron Habermas

NOTES

1. Robert W. Pazmiño, *Foundational Issues in Christian Education: An Introduction in Evangelical Perspective* (Grand Rapids: Baker, 1988), 40.
2. Inadvertently, in this book the second and third categories were switched. Consequently, chapter 15 deals with Service and chapter 16 focuses on Fellowship Community.
3. All quotations attributed to Dietrich Bonhoeffer hereafter are from *Life Together* (New York: Harper and Row, 1954).

Part 1

FOUNDATIONS TO RESTORATION

Teleological Foundations

Theological and Social Science Foundations

Teleological Foundations

Chapter 1

MAPS, SIGNS, AND CHOICES

Recently, while traveling for work, I discovered that I had forgotten to pack a dress shirt that I needed for a presentation I would make that evening, so I asked my host to drop me off at a shopping mall. There is little that is more frustrating than an unfamiliar place in a distant city and too little time. I needed the shirt and I needed it fast. But the mall was a crowded, deafening, teeming maze of stores that all looked alike. To make matters worse, I was exhausted from traveling, so sorting through the confusion was difficult.

When I was about to give up and start constructing amusing stories for my audience about why I was wearing a Michigan State Spartans tee shirt under my tailored jacket, I suddenly spotted a large pedestal map in the walkway; it was the mall directory.

"YOU ARE HERE," the bold, capital letters declared reassuringly. A large red arrow pointed to the very spot where I stood.

I sighed, relieved and relaxed. I was instantly filled with confidence and renewed energy. After a quick study, without having to move, I was completely oriented. I located the store I needed and knew how to get there in the shortest possible time with no mistakes.

This book will serve you the same way the map at the mall served me. But instead of helping you locate yourself and point you toward a specific store, it will give you guidelines for your Christian life. And just like the map at the mall, this spiritual map will be accurate, comprehensive, and practical. It will lead you directly to the way God wants you to live.

You can think of this book's map as a Life Plan. The table of contents identifies chapters 1 – 2 as the *teleological* foundations for this resource, meaning that each chapter discusses the significant subject of life purpose.

Signs That Point the Way Home

When you're on a trip, there's nothing so useful as a good map, even if it's a hastily printed one from Mapquest or Google. Clear directions and accurate routes allow you to get from one point to another with the least amount of effort and frustration. When you have a good map and you're skilled at reading it, you can eliminate aimless wandering, frantic searching, and asking strangers for directions that may or may not bear any resemblance to reality. Frankly, without clear directions and accurate routes, you may never locate your destination.

One of the most famous of all "wanderers" was Christopher Columbus (1451 – 1506), a map-making Italian mariner whose mission was to reach the East Indies (India and China) — all east of Europe — by sailing his fleets west. He successfully arrived at the "New World" (the Bahamas, Cuba, the Caribbean, and South and Central America) several times but never abandoned his stubborn belief that he had really reached an island in the East Indies and been very close to Japan and China. Why was there such obvious discrepancy? His maps were inaccurate because he was calculating his mileage with the wrong formula. He had no Google Earth or GPS system to check his calculations. *Columbus got somewhere, but not where he thought.* This is why he is known as a famous explorer, not a famous navigator.

There is even a fictitious award in Columbus's honor for people who can't find their way:

The Christopher Columbus Award

Citation: This award goes to those who, like good old Chris, when they set out to do something, don't know where they are going; neither do they know how to get there. When they arrive, they don't know where they are, and when they return, they don't know where they've been.[1]

Was there ever a time in your life when *you* might have been a candidate for the Christopher Columbus Award?

Pointing Out What We Once Had

It is reassuring to have an up-to-date map exclaim: "YOU ARE HERE!" However, when it comes to a Christian life map, we must first locate an older, equally accurate map that announces: "BUT YOU *WERE* HERE!"

Every saint must understand his or her roots.

In the beginning, we received the breath of God along with his image. In my attempts to discover the functional meanings of those two abstract ideas, I formulated the three Eden legacies — each of which links to our core communion with the Creator (figure 1.1):

- Family Name (Character)

- Family Business (Calling)
- Family Ties (Community)[2]

Another way to understand our original Eden legacies is to think of them as our three-way partnership with the Creator. We once served perfectly as "junior" partners with the Maker of the universe.

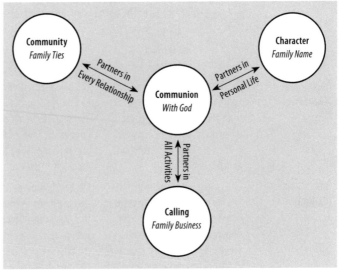

FIGURE 1.1 — Eden's Legacies as Partnerships with the Creator

Pointing Out What We Lost

Following the first human sin, everything became distorted. Familiar biblical word pictures come to mind when we describe sin. Many of us have heard terms for sin like "blindness," "stiff-necked," and "missing the mark." When we maintain the biblical analogy of highway, there are additional words for our rebellion. Opposition to God's way reminds us of concepts such as "wanderer," "wayward," and "waywardness."

When we persistently choose wayward paths today, our chances of personal devastation quickly increase. Playing with sin makes about as much sense as playing Russian roulette. These scary outcomes can potentially occur because selfish rebellion always runs contrary to the original design of creation. Waywardness is like intentionally leaping from a tall building (rebelling against God's natural design), then desperately praying for God's protection all the way down! Our Maker still upholds his natural laws (like gravity and inertia), just as he does all of his laws (e.g., the Ten Commandments).

In sum, rebellious sin is "not the way it was supposed to be," according to Neal Plantinga.[3] Sin is *anti*-Creation. Sin deforms the image of God in us. Sin makes us *less human* when compared to the pre-sin lives of our first parents.

Think about creation and the fall as the first two (of three) acts in God's human drama. Notice how these two acts relate to our three Eden legacies in chart 1.1.

Pointing Out What We Regained in Christ

It would be depressing to end this chapter on the note of universal sin, human despair, and wandering. So I want to be quite clear: *God has always had a plan.* And it was always based on Jesus Christ. God was neither surprised by our Eden rebellion nor at a loss for what he would do next. For that matter, because the Trinity has never been bound by time, Scripture notes that the key doctrines such as Christ's sacrifice

CHART 1.1 — Eden's Legacies and God's Human Drama

The Three Acts of the Human Drama			
	Act 1 What We *Had* **(Creation)**	Act 2 What We *Lost* **(Fall)**	Act 3 What We *Regain* in Christ **(Restoration)**
Family Name **(Character)**	The image of God presents God's righteousness in each person. This truth of bearing his holy Name is illustrated by fellowship walks in Eden between the Creator and perfect people.	The holy Family Name was rejected by God's people. Sin's consequences (especially from Cain's rebellion) left people "hidden" from God's presence, indicating the unholy nature of all people.	By Jesus' reconciling work, believers again receive their status of holy Family Name. We are actually new people through our restored communion with God: brothers and sisters of Christ himself.
Family Business **(Calling)**	God's image means human partnership with the Trinity to perform duties of dominion and care for creation. This fact is lovingly expressed by the Creator's assistance in Adam's first chore to name the animals.	The Family Business turned chaotic because humanity rebelled so that God could no longer partner with people. Sin's consequence of "restless wander" is symbolized by Cain's dramatic vocational shift from agricultural work to nomadic herding.	After their own salvation in Jesus, believers are to spread this good news. We are also given the vocational insight of God's will, partnering again with Christ in the Family Business. These blessings represent how we should live, through our Calling.
Family Ties **(Community)**	Image of God finally means intimate affinity between God and people. This legacy is displayed by the Creator's inaugural institution of marriage in Eden. That model of selfless love was to typify all relationships.	The once-perfect interpersonal bond between God and people is broken by defiance, then murder. Sin's consequence from these image-despising acts reaps distortions in every single relationship thereafter.	Through Jesus' redemption, a newfound relationship is struck between all believers. Christians are fellow members of a new community, Christ's body. Our Family Ties are fully restored.

for sin and the election of all saints actually occurred — in God's plan — "from the foundation of the world" (see Matt. 25:34 KJV; Heb. 4:3; 9:26; Rev. 13:8; 17:8). So, when the time came for Jesus' life and sacrifice, all of God's "reborn" children regained what was distorted by the fall — and much more. Chart 1.1 informs us that, besides our immediate gift of eternal life (see John 5:24), all believers regained their three legacies from Eden.[4]

Present-Day Signs

Our faithful Father has always posted clear markers for his people. And he continues that pattern today. Just as God's signs are accurate, God's purpose is consistent: *his signs point us Home.*

Our Maker's signs are everywhere! Besides the signs of God's law and miracles, additional signs are positioned in necessary and difficult places: at "forks in the road" of our lives, at major intersections of distraction or temptation, at unexpected roadblocks, and at frustrating detours. In these prominent places — if we truly desire the best — we must carefully read and apply the truths revealed through the Word of God and the Holy Spirit's guidance.

It's crucial to note that God also expresses himself through less obvious symbols. These markers are indirect and more subjective, but they're quite real. Five of these lesser-known signs are described below. To help you personalize each category, think about one specific example for all five indicators, preferably based on your personal experience.

1. *The world's natural beauty.* My middle daughter went to the Grand Canyon on her honeymoon. An artist, she sent gorgeous photos back to us with this disclaimer: "These pictures really don't do justice to these scenes!" When the talkative, imaginative orphan Anne of Green Gables saw Newbridge's "Avenue" on the way to her new home in Avonlea, its beauty stopped her mid-sentence. When she found her tongue again, she announced it was the first thing she had ever seen that imagination could not improve.

God-shaped signs thrill our hearts. A rainbow that arches across the sky after a storm. A colorful sunrise that slowly overtakes the dark of night. The pleasurable sound of the wind. The smell of clean air. The taste of a freshly picked blueberry. The stirring expanse of the ocean. The majesty of a snowcapped mountain. The magnitude of the universe and the infinitesimal intricacies of life.

Some of us appreciate these beauty signs silently. Others express in art the emotions they trigger. Still others preserve a memory in a journal, a postcard, a photo, or a video. Yet every human attempt to capture the imagery is merely a replica — and a poor one at that. We can never duplicate it, because there is absolutely nothing like the original. Still, these earthly beauties — our replicas, but especially God's original — are invaluable because they portray the "good" on earth, which points to the "best" in heaven.

Just imagine: Because we have the capacity to enjoy earth's breathtaking beauties, we will be ecstatic — enraptured with joy — over the wonders of heaven!

2. *The world's ugliness.* At the other extreme, we know intuitively that something's not right in this world … *significantly* not right. These are the Creator's caution signs. They point to things that are out of place, even dangerous. Signs that announce, "Watch for falling rocks," "Slippery when wet," or "No shoulders ahead," warn us that the way is not safe — *not* as it was created to be.

"The whole range of human miseries, from restlessness and estrangement through shame and guilt to the agonies of daytime television — all of them tell us that things in human life are not as they ought to be," says Neal Plantinga.[5]

We are all too aware of the cancerous effects of sin in the world. We sense this throughout life's oppressive suffering and fear. We experience it when a loved one dies: something in us knows that we were not originally made to die. We know it when a friend breaks a promise, when our kindness is abused, when our loyalty is betrayed. This is not what relationships should be. We know it when children go hungry and spouses go astray. Injustice prevails, the wicked take power, and our hearts break for ourselves or for others.

C. S. Lewis said nobody can recognize a crooked line unless he possesses knowledge of a straight line. Ours is a God of straight lines. We want our Maker to obliterate the crooked lines and to make way for the new world in which all will be straight again — straight lines that connect to our Home.

Because God promises it, heaven has no more ugliness: no more death, no more hunger, no more perversion, no more tears. When you encounter any "crooked line" in this life, contemplate its opposite. What does the straight version of that twisted reality look like? Hope and pray for the day when all crookedness will end. Remind yourself — while standing waist-deep in this world's rubbish — it's *never* a matter of *if* we Christians will arrive in heaven. It's always *when* we get there. Face ugliness with that certainty!

3. Heaven's buried treasures in the earth. "The kingdom of heaven is like treasure hidden in a field," Jesus said, and the man who found it was filled with joy. He quickly recognized that possessing the treasure was worth selling everything he had (Matt. 13:44). Every once in a while we experience what it's like to discover a long-buried treasure, the stuff of fairy tales and legend. In an imperfect marriage, we have moments of true union. In a difficult job, we have rewarding days and the satisfying exhaustion of real productivity. We hold a new baby, shed tears at a wedding, embrace a loved one returned from a long absence. When we look carefully, we find God's grace everywhere on earth. When we patiently take an even longer look, we see God's grace working overtime.

Think of a moment when you felt unexpectedly close to God or at peace in a relationship or satisfied with a personal accomplishment. *These* are the treasure signs of God's kingdom, priceless gifts buried under the rubble of sin's ruin. Though dusty and distorted, they are nonetheless a real, shining, and valuable part of this world. Ask the Holy Spirit to regularly train your senses, your intellect, and your heart to detect God's treasure signs in this life — and to reject the junk you find as you unearth the real value. Treasures are often human qualities that transcend culture and time.

These signs point us to meaningful realities larger than ourselves. They point us to our Creator's fingerprint on humanity. These signs include connecting emotions like love, joy, grief, and anger. They are also part of our common physical traits, like seeing glimpses of God through human eyes or smiles. These linkages might spring from behaviors, like unexpected signs of kindness or genuine sacrifice. They also tie us with others made in the Creator's image. They bond us cross-culturally, reminding us that we share commonalities of a grand design and destiny not confined to language, territory, culture, or history.

4. Human hungers. Each of us is born with ravenous appetites that demand to be satisfied. While physical appetite is the first that comes to mind, there are others. As we shall see in chapter 3, we all have lifelong questions that become the quests that drive us, such as: Who am I? What am I supposed to do? What does my future hold? Sometimes we attempt to answer these questions by pursuing seemingly worthy goals. We might even achieve illusory success: wealth, fame, power, or self-sufficiency. Yet we are still left unsatisfied. Or we might fail completely to answer our questions and find ourselves in the uncharted territories of frustration, anxiety, and depression. But Christians who are sensitive to the quiet voice of the Holy Spirit recognize these questions as God-given yearnings. Only the Creator provides correct answers to his own questions. Only he gives complete satisfaction. As we align ourselves with his answers, we are enabled to lead the most fulfilling lives — as well as experience something of heaven's ultimate satisfaction. C. S. Lewis wrote, "If I find in myself a desire which no experience in this world can satisfy, the most probable explanation is that I was made for another world."[6]

God deliberately pointed our hungers toward Home by creating inside us only eternal (vs. temporal) satisfaction. This world will *always* leave us wanting; there is no other way to say it. This is why Jesus' offer to the Samaritan woman at the well was so poignant: "Everyone who drinks this water will be thirsty again, but whoever drinks the water I give him will never thirst" (John 4:13 – 14a).

Jesus was not trying to be a punster. He was saying, *I know what deep longing you really have, and you won't find satisfaction for it in this worldly well. But I can satisfy your thirst forever and always.* God alone meets our human hungers with eternal satisfaction, and he offers that to us today: "Indeed, the water I give him will become in him a spring of water welling up to eternal life" (John 4:14b).

5. Human hopes. This last God-created sign that points us to heaven is an unshaken confidence that our Maker has embedded in all his creatures. It must not be confused with humanism, even though some similarities exist. This sign includes all universal human expectations that one day good thoroughly triumphs over evil, order totally trumps chaos, and justice once and for all conquers unfairness. "That's not fair!" is not simply the cry of a snubbed child but the cry of every human heart, for all are subject to the Creator's restoration rules within this broken world. As we experience fragmented bits of good, order, and justice here, we intuitively know that much more is yet to come. And we gain greater confidence to hope for the best of the best on heaven's grandest scale.

Now You Choose

Imagine that you find yourself back in front of the mall map where we started. Now *you* have a choice. Do you choose to follow the map in front of you? Choose another map? Ask somebody for help? Wander around without a map? Or do nothing at all?

They say there are only two certainties in life: death and taxes. But in fact, there are at least two more: *a life plan* and *human choice*. Somewhere in early childhood all youngsters start constructing their view of the world. Concurrently, they make personal choices about their views. It doesn't matter that they don't know technical philosophical words like "epistemology" or that they are clueless as to who Plato was.

You can bank on this: *Everybody has a life plan, and everybody has a choice.* Ever since God breathed his breath into humankind, all people have reflected the Creator. That reflection is called *imago Dei* (image of God). Among other exhilarating qualities, God's image has always included these two certainties: the human need to serve (someone or something), and the human privilege and responsibility to choose. James Sire came to this accurate assessment:

> We are given the ability by God to make responsible decisions and to act on them. What kind of decisions should we make? The sorts of decisions God would make. Of course, when Adam and Eve failed to obey God, they destroyed our ability as men and women to rightly reflect God's glory, and they brought all of humanity under God's judgment. It took the Son of God, Jesus Christ, to show us again what God is really like and how he wants us to act.[7]

The serpent's temptation in Eden features both of these traits of the image of God in our first parents. Eve and Adam were created to serve God, but they were also sculpted to cast their personal votes. They began by voluntarily choosing to submit and to obey their Maker. Of course, they eventually decided to rebel. Another way to combine these two factors is to say *everybody chooses to serve some life plan* — whether godly or not.

Technically, we become slaves to what or who we choose.[8] For those of us with a more aggressive, rebellious streak, remember that to defiantly choose to *not* choose is also a choice! Joshua's famous challenge to Israel centered on this very simple pairing of certainties: "Choose for yourselves this day whom you will serve" (Josh. 24:15a).

"Plato once defined a slave as the person who ... is enslaved to his own blind desires."

— JOHN DEWEY (1938)

Conclusion

This chapter boils down to the last word in its title: choices. Ever since our creation in God's image, all people have had the obligation and the privilege of *service* and *choice*. Each individual serves someone or something; consequently, everyone has some type of related life plan. And each person's plan is linked to a personal choice.

There are many makes and brands of life plans bidding for attention and commitment. Some are very compelling. If you don't believe me, watch a couple hours of TV — especially the commercials. Jot down the "gods" that these ads want you to serve. If you're perceptive, it won't take long before you've recorded these top ten idols — the *real* "American Idols":

- The god of beauty
- The god of sex
- The god of self-centeredness
- The god of success
- The god of fortune
- The god of leisure
- The god of consumerism
- The god of "brains"
- The god of fame
- The god of power

Each of these idols longs for your worship. For some of these, the lure is strong.

But there is another way. Another choice. Throughout the Old Testament and into the New, God has prepared this message of hope: *The way of the Lord Jesus is straight and it brings salvation.* One excellent example of this promise starts in Isaiah 40:1 – 5 and is fulfilled in Luke 3:4 – 6: Jesus' coming makes the crooked roads "straight," which essentially parallels the truth that "all mankind will see God's salvation."

God's promised hope is true. It leads to salvation. What magnificent grace! What undeserved mercy! And our Creator has always provided that hope. This final reference to John the Baptist's message points out that God's way is also accurate. It is "straight." It can be trusted.

That's why, in John 14:6, Jesus personifies God's marvelous plan and path of the ages: "I am the way and the truth and the life. No one comes to the Father except through me."

It's up to each person to decide whom he or she will worship.

NOTES

1. Source unknown. Cited in Jim Berg's *Changed into His Image* (Greenville, SC: Bob Jones University Press, 1999), 1.
2. Ronald T. Habermas, *The Complete Disciple: A Model for Cultivating God's Image in Us* (Colorado Springs: Chariot Victor, 2003), 40.
3. Cornelius Plantinga Jr., *Not the Way It's Supposed to Be: A Breviary of Sin* (Grand Rapids: Eerdmans, 1995).
4. Habermas, *Complete Disciple*, 53.
5. Plantinga, *Not the Way*, 5.
6. C. S. Lewis. *Mere Christianity* (New York: Macmillan, 1952), 105.
7. James Sire, *Discipleship of the Mind* (Downers Grove, IL: InterVarsity Press, 1990), 69.

8. Paul often refers to himself and other Christian leaders as "slaves" or "servants" (see Rom. 6:19b and 22, along with Rom. 1:1; Col. 1:23; see also Rev. 19:10). Nonbelievers are also described as slaves or servants — to sin (Rom. 6:16). Second Peter 2:19 refers to "slaves of depravity." Romans 6:20 issues a provocative phrase, "When you were slaves to sin, you were *free from the control of righteousness.*"

Chapter 2

THE TRINITY RELAY:
THE WAY OF RESTORATION

Young Justin finally figured it all out. It came together for the precocious four-year-old one Saturday afternoon when he heard familiar snoring after his father's stressful work week. In his best attempt at whispering his most exciting discovery ever, Justin shouted to his mom: "Me and Dad do the same things! We eat and play and sleep!"

Ah, such innocent insights come, as Scripture notes, "from the lips of children and infants" (Ps. 8:2). If only our life's purpose was as simple as Justin's findings.

God's Three Purposes

When we investigate God's awesome perspectives of our life plan, we would do well not to rush closure. So it is helpful to look at our Maker's three-part desires for creation through the three lenses seen in figure 2.1 below. These lenses signal God's distinguishable purpose for three aspects of creation.[1] Each sharpens our view of God's central desire to eventually "restore everything" through Christ (Acts 3:21).

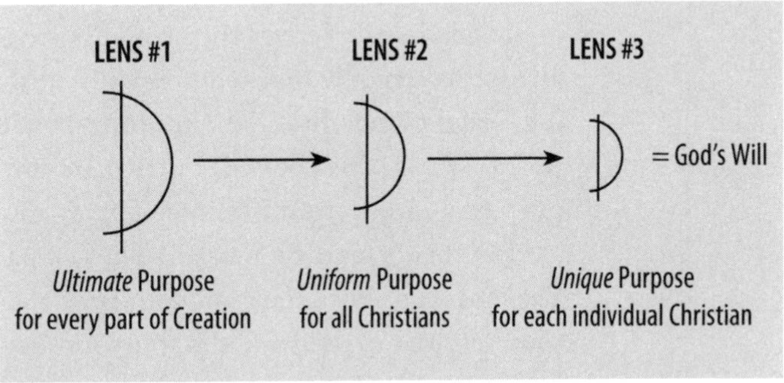

The first lens, God's *ultimate* purpose, is by far the largest in scope. It includes the Creator's intentions for *all of creation* — but it even encompasses pre-human creation. For this reason, parts of this category are incomprehensible for humans, because it stores some of God's great and unfathomable mysteries. For instance, examples of God's ultimate purpose include the diverse ways that majestic redwoods, heavenly cherubim, and delightful

FIGURE 2.1 — The Three Lenses of God's Will

LENS #1   LENS #2   LENS #3

= God's Will

Ultimate Purpose for every part of Creation

Uniform Purpose for all Christians

Unique Purpose for each individual Christian

lightning bugs praise him. This ultimate purpose also features God's intimate relationships with seemingly inert objects like stars (Ps. 147:4) and stones (Josh. 24:27; Luke 19:40).

God's ultimate purpose, then, is identified by two precise statements. First, Jesus predicts that "when the Son of Man sits on his glorious throne" the "renewal of all things" will occur (Matt. 19:28). Second, on a similar note, Peter preaches soon after Pentecost that when Jesus returns to earth, God the Father will "restore everything, as he promised long ago through his holy prophets" (Acts 3:21).

Since each of the subsequent lenses is contained within the lens that is immediately prior, the second lens (God's *uniform* purpose) is subsumed within the Creator's ultimate intentions. This second category is restricted to the life plan for *all* people since it runs the gamut of human history: the Creator's uniform purpose begins chronologically with our Eden ancestors, then incorporates the fall, the Father's work in the Old Testament, the human life of Jesus (especially his death, burial, and resurrection), the Holy Spirit's ongoing ministries during this present church age, and finally the believers' entry into heaven.

This uniform purpose, then, incorporates the third category of God's *unique* purpose, which features the Maker's customized life plan for *each* saint. Consider this comparison: the uniform purpose equals our Maker's *broad* goals for the entire church, whereas God's unique purpose represents his *particular* goals for each believer. Components that shape the contents of this third lens involve God's special giftedness of each saint, distinct personalities, one-of-a-kind life experiences, and solitary callings to a particular life task.

An excellent biblical contrast of uniform and unique purposes emerges from Acts 15. Verses 1–34 detail the Jerusalem Council, which explicitly convened to discern the uniform purpose for all Christians, asking, "What does God expect every Christ-follower to do?" Representatives assembled from the Jewish-Christian sector and from the Gentile-Christian population to determine God's purpose for all. Of the many possible directives they could have formulated, these church leaders eventually settled on only four requirements: abstaining from food offered to idols, avoiding sexual immorality, and refraining from eating both blood and strangled animals (v. 29). Thus, this council, for that period of history, determined God's uniform purposes — the lowest common denominator — for all saints.

But there's more to Acts 15. The last part of the chapter indicates that Paul and Barnabas continued their joint ministry of teaching and preaching (vv. 35–41). They soon resolved to return to the churches they earlier served. It was then that a debate broke out — which could *not* be resolved — a debate over who would be invited to join them in their follow-up trip. The argument particularly centers on young John Mark (Barnabas's cousin), who had deserted them on their previous mission trip. Scripture records that "a sharp disagreement" surged between Paul and Barnabas — until their conflicting views hit a fever pitch (v. 39). Tragically, Paul and Barnabas ended their partnership, and the latter is never heard from again.

Why did this apparent disaster occur? There are no simple answers, but one fact is certain: when it came to John Mark, each godly man possessed a powerful and unshakable sense of God's *unique* purpose. The personalized view of God's goal that each of these two men held was so real and so strong that it caused an irreparable rift between the very first missionary team!

The Trinity Relay for Restoration

Why is it that almost everybody on the planet values the second word over the first word in each of the following pairs?

- Chaos to order
- War to peace
- Unfairness to justice
- Brokenness to repair
- Illness to health
- Despair to hope
- Inefficiency to efficiency
- Ugliness to beauty
- Uneducated to schooled
- Dirty to clean
- Tired to rested
- Captivity to liberation
- Abandoned to reunited
- Indebtedness to financial freedom
- Weak to strong
- Hungry to fed
- Thirsty to hydrated
- Immorality to morality

Simple Answer: With every few exceptions, every person longs for completeness and wholeness. We all want Humpty-Dumpty put together again.

Complex Answer: All people are created in God's flawless image. All have experienced sin too. Humans usually realize intuitively there is an enormous gap between those two realities — what some call the capacity for tremendous good within individuals *and* the sobering potential for frightening evil. Deep down, all people feel at a loss in their souls. But we believers also have great hope. St. Augustine refers to this blended sensation as a "void" that only the Creator can satisfy. As distorted image-bearers, our collective DNA cries out for something better than chaos, unfairness, illness, and weakness.

We yearn for restoration.

Total restoration is exactly what the loving grace of God gives us. The Creator intervenes — in the form of a "Trinity Relay for Restoration" — as each member of the Godhead actively engages destitute humankind throughout the span of history:

- The Father introduces the promised Messiah all the way back in Eden (Gen. 3:15), then he paves the way of righteousness throughout the Old Testament.
- The Son is incarnated as the God-Man, claiming to be *"the* way" back to the Father. He lives for thirty-three years on earth, then voluntarily sacrifices his life so that we can be redeemed — brought back to righteousness.
- The Holy Spirit, who permanently indwells believers since the day of Pentecost in Acts 2, empowers every saint as "followers of the Way."

Two superb biblical examples testify of the Trinity Relay for Restoration, each within a single verse of Scripture. The first is John 16:15, when Jesus provides last-minute instructions and promises to his disciples:

- "All that belongs to the Father is mine." (v. 15a)
- "That is why I said the Spirit will take from what is mine" (v. 15b)
- "and make it known to you." (v. 15c)

The second single verse summary of this relay springs from 2 Corinthians 5:19. The apostle Paul previously claimed that "if anyone is in Christ, he is a new creation" (v. 17). Next he notes that we disciples have been given "the ministry of reconciliation" (v. 18). Then, verse 19 provides an overview of that restorative ministry of ours:

- "God was reconciling the world to himself in Christ" (v. 19a)
- "not counting men's sins against them." (v. 19b)
- "And he has committed to us [and to the Holy Spirit indwelling us] the message of reconciliation." (v. 19c)

Even though all three persons of the Trinity advance restoration, each does so through his own particular contribution. In sum, it can be said that:

- God the Father *initiates* restoration.
- God the Son *incarnates* restoration.
- God the Holy Spirit *individualizes* restoration.

God the Father's Commitment to Total Restoration

Our Maker always votes for total, vibrant, and fulfilling life. It does not matter if the focus pertains to his entire creation or just to one person. The Father always values the thoroughness of holistic health. When he initially stamps his image on all people, for instance, the first person of the Trinity invests many intricate traits within each person to affirm his commitment to human wonder and completeness. After all, each trait captures some reflective aspect of who he is. Each trait also possesses something like a techno-chip to remind us not just *what* we had at creation but the *quality* of what we had.

On the wider scale, in order to maintain Eden's perfect ecosystem, the Creator established an unusual job description for our first parents. It is as though our Maker said to Adam and Eve: "I have good news and I have bad news. The good new is that you have *only one job* to do. The bad news is that you must rule over and care for *all creation!*" (Gen. 1:26, 28; 2:15). Theologically, that job is known as the Cultural Mandate.

Of course, our parents' sin causes them to be evicted from the garden, and every aspect of creation is totally contaminated. But there remains one important fact that about 95 percent of all Christians seem to miss from this early point in time: *the Cultural Mandate has always remained*. Nowhere in Scripture does the Creator cancel this premier human duty. It is still part of his *uniform* purpose for all believers. We are still expected to serve as God's ambassadors in the areas of leadership, stewardship, wisdom, kindness, care, and so forth. Consequently, when Christ finally entered our world as Messiah, our job description as God's children was ratcheted several notches higher in responsibility — higher than most believers understand.

Again, the Father always desires total wellness for his people and wholeness throughout his creation. The sinful fall of humankind never changes that standing desire, but it now requires drastic foundational repair in people. The Father initiates, as early as Genesis 3:15, a plan of loving sacrifice and lifelong ministry through the Son. Respectively, this plan brings to believers the *redemption* of the inner person along with *rejuvenation* of the outer person.

But here's the key: our present-day focus on restoration in Christ through the Gospel Mandate builds upon the Cultural Mandate, because *both responsibilities emphasize human completeness and well-being.*

We should not be surprised, then, to discover that the Father initiates plans for full restoration in the Old Testament. The first person of the Trinity paves the holy way, then faithfully maintains that path throughout history. Here are a handful of Scriptures that cite this consistent grace: it is the Creator's intention for his people to "walk in that Way" (Isa. 35:8), recalling that God's "ways are eternal" (Hab. 3:6) and are "just and true" (Rev. 15:3). They are also "straight paths" (Prov. 2:13; 3:6) and represent the "right way to live" (1 Kings 8:36).

Many of us have heard the Old Testament truths ever since we were young. However, when these independent passages are combined, some wonderful — and perhaps unfamiliar — rewards for faithful travelers on the King's Highway are revealed:

+ Prosperous and prolonged life (Deut. 5:33; 1 Kings 2:3)

- Sustenance that is more important than "daily bread" (Job 23:10 – 12)
- "Health to your body and nourishment to your bones" (Prov. 3:8)

Indeed, God the Father shows concern for his children's ongoing holistic restoration. The metaphor of daily pilgrimage represents one of the best pictures of this life plan throughout the Bible.

King David's Psalm 40:6 – 10 prayer proclaims, "I desire to do *your will*, O my God" (v. 8). Many believers today would say David is committing his total life to Jehovah. But more is involved. David actually quotes from the Law in Exodus 21:5 – 6, which refers to the proper treatment of Hebrew slaves. In particular, when it came time for a Hebrew slave to be legally released by a fellow Israelite, the slave is given the option of returning to his master. To select that option, the slave makes a one-time choice leading to a lifetime of loyal commitment. To indicate this significant decision, *the slave has his ear pierced.*

In Psalm 40:9 – 10, David outlines the strategy he has devised for making a similar public decision to serve God. He customizes his own application of Exodus 21 by confessing three times that he refuses to keep secret his unmitigated commitment to God. David specifically identifies several qualities of his Maker that he intends to publicize:

- God's righteousness
- God's faithfulness
- God's salvation
- God's love
- God's truth

What ties these two passages (Exodus 21 and Psalm 40) with the Father's redemption plan is how the New Testament repeats this exact theme and prayer of the Son's life. Hebrews 10:5 – 7 quotes Psalm 40:6 – 8, revealing how Christ ultimately fulfills David's petition. That is, Jesus similarly submits himself to be a servant to his Father's plans and to be sacrificed for the world's sins.[2]

All that said, the Father is seen as the one who starts building the solid foundation for complete restoration in the Old Testament. He advocates holy lifelong commitment for each family member — beginning with laws about the freed slave's deliberate choice to serve his master, continuing with King David's total desire to serve God the same way, and finally, establishing the prototype of Christ's voluntary commitment to the Father, which will bring the message of complete restoration to humankind.

God the Son's Commitment to Total Restoration

The basic meaning of the phrases "God's work," "the Way," and "the will of God" overlap so much that they are virtually synonymous in the Gospels. That's because that combination of words correlates with the fact that the biblical restoration that the Father *initiates* is what the Son *incarnates*. We've noted how Jesus' exclusive claim as "the Way" (in John 14:6) complements the many Old Testament predictions tied to the Father's Way of Righteousness. In fact, Tinsley makes this linkage: "Sin is *turning aside from the Way*" of God, whereas "repentance is *turning back into the Way*."[3]

In the gospel of John alone, Jesus not only uses God's "will" and "work" interchangeably, but *he describes his own work as precisely his Father's will and work*. Recall the Son's personal contributions to this restoration objective:

+ John 6:38 – 40 — "For I have come down from heaven *not to do my will* but to do the *will of him* who sent me. And *this* is the *will of him who sent me* ... that everyone who looks to the Son and believes in him shall have eternal life, and I will raise him up at the last day."
+ John 9:3 – 5 — "'Neither this man nor his parents sinned,' said Jesus, 'but this happened so that *the work of God* might be displayed in his life. As long as it is day, *we must do the work of him who sent me*. Night is coming, when no one can work. While I am in the world, I am the light of the world.'"
+ John 14:31a — "but the world must learn that I love the Father and that *I do exactly what my Father* has commanded me."
+ John 17:4 — "I have brought you [Father] glory on earth *by completing the work you gave me* to do."

The previous section shows how Jesus Christ ultimately fulfills David's Psalm 40 prayer from Hebrews 10:5 – 7. That is, Jesus comes to earth to exclusively "do your will, O God" (v. 7b). John 6:38 – 40 supplies more detail. The Son's desire is only to do the Father's plan: to sacrificially die for our sins and to provide saints with eternal life (see also John 4:34; Matt. 26:39). Hebrews 10:9 – 10 further explain that, because of Jesus' loyal commitment to the Father's will, "we have been made holy through the sacrifice of the body of Jesus Christ once for all." Verse 14 then adds a curious conclusion — that by this sacrifice, Christ "*has made perfect* forever those *who are being made holy*." The following section on the Holy Spirit further analyzes this matter.

God the Holy Spirit's Commitment to Total Restoration

There is an important transition between the Father's initiation of the Way and the Son's incarnation of that same Way. This time period is generally thought of as the end of the Old Testament and the start of the New. More specifically, this is tied to the ministry of John the Baptist, who prepares the way for Jesus.

There is another significant shift between the end of the Gospels and the start of the book of Acts. This second transition moves the Trinity Restoration Relay from the second person to the third person of the Godhead. The day of Pentecost in Acts 2 officially commences this part of the Holy Spirit's work because — for the first time in history — each person who accepts Jesus as his personal Savior is permanently indwelt by the Holy Spirit (see 1 Cor. 6:19 – 20; 2 Cor. 5:5; Eph. 1:11 – 14; 4:30). In other words, the Spirit *individualizes* the Trinity's restoration plan. He customizes his renewing work within each believer so that any thought of spiritual cloning is completely out of the question.

Two supportive subtopics undergird this third segment of the Relay: the introduction of the Holy Spirit's *new role* within believers, and the disciples' replication of the Son's three-part ministry as they assume that (same) *new task*. John 14:26 provides a magnificent perspective of the Trinity in this regard, because Christ predicts the Father would soon send the Holy Spirit as a Counselor to each believer in the name of Jesus.[4]

Certain aspects of the Holy Spirit's *new role* are predicted and delineated by Jesus, including: (1) that the Spirit will remind disciples what Jesus has already said (John 14:26b; see Luke 12:11 – 12 for one helpful illustration); (2) that the Spirit will testify the truth about Jesus, which the disciples will subsequently proclaim (John 15:26 – 27); (3) that the Spirit will teach additional truths to the disciples, which they are not currently ready to hear (John 16:12 – 13a); (4) that the Spirit will speak "only what he [the Holy Spirit] hears" from Jesus, not his own thoughts (recall how Jesus, in John 14:10, assumed this same submissive role to the Father); and (5) that the Spirit will glorify Jesus (John 16:14a).

The *new task* of the very first Christians was the same task that Jesus did throughout his entire life — and the same earlier work of the Father in the Old Testament. All three persons of the Trinity actively participated in the ministry of complete restoration. This complementary pattern is documented in the Gospels (under Jesus' supervision) and in the book of Acts. Jesus' twelve disciples extend his three tasks of teaching, preaching, and healing (Luke 9:1 – 6), as did the seventy-two disciples who were sent out soon thereafter (Luke 10:1 – 17).[5]

In the Spirit-led context of Acts 3:17 – 21, an outstanding overview of the Trinity Relay for Restoration is highlighted. All three phases are featured in Peter's preaching. Furthermore, this apostle concludes that, at the Father's appointed time, God will "restore everything." What a glorious culmination of history that will be!

Now let's return to that rather curious conclusion from Hebrews 10:14 that Christ's sacrifice "*has made* perfect forever those who are *being made* holy." The first italicized phase is a one-time-and-it's-done look at holiness. Theologians call this "positional holiness," meaning that when a person trusts Jesus as Savior, he or she immediately becomes a born-again child of God. The Holy Spirit immediately indwells them, and they immediately receive a new spiritual "position" of righteousness.

The second italicized phase centers on the saint's need to cooperate with the Holy Spirit for daily decisions to remain holy. Unlike the first phase, this second one is an ongoing process empowered by the indwelling Spirit, and it is sometimes referred to as "experiential holiness."

The best human analogy for both holiness phases is marriage. All marriages that adhere to biblical guidelines contain these same two phases: a one-time decision to say "yes" to one's spouse as well as daily "yes" decisions to remain faithful. Both of these "yes" decisions are necessary, invaluable, and complementary to each other.

Summary of the Trinity Restoration Relay

A harmonious blend of Trinitarian efforts consistently restores God's people from Genesis through Revelation. In each case restoration also occurs because of deliberate human choices to follow God's plans. As in marriage, believers need to regularly commit themselves to Christ by the Spirit's power. In this light, the Old Testament picture of the freed slave's one-time choice for lifelong service is remarkably helpful and relevant for the contemporary believer who desires Jesus to be both his Savior and his Lord.

Scripture, then, records that each person of the Trinity holds a particular responsibility when it comes to the consistent way of restoration:

+ God the Father *initiates* total restoration at the core of his personal will, designating the Holy Highway that his people must take;
+ God the Son *incarnates* total restoration through the Father's call to provide redemption and rejuvenation;
+ God the Holy Spirit *individualizes* total restoration by permanently living within every believer who accepts Jesus as Savior (positional holiness) and by encouraging daily maturity (experiential holiness).

Finally, chart 2.1 highlights eight specific restoration targets. It starts with Eden's perfect setting, then moves to the consequences of the fall. The third column portrays, besides the Creator's purposes, what each Christ-follower should also confront.

CHART 2.1 — Practical Goals of Image Restoration

Pre-Fall Facts	Sin's Consequences	God's Goals of Restoration
1. God created male and female to express complete humanity (Gen. 1:26 – 27).	Antagonism grows between genders; sexism and exploitation emerge.	To reintroduce dignity, harmony, and complementariness between men and women.
2. God commands man and woman to "be fruitful and increase in number" (1:28a; also 2:20 – 25).	Parenthood is devalued; children are marginalized; parental roles are confused.	To affirm the proper place of the home; to see parenting as a divine calling.
3. God tells Adam and Eve to "subdue" the earth (1:28b).	The earth (and its creatures) is misused. God's ownership and imperative are denied.	To attend to challenges of stewardship throughout creation, via sciences, technology, and business.

Continued on next page...

Pre-Fall Facts	Sin's Consequences	God's Goals of Restoration
4. God models Sabbath rest for all creation (2:2 – 3).	Rest and reflection are substituted by busyness and stress.	To balance work with leisure; to reestablish recreation and worship.
5. God provides people with meaningful sensory experiences (2:9 — sight and taste; 2:12 — smell).	Human senses are employed for selfish and sinful ends.	To restore appropriate use of sensory learning, aesthetics, and the arts.
6. God directs man and woman to work the garden and to care for it (2:15).	Work is misunderstood as a "curse"; food resources are wrongly distributed; pollution increases.	To perceive work as God's "calling"; to address ecological concerns; to seek equitable food production and distribution.
7. God declares that it was "not good for the man to be alone" (2:18).	"Aloneness" is perpetuated through unhealthy isolationism, hatred, and racism.	To reassure the value of personal and interpersonal well-being; to affirm disciplines like social sciences (e.g., sociology).
8. God regularly fellowships with Adam and Eve (inferred in 3:8).	Unsuitable replacements for spirituality range from atheism to polytheism.	To rejuvenate fellowship with and worship of the Creator.

NOTES

1. This chapter lays the broad foundational issues pertaining to God's purposes for all creation. Chapter 12 raises a similar, yet different, topic as it focuses on the more particular details of God's will.
2. The author of Hebrews is led to follow the Septuagint, a Greek translation of the Bible written before Christ's time, which exchanges the phrase "pierced ear" for "a prepared body," indicating the servant's *total* commitment.
3. E. J. Tinsley, *The Imitations of God in Christ* (Philadelphia: Westminster, 1960), 33.
4. Because of religious groups that deny the doctrine of the Trinity, it is important to take mental notes of single verses like these, which identify the Triune God as three distinct persons.
5. Also recall the correlation of inspired records that cite Jesus' call for workers (in Luke 10:2 and Matt. 9:35 – 38), each of which begins with the example of Jesus' own three-part ministry. Acts 3 portrays the Spirit-led disciples' version of John 9: in John 9, the Twelve were dependent on Jesus' lead; whereas Acts 3 shifts the dependence of Peter and John directly to the Holy Spirit. Both passages reveal the same restorative blend of ministries through teaching, preaching, and healing.

Theological and Social Science Foundations

Chapter 3

THE TOTAL PERSON:
INTEGRATING THEOLOGY AND ANTHROPOLOGY

I occasionally ask my students to recall *every prayer* they've ever heard. Seriously. They don't need to remember every detail — like prayer "for Aunt Rita's ingrown toenail" — just the basic categories (i.e., Rita's health).

After about five minutes, the class comes up with a list of categories like:

- Health
- Wisdom for decisions
- Relationships (from casual ties to marriages)
- Job needs
- Finances
- People who need salvation
- Consequences of natural catastrophes (hurricanes)
- Worldwide illnesses (AIDS)
- Worldwide problems (war, homelessness)
- Guidance for several types of leaders
- Boldness to evangelize
- Protection (during travel)
- For kingdom virtues to be found in the world (justice, peace)
- Christ's return
- Revival and growth among believers
- Transportation needs
- Interpersonal communication (confession, conflict resolution)
- Living and housing arrangements
- Weather concerns
- Freedom of/tolerance for personal beliefs

After allowing some time for personal reflection, I conclude with these comments:

- Apart from explicitly Christian prayer requests, like prayers for salvation, all people generally "pray" for the same basic concerns.
- Consequently, even though we will not all use the same terminology, when it comes to our prayers, Christians are much more like non-Christians regarding their human makeup and needs than most of us realize.[1]
- What is the common denominator?[2] Christ-followers can attribute a generous portion of this to the fact that all people possess God's breath and reflect our Creator as image-bearers.

With so much in common, it would make sense to investigate other possible similarities. When we do, we discover significant overlap in the fields of theology and anthropology in comprehending who people are.

A Common Look

With some notable differences, all people share the same "look," as figure 3.1 indicates. We saints share the same inner and outer structures as everyone, with the exceptions of the believer's new "inner person" and the permanent residency of the Holy Spirit.

Figure 3.1 details our shared personhood, from:

- Our *innermost* self (our human spirit and will, which is the source for making decisions, trusting, and having faith)

FIGURE 3.1 — Illustration of People and the World (starting w/inside ring)

1. **Innermost Person** — First ring portrays the individual's core personality (e.g., "heart of hearts").

2. **Interior Person** — Head and Heart reflect the next complementary, inner areas. (*Mark 1:40 – 42 offers a biblical synthesis of these first two categories within Christ's life.*)

3. **Outer Person** — This next circle represents the physical body.

4. **Total Person** — The soul is the combination of all rings up to this point.

5. **Natural World** — This ring includes all physical realities that are external to people.

6. **Spiritual World** — The last ring includes all godly and ungodly realities.

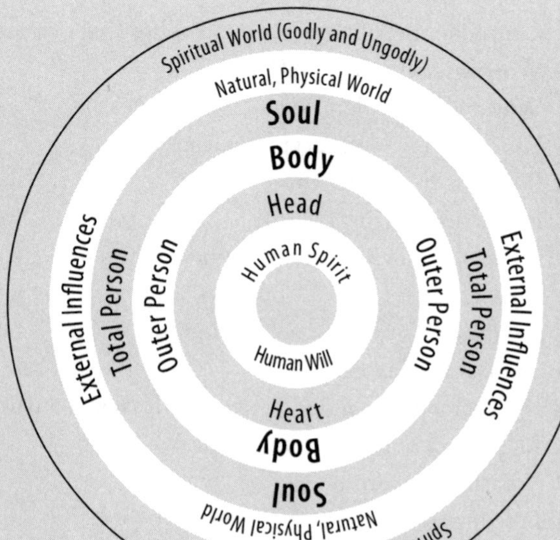

Rabbi Jehudah, the son of Tema, says: "At five years of age, reading of the Bible; at ten years, learning the Mishnah; at thirteen years, bound to the commandments; at fifteen years, the study of the Talmud; at eighteen years, marriage; at twenty, the pursuit of trade or business (active life); at thirty years, full vigour; at forty, maturity of reason; at fifty, of counsel; at sixty, commencement of agedness; at seventy, grey age; at eighty, advanced old age; at ninety, bowed down; at a hundred, as if he were dead and gone, and taken from the world."

— FROM THE MISHNA (*ABOTH.* V. 21)

- Our *interior* self (the blend of our thinking and feeling)
- Our *outer* or *exterior* self (our body or "hand," highlighting our external behaviors)

Acts 2:37 identifies the previous two categories, but something is still missing — what is it? "When the people *heard* this [Peter's sermon at Pentecost], they were cut to the *heart* and said to Peter and the other apostles, 'Brothers, what shall we *do*?'" These three italicized words represent the "head, heart, and hand" of every human. But the crowd ached for something else.

Peter's answer in verse 38 is for them to "repent" — a volitional duty of the human will, from the innermost domain — and then be baptized "in the name of Jesus for the forgiveness of your sins," which would bring them the permanent, indwelling "gift of the Holy Spirit."

Besides these first three rings, then, comes our *total* self — the soul. This is the combination of all the "rings" to this point. Recall Matthew 16:26, "What good will it be for a man if he gains the whole world, yet forfeits his soul?" In other words, Jesus speaks of a tradeoff of the "whole world" for the "whole person."

Anthropological Findings

Just prior to the midpoint of the last century, extensive international research began to ascertain the *common* characteristics of every people group in the world. Before that time, anthropological studies primarily focused on the opposite goal: what is *unique* among international peoples?

In 1945, George Peter Murdock publicly pioneered this new trend, which later became known as the common qualities of Universal People. By the second page of his groundbreaking chapter entitled "The Common Denominator of Cultures," Murdock displays an impressive, yet admittedly "partial" list of seventy-three universal human characteristics, in alphabetical order:

Age grading, athletic sports, bodily adornment, calendar, cleanliness training, community organization, cooking, cooperative labor, cosmology, courtship, dancing, decorative art, divination, division of labor, dream interpretation, education, eschatology, ethics, ethnobotany, etiquette, faith healing, family, feasting, fire making, folklore, food taboos, funeral rites, games, gestures, gift giving, government, greetings, hair styles, hospitality, housing, hygiene, incest taboos, inheritance rules, joking, kin-groups, kinship nomenclature, language, law, luck superstition, magic, marriage, mealtimes, medicine, modesty concerning natural functions, mourning, music, mythology, numerals, obstetrics, penal sanctions, personal names, population policy, postnatal care, pregnancy usages, property rights, propitiation of supernatural beings, puberty customs, religious ritual, residence rules, sexual restrictions, soul concepts, status differentiation, surgery, took making, trade, visiting, weaning, and weather control.[3]

Besides Murdock, many of the major contributions to the field of Universal People studies in the past half-century include the works of Lionel Tiger and Robin Fox,[4] Charles F. Hockett (1973),[5] and Donald E. Brown (1991).[6] For the most part, a significant subject overlap exists between these four research teams, especially the efforts of Tiger and Fox, as well as Hockett,[7] who offer the fewest number of universal characteristics.[8]

Detecting Common Themes

Two primary subpoints of this entire listing (in terms of their frequency) center on *individuals* (from babies to older adults) and on *groups* of people (family, leaders, neighbors, and so forth). Beyond that, it appears that what people *do* (eating, division of labor for tasks, tool-making, etc.) and their collective *background* (folklore, inheritance rules, puberty customs) are the strongest remaining subcategories. Finally, *belief systems* — ranging from origins ("cosmology" and "soul concepts") to the afterlife ("position death customs," "eschatology," and "funeral rites") — emerge as relatively prominent factors. All four research findings, for instance, identify "worldviews" or the "supernatural" as realities that exist among all people. Thus, one could conclude that all universal topics that people deal with can be reduced to five themes:

- The start of human life (individual and collective)
- The historical/cultures background of humanity
- The individual human makeup
- The tasks of life (individual and collective)
- The end (or future) of humanity

Locating Universal Questions

Finally, when these five themes are further refined to five specific and personal inquiries, all people raise these inquiries throughout their lives:

1. Question of Origin, or **Creation**: "*Where* did I come from?"
2. Question of **History** and Culture: "*What* is my background?"
3. Question of **Identity**: "*Who* am I?"
4. Question of **Lifework**: "*Why* am I here?"
5. Question of **Destiny**: "*How* do I get to where I must go?"

In sum, the acrostic C.H.I.L.D. synthesizes these five lifelong queries: Creation, History, Identity, Lifework, and Destiny.

Theological Findings

The complementary question, "How does Scripture inform these five universal questions?" poses an inviting and pertinent task of contemplation, yet this challenge is impossible to address without some restrictions. For the purposes of this resource, those five questions are deliberately viewed through the theological perspective of *imago Dei* in chart 3.1.

CHART 3.1 — 33 "Flavors" of Sinless Image Reflections (from Genesis 1–3)

1. HONORABLE (1:27–28a)	Male and female are blessed by the Creator, both as individuals and as a collective representation of God.
2. FAMILIAL (1:28b)	People are commanded to "be fruitful and increase" as a family, which identifies one of God's early goals of the first institution of family.
3. CULTURAL (1:28c)	The command to "fill the earth" anticipates multiple cultures and nations of humanity as God's purposes unfold.
4. REGAL (1:28d)	Commands to "subdue" and to "rule over" the earth as God's representatives speak of the dominion Adam and Eve were to exercise.
5. HEALTHFUL (1:29)	Adam and Eve were to eat the "food" their Creator gave them, in order to be nourished and healthy.
6. INCORRUPTIBLE (1:31)	"Very good" means humans were perfect in every sense, including sinlessness, which is later matched by the phrase "no shame" (2:25).
7. RESTFUL (2:2–3, *implied*)	The first explicit reference to humanity's need to emulate their Creator through rest does not surface until later (Deut. 5:12ff.), but that need may be implied here.
8. WORSHIPFUL (2:2–3, *implied*)	Some say that Genesis 2:15 ("work" and "care") also includes "worship and serve." Again, the first explicit citation to worship comes from Deuteronomy 5:14.
9. PHYSICAL (or material) (2:7a)	Part of the human composition and makeup is the "dust" from the ground.
10. SOUL-ful (or immaterial) (2:7b)	Another part of the human makeup is God's "breath of life," which was "breathed into his nostrils."
11. BEAUTY-ful (2:9)	People are able to value beauty: "trees that were pleasing to the eye."
12. SENSE-sational (2:9)	People are capable of using all five senses (also 2:12, 16–17, 23–25).
13. CAREFUL (2:15)	People are capable of care, attention, and nurture in their work.

Continued on next page...

14. MORAL (2:17)	People are capable of knowing right from wrong.
15. VOLITIONAL (2:17)	People are capable of making decisions and choices (see also 2:20; 3:6).
16. TEACHABLE (2:17)	People are able to learn new knowledge like consequences of decisions (2:19 – 20 also specifically focuses on learning from observation and study).
17. SELF-CONTROLLABLE (2:17)	They are able to be self-disciplined in regard to personal desires.
18. RESTRAINABLE (2:17)	People are capable of living within limits and restrictions.
19. SEXUAL (2:18)	The complete image of God requires both male and female people.
20. SPOUSAL (2:18)	The wife completes the husband in their family partnership.
21. PEDAGOGICAL (2:19 – 20)	People are able to effectively teach what they have learned.
22. REASONABLE (2:20)	People are able to use both inductive and deductive reasoning.
23. RESOURCEFUL (2:20)	People are able to creatively name the animals, just as the Creator earlier models this ability, by calling the stars by name in Psalm 147:4.
24. LOGICAL (2:20)	People are able to distinguish and to organize wild from domestic animals.
25. RESPONSIBLE (2:20)	People are capable of being trusted to accomplish tasks (see 1:26).
26. ASSESSABLE (2:20)	People are capable of evaluating personal needs, just as Adam could not find a "suitable helper" among the animals.
27. DISPLEASUREABLE (2:20b, *implied*)	People are able to express disappointment, Adam's likely response in the previous point (see Gen. 6:6).
28. VERBAL (2:23)	People are able to communicate effectively with spouse and with God (3:8).
29. JOYFUL (2:23)	People are capable of experiencing and expressing celebration.
30. INDIVISIBLE (2:23 – 24)	People are united as husband and wife, and "two become one."
31. TEMPTABLE (3:6c)	People are able to anticipate something "desirable" and to choose evil.
32. IMPRESSIONABLE (3:6d)	People are capable of succumbing to external influence.
33. COMMUNAL (3:8, *implied*)	People are capable of fellowship "walks" with God.

Chart 3.1 lists, in sequence, thirty-three qualities of God's image in all people. They represent sinless humanity at the time of creation. When the contents of chart 3.1 (including Scriptures) merge with the universal questions outlined above, all five categories discussed below feature a single theological truth that is rarely associated with human creation and our Maker — *pleasure*.

In one particularly brilliant episode of *The Simpsons*, token and oft-mocked Christian Ned Flanders builds an amusement park in honor of his late wife, Maude. The rather unamusing "Praiseland" features Whack-a-Satan (similar to the Whack-a-Mole carnival game), King David's Wild Ride (a spook house in which children are forced to listen to all 150 psalms), a Rockin' Ark, a Tower of Babel slide, a candy kiosk in which all candies are the same flavor ("plain"), and a tithing pond. A statue to Maude Flanders stands in the center of the park over a plaque that reads, "She taught us the joy of shame and the shame of joy."

As funny as the episode is for those of us who can laugh at ourselves, it touches on a sad truth: Many who call themselves Christians seem to value Maude's legacy. As Peter Kreeft wrote in reference to C. S. Lewis: "To find a joyful Christian is so unusual that when we find one, we entitle an anthology of his writings *The Joyful Christian* precisely because he is so distinctive."[9] Many believers are notable for their generally joyless outlook on the world, their sober (and sobering) attitudes, and their suspicion of pleasure. Pleasure gets a bad rap. It's taboo, worldly, sinful. And of course sometimes it is. But real pleasure, delight as God created it, is exactly the opposite. Why are we often unable to distinguish between the two?

CREATION: "Where did I come from?"

All people were created in God's image (Gen. 1:26 – 27), given life by God's breath (Gen. 2:7). We are "fearfully and wonderfully made" (Ps. 139:14). Adam and Eve both had to be present for humanity to be complete and for the image of God to be fully represented (Gen. 1:26 – 28 and 2:18 – 25). People are made of both material ("dust") and immaterial qualities (breath of God) (Gen. 2:7). We have a finite past but an infinite future, which is essentially what "living being" means (Gen. 2:7 and Dan. 12:2).

Adam and Even were perfect, but they were each given a will to choose who they would serve and worship (Gen. 2:16 – 17).

People were placed in the Garden of Eden, which literally means a "hedging around delight" (Gen. 2:8). They were specifically blessed by God: to increase, to subdue the earth, and to rule over the earth (Gen. 1:28).

Even in this perfect setting, God never intended people to "do anything they wanted." That is, Adam and Eve were so created that their obedience to the Maker's one and only prohibition (not to eat from the Tree of Knowledge of Good and Evil) was *infinitely better for them* than their disobedience. This is true because

- God established this only prohibition
- Obedience is always better than disobedience
- In choosing to obey, they wouldn't die, as God promised

These three answers are true and excellent. But they don't identify the most unknown trait of our pre-fall character: we are only really happy when we are living in obedience to God's law. See if this story helps. In an article titled "Pursuit of [Real] Happiness," Carli Conklin cites an ad that features a happy hula-hooping woman and this caption: "The pursuit of happiness. Nice work, forefathers." The ad touts services "to help your pursuit of, whatever." Professor Conklin writes:

> The pursuit of happiness language comes from the *Declaration of Independence*
> and, to be honest, it never seemed quite right to me.... Life and liberty I can

understand. But to risk everything for the pursuit of happiness? To give up one's life for the "pursuit of, whatever"? It never made sense to me. As it turns out, it wouldn't have made sense to the forefathers, either. The true meaning of "pursuit of happiness" can be found in William Blackstone's *Commentaries on the Law of England*, one of the most authoritative legal texts of the time.

… According to Blackstone, to pursue your own happiness is to pursue the laws of your Creator. The Creator "has so intimately connected, so inseparably interwoven the laws of eternal justice with the happiness of each individual, that the latter cannot be attained but by observing the former; and, if the former be punctually obeyed, it cannot but induce the latter." Did you catch that? According to Blackstone, we can *only* be happy by following the laws of eternal justice, and if we observe the laws of eternal justice, we cannot *help* but be happy.[10]

The most unknown trait of our nature in the image of God starts by realizing that our Maker set our first ancestors into a garden that literally means a "hedging around delight." Furthermore, our Creator set us within a *symbolic hedging*, where we were deliberately told we could *not* "do everything" — contrary to what many believers think that both Eden was like and that heaven will be like. In other words, the Creator made us so we would be most complete and at peace when we obediently lived within his purposeful design of *human limitations*.

To summarize the Lord God's response to the first universal human question, "Where did I come from?" — along with Professor Conklin's godly insights — we must conclude: All humans are made by a loving God who ties our personally created lives to the eternal kingdom laws of justice so that only by and through those predetermined confines are we able to be most thoroughly satisfied and "happy" in life!

<u>HISTORY</u>: "What is my background?"

A study of Genesis 1 – 3 does not reveal any newfangled insights about human culture. Essentially Scripture tells us:

- We are commanded by God to "Be fruitful … and fill the earth" (Gen. 1:28)
- We are commanded to "rule over" all creation (Gen. 1:28) and work/care for it (2:15)
- We have problem-solving skills of creativity/reason (Gen. 2:19 – 20)
- We have abilities to learn and to teach (Gen. 2:15 – 23)
- We have a communication range of rational to emotional expressions, including disappointment (implied in Gen. 2:20b) and celebration (Gen. 2:23)

How does the theme of pleasure fit into human history and culture? Start with the fact that godly pleasures and selfish pleasures are worlds apart. They always have been and always will be.

"We have won many a soul through pleasure," the demon Screwtape tells his nephew in C. S. Lewis's *Screwtape Letters*. "All the same, it is his invention, not ours. He made the pleasures: all our research so far has not enabled us to produce one. All we can do is to encourage the humans to take the pleasures which our Enemy has produced, at times, or in ways, or in degrees, which he has forbidden." The demons' strategy is to distort the original condition of God's pleasures so that they become the least natural and least pleasurable. "An ever increasing craving for an ever diminishing pleasure is the formula," Screwtape claims.[11]

Sinful pleasures are selfish goals, and they are "least natural" and "ever diminishing." They are escapes *from* our reality (which includes chaos, noise, and conflict) rather than an escape *to* God's reality (which includes peace, rest, and beauty). The more we pursue worldly pleasures, the less we are fulfilled, the less human we become, and the farther we get from God's pure joy for us.

True pleasure has always been — and remains — God's "invention."

IDENTITY: "Who am I?"

Again, Genesis 1 – 3 unequivocally asserts the nature of individual people:

+ We are a reflection of God the Creator (Gen. 1:26 – 27)
+ We are either male or female — as individuals (Gen. 2:7; 2:21 – 22)
+ We are part of humankind — as a collective group (Gen. 1:26 – 30; 2:18)
+ We are able and responsible to make choices (Gen. 2:16 – 17)
+ We are both physical and spiritual beings (Gen. 2:7)
+ We are capable of solving problems (Gen. 2:19 – 20)
+ We are capable of learning and teaching (Gen. 2:15 – 23)
+ We are capable of a range of communication (Gen 2:20b; 23)

How does true godly pleasure fit into a theological understanding of the individual God made? This complex and controversial subject has to be one of the most difficult waters we Christ-followers are called to navigate.

Many of us have made the error of rejecting pleasure in its entirety, not only in its corrupted form. Austerity might not be fun, but at least it's safe. Self-denial might be bland, but at least it's not poison. Pleasure just isn't worth the risk, especially in this age when the prevailing definition of *joy* or *pleasure* or *happiness* seems to be "whatever feels good." That can't ever be right, we reason; let's steer clear. We might evade Screwtape's trap this way, but the unfortunate result is that we also develop decreasing cravings for genuine pleasures and a false sense of shame when we encounter them — as Maude Flanders would have it.

We have biblical grounds for this safe, anti-pleasure attitude. Scripture warns against being "lovers of pleasure rather than lovers of God" (2 Tim. 3:1 – 5). Moses was praised for choosing "to be mistreated along with the people of God rather than to enjoy the pleasures of sin for a short time" and for regarding "disgrace for the sake of Christ as of greater value than the treasures of Egypt" (Heb. 11:25 – 26).

So I'm not about to suggest that we throw out these cautions and run full tilt into lives of carousing and gluttony. I wholeheartedly agree that "whatever feels good" is not God's idea of true pleasure. Neither is the strange amalgam of trendy religious attitudes that sociologists Christian Smith and Melinda Lundquist Denton call "Moralistic Therapeutic Deism," that is, the increasingly popular idea in Western culture that the aim of the Christian life is to do good and be happy, guarded by an aloof Creator whose purpose is to make us feel better and more secure about ourselves.[12]

There is no shortage of twisted notions about pleasure. Besides pleasure's "sinfulness," some of us think real pleasure is going to cost us something, like an unaffordable admission ticket to Disneyland.

When our youngest daughter, Susan, was three, I took her trick-or-treating for the very first time. Because there was a downpour, I decided to take her by car. Fishing her out of the backseat at our first stop, I cradled her in one arm and balanced her bag and a large umbrella in the other. We dashed for the neighbor's door, fetched some candy, and then dashed back to the car, getting soaked in spite of the umbrella. I drove to the next house, parked, and began to repeat the routine. As I leaned back to get her she squealed with surprised excitement and said, *We get to go again?!* Her delight thrilled my father heart and made the spirit-wilting rain an unimportant detail. The outing brought both of us tremendous pleasure, for completely differing reasons.

"God ... richly provides us with *everything* for our *enjoyment*," Paul wrote (1 Tim. 6:17). He fills our lives with good and perfect gifts (James 1:16 – 17). And God himself is pleased to give us the kingdom (Luke 12:32). Why? Because God's pleasures always extend from his eternal goodness.

We must live by that blended axiom of God's goodness and pleasures for us. Our loving Father calls us to go back — again and again — to enjoy his very, very good pleasures.

<u>L</u>IFEWORK: "Why am I here?"

Our job description from Eden is clear. No need to bring in experts to state the obvious. These tasks are traditionally known as the Cultural Mandate, which says:

1. We are to "rule over" all creation (Gen. 1:28; Ps. 8:6 – 8)
2. We are to "work" the garden of Eden (Gen. 2:15)
3. We are to "take care" of the garden (Gen. 2:15)
4. We are to work, rest, and worship (*implied* Gen. 2:2 – 3; 19 – 20a; 3:8)

In short, we are to serve God in all of life. And obedience to him frequently yields pleasure.

Pleasure as defined in Scripture is a win-win, complementary experience between God and us. The attitude of Olympian Eric Liddell, as shown in the film *Chariots of Fire*, comes to mind. Explaining why running brought him so much joy, Eric said, "When I run, I feel his pleasure!"[13] God delights in the gifts he gave to Eric, the sheer thrill of running like the wind among them. That's why we must rediscover this simple truth: *Our gratitude for his delight in us is best expressed by our delight in Him.*

Conversely, some of us think that anything involving self or self-care, as pleasure does, is inherently selfish. When Katie, a talented artist, went through a period of financial hardship, she reacted by working long hours and denying herself the pleasure and necessity of rest. Why? Because, she reasoned, "if I do the absolutely unpardonable (which is to not work every minute I'm awake), then I'll be deemed 'lazy,' and of course lazy people are not to be supported in their laxity, and therefore God will be under no obligation to pay for my upkeep." These notions could not be farther from the truth.

"If there lurks in most modern minds the notion that to desire our own good and earnestly to hope for the enjoyment of it is a bad thing, I submit that this notion … is not part of the Christian faith," wrote C. S. Lewis in *The Weight of Glory*. "Indeed, if we consider the unblushing promises of reward and the staggering nature of the rewards promised in the Gospels, it would seem that Our Lord finds our desires not too strong, but too weak."[14]

In sum, God's pleasures are unlike any other pleasure — and they are explicitly there for us to enjoy, thus honoring our Maker.

DESTINY: "How do I get to where I must go?"

In brief, here's our Maker's reply to how we must face the future.

+ We are to live in faithful obedience toward our Creator (Gen. 1:28; 2:15; 2:19b)
+ We are to realize that we live eternally now (Dan. 12:2; Matt. 25:34, 41, 46)
+ We are to be thankful for our wonderful personal creation, motivated by God's innumerable "precious" thoughts toward us, realizing he has fore-ordained "all the days" of our lives (Ps. 139:13 – 18)

Many believers know that a primary purpose for our life on earth is to glorify God. However, we often forget that one of the ways we do that is by bringing pleasure to our heavenly Father, just as we do for our parents. One passage that emphasizes this aim, whether it is here or in heaven is 2 Corinthians 5:9: "So we make it our goal *to please him*, whether we are at home in the body or away from it."

We are maturing in our faith and life, in which we understand that God's pleasure, the source of our true happiness, extends from doing his will. Heavenly pleasures experienced on earth affirm that we're moving in the right direction: "Offer your bodies as living sacrifices, holy and pleasing to God — this is your spiritual act of worship. Do not conform any longer to the pattern of this world, but be transformed by the renewing of your mind. Then you will be able to test and approve what God's will is — his good, *pleasing* and perfect will" (Rom. 12:1 – 2).

When our lives are in alignment with God's will — like a plumb line, which tests vertical straightness in construction — our earth-bound experiences are filled with true happiness and contentment. His desires become our desires. His delight becomes ours, and ours his. Our joy becomes a living, breathing, expanding beauty. "A man can do nothing better than to eat and drink and find satisfaction in his work. This too, I see, is from the hand of God, for without him, who can eat or find enjoyment? … Go, eat your food with gladness, and drink your wine with a joyful heart, for it is now that God favors what you do" (Eccl. 2:24; 9:7).

How do we please God? By aligning our lives with his commands. I am not talking about ordinary, law-abiding, you'd-better-do-this-or-else obedience. That's too superficial, too legalistic, and too Pavlovian. I'm talking about an otherworldly cause and effect, a reality outside our limited human experience. God's gracious plan for our lives, which involves obedience to the Word, connects deeply with our souls and infuses our lives with an indescribable joy.

Even the beginning of Jesus' ministry on earth is marked by pleasure. His first miracle took place at a party, and he contributed to the guests' merriment by creating the best wine to be offered there. Close to the time of his death, Jesus promised his disciples at his last Passover feast that, although that celebration was coming to an end, he would drink wine "anew in the kingdom of God" (Mark 14:25).

How will it all end? What is the place of pleasure as we head for eternity? How does our destiny shape our thoughts and values now? God delights in us, his creation, all the way to the last chapter of the Bible. He wants us to enjoy his pleasures now, here on earth. And he wants to do so in heaven. His delight is not elitist or exclusive because God offers this pleasure freely, generously, and "without cost" to everyone who seeks it in him. The fifth from the last verse in the entire Bible invites all people: "'Come!' Whoever is thirsty, let him come; and whoever wishes, let him take the free gift of the water of life" (Rev. 22:17b).

That passage builds upon a similar prediction from the Old Testament. Listen to these consistent and inviting words of peace, contentment, and pleasure:

> Come, all you who are thirsty,
> come to the waters;
> and you who have no money,
> come, buy and eat!
> Come, buy wine and milk
> without money and without cost.

Why spend money on what is not bread,
and your labor on what does not satisfy?
Listen, listen to me, and eat what is good,
and your soul will delight in the richest of fare. (Isa. 55:1 – 2)

What a beautiful truth to claim. Our Father thrills to give us his pleasures freely throughout eternity!

Conclusion

These five universal questions are so important that they shape much of the content in Part II, where the human Jesus intentionally takes on five prominent roles in his earthly life besides that of Savior. Each role is deliberately fashioned to thoroughly answer every lifelong human inquiry. Here's a preview of those questions matched to five roles:

- *"Where* did I come from?" and Jesus' Role of Master Teacher
- *"What* is my background?" and Jesus' Role of Faithful Learner
- *"Who* am I?" and Jesus' Role of Son of Man
- *"Why* am I here?" and Jesus' Role of Great Physician
- *"How* do I get to where I must go?" and Jesus' Role of Submissive Servant

---

NOTES

1. In the first practical insight at the end of chapter 5, John Dettoni similarly concludes, "People are more alike than dissimilar."
2. Donald E. Brown frames his own anthropological observations and this same query:

   "Once one has absorbed the lesson of cultural relativity, what was initially astonishing becomes mundane or fully expectable. It poses no great problem for explanation. Indeed, any outrageously different custom or belief can get the same explanation: it's because of their culture. But when the kaleidoscope of world cultures becomes normal, then the fixed points, the universals, stand out as curiosities. And the explanation that it is because of their culture becomes meaningless. A new question emerges: given the inherent tendency for disparate peoples to develop disparate cultures, *how on earth can some things be the same everywhere?"* (*Human Universals* [New York: McGraw-Hill, 1991], 88; emphasis added).

3. Murdock's chapter was part of editor Ralph Linton's book, *The Science of Man in the World Crisis* (New York: Columbia University Press, 1945), 124.
4. Primarily, Lionel Tiger and Robin Fox, *The Imperial Animal* (New York: Rinehart & Winston, 1971).
5. Primarily, Charles F. Hockett, *Man's Place in Nature* (New York: McGraw-Hill, 1973), 276 – 79.
6. Primarily, Brown, *Human Universals,* 130 – 41.
7. About thirty themes from Tiger and Fox include "adornment (of young females); adultery; children's play; courtship; culture; dance; dominant individuals a focus of attention; flirt-

ing; games of skill and chance; homicide; homosexuality; incest regulation; juvenile delinquency; loyalty; male activities that exclude females and/or are secret; male dominance (in political arena); marriage; myths and legends; obligations to give, receive, and repay; persons who attempt (or pretend) to cure the ill; property; psychoses and neuroses; rules; self-deception; senility; sexual division of labor; statuses; suicide; supernatural (deference to and attempts to control); taboos (and avoidances); and traditional restraints on the rebelliousness of young men" (from Donald E. Brown's resource list on p. 196).

Hockett's list of just over forty characteristics includes these universals: "sociality and social structure, social structure influenced by sex and age, age grading, social structure influenced by accumulated information, leadership, collective decision making, consultation in collective decision making, informal vs. formal consultation, moderator-type leader, band (or derivative organization) distinct from family, nonlocalized social groups, intimate property vs. nonproperty, loose property, inheritance rules, equation of social and physiological maternity, prohibition of mother-son incest, other incest prohibitions that yield exogamous groups, dominant household dyad includes at least one adult, dyadic conflict, modeling transactions with remote (and larger) groupings on those in intimate (small) social groups, personality apart from social role, mutual influence of personality and social role, ascribed vs. achieved status, a pool of 'state parameters' (degrees of uncertainty, freedom of choice, urgency, pleasantness, anxiety, and seriosity) that characterize or govern the actors in a dyad, quandary, boredom, sleep, dreaming, ritual, play, games, joking, affection, submissiveness, hostility, worldview, worldview involving entities not directly observed or observable, curiosity about one's nature, positive death customs, knowledge of relationship between sickness and death, care of ill or injured, creativity, and creative arts (always including literature)" (from Donald E. Brown's resource list on p. 176).

8. The appendices for chapter 3 include Donald E. Brown's list of seventy-nine traits from chapter 6, "The Universal People," of his *Human Universals*, 130 – 31.

9. Peter Kreeft, *Everything You Ever Wanted to Know about Heaven … But Never Dreamed of Asking* (San Francisco: Ignatius Press, 1990), 195.

10. From the John Brown University student newspaper, *The Threefold Advocate*, 10/24/05. Used by permission of Professor Conklin.

11. C. S. Lewis, *The Screwtape Letters* (San Francisco: HarperSanFrancisco, 1942), 44.

12. Christian Smith and Melinda Lundquist Denton, *Soul Searching: The Religious and Spiritual Lives of American Teenagers* (New York: Oxford University Press, 2005), 163 – 71.

13. *Chariots of Fire*, Enigma Productions, directed by Hugh Hudson, 1981.

14. C. S. Lewis, *The Weight of Glory and Other Addresses* (San Francisco: HarperSanFrancisco, 1949), 25.

Chapter 4

THE MATURING PERSON:
ANALYZING HOW JESUS GREW HOLISTICALLY

Psychologist-educator John Dewey made this prudent contrast: "Experience and education cannot be directly equated to each other. For some experiences are mis-educative. Any experience is mis-educative that has the effect of arresting or distorting the growth of further experience."[1]

One of my all-time favorite *mis-educative* Sunday school stories goes something like this: Mrs. Brown thinks it's about time to try a new instructional method at the start of her third-grade class, just to be different, so she chooses a riddle:

"Okay, who can tell me what's small, brown, has four legs, and a furry tail?"

All fourteen girls, to a person, wonder if they've wandered onto the set of the sci-fi channel. A few kids — farthest from Mrs. Brown — boldly yet quietly whisper, "What's goin' on?" and "What does that weird question have to do with Sunday school?"

Undaunted, the teacher pursues, "It loves nuts and it lives in trees."

Again, the class shoots perplexing looks at each other. They unconsciously stiffen and pull back, as though avoiding something contagious from their leader.

"Oh, come on, you guys all know this! It's not that hard!"

Gwyn, sitting closer to the front, takes a chance. "Well, Mrs. Brown, all of us know you're describing a squirrel. But just to be on the safe side, I'm guessin' the answer's 'Jesus'!"

How many other mis-educative stories from Christian education settings do you recall?

Dewey continues his critique of mis-education in public institutions, which we must hold alongside church education: "Almost everyone has had the occasion to look back upon his school days and wonder what has become of the knowledge he was supposed to have amassed."

Now that one hits too close for comfort, including both my third-grade Sunday school and some of my seminary days.

But Dewey's not done. Just when I thought so, he launches this last symbolic mortar shell: "Indeed, he is lucky who does not find that in order *to make progress*, in order *to go ahead* intellectually, he does not have *to unlearn much of what he learned in school*."[2]

That's a solid evaluation of most formal education. But these assessments are especially insightful, considering they were made seventy years ago.

The Objective of Christian Education-Formation

The objective of every believer's life and ministry is holistic, biblical restoration. We share the Trinity's highest aspiration for people to be totally whole and for Christ-followers to be Christlike.

But there's one prominent factor that we usually bypass: Christlikeness is not only a *goal;* it is a *process.* Jesus was *fully human* from his birth — but he was not *totally complete or mature* until the end of his life. That's because the Father's purpose for his human Son was to help him become mature, specifically to prepare him for the cross, the "Last Hurdle" in his holistic growth. Several aspects of Jesus' maturation process are relevant for our own maturation.

The Pivotal Contribution of Hebrews 5:7 – 10

The most concise Scripture on the "Last Hurdle" is Hebrews 5:7 – 10. In four verses, we receive inspired truths concerning Jesus' final hours on earth, the excruciating pain he endured for us, and the "learned obedience" that enabled him to mature — which leads to the marvelous consequence that Jesus is "made perfect."

All of this means that the Son is now ready, according to the Father's plans, to become the once-for-all Savior "for all who obey him." Furthermore, the Father assigns Jesus the ongoing task of high priest, on our behalf.

Carefully read Hebrews 5:7 – 10. In fact, read those four verses twice. Here is a paraphrase, along with extra comments in brackets:

"While on earth, Jesus seriously prays — with resounding cries and tears — to the Father, the only one who can spare him from his calling: death on the cross![3] And the Father hears his Son because of his reverent submission and fear.[4]

"Even though Jesus is God's Son — he *learns.* [What an incredible statement about Christ's total humanity. He learns to *obey!*] Jesus learns to obey the Father and the Father's will. Moreover, Jesus learns obedience through this source of suffering [another potential blessing we can have from our suffering].

"All of this — his learned obedience from suffering — makes Jesus *fully mature.* ["Perfect" is an unfortunate English translation here, because it may imply to some that Jesus actually sins — which is not true. That is, it may convey that he had to be "*imperfect*" prior to this "fully mature" time.[5]] Now that Jesus is fully mature, according to the Father's standards for him, he is finally able to become the one and only Savior, who supplies eternal salvation for everyone who *obeys*. The Father also gives his Son the permanent title of Great High Priest, similar to Melchizedek, an early illustration of Christ in the Old Testament. The title of Savior is based on Jesus' once-for-all sacrifice that redeemed God's children. The title of Great High Priest represents Jesus' constant service for all the redeemed — right now — based on his total human life, experiencing every temptation we do. Our Lord is just the person for this job — the only person — because he is completely empathetic to our struggles, taking those very needs to the Father."

This process that leads Jesus to full maturity incorporates what I have labeled the "Last Hurdle." In particular, it is Jesus' submission of his own will to the Father's will that produces *learned obedience*, the last step in the Father's strategy for the Son to become "complete." Now Jesus is ready to serve as our Savior and our High Priest (v. 10).

For many Christ-followers, that same personal submission to and trust in God is our "last hurdle" as well. Our daily task requires jumping that same hurdle of trust by regularly submitting our will to the Father's will, just as the Lord's Prayer explicitly tells us: "Your kingdom come, your will be done on earth as it is in heaven" (Matt. 6:10).

A Bird's-Eye View of Holistic Maturity

Figure 4.1 offers visual insights into Jesus' total growth, especially featuring concepts that pertain to our lives. The Last Hurdle passage of Hebrews 5 pinpoints the biblical target of *holistic maturation* through its use of the word "perfect," or complete or totally mature. Learning — particularly learning that yields this total maturation — provides the entire backdrop for figure 4.1. Then two axes are displayed:

FIGURE 4.1 — Life Components of Suffering That God Can Turn into Maturity (Based on Hebrews 5:7 – 10)

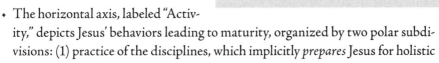

- The horizontal axis, labeled "Activity," depicts Jesus' behaviors leading to maturity, organized by two polar subdivisions: (1) practice of the disciplines, which implicitly *prepares* Jesus for holistic maturation,[6] and (2) obedience of God's will — including suffering — in which Jesus explicitly *participates*.

- The vertical axis emphasizes "Motivation," answering the question, "What are the factors that compel Jesus' desire for total maturity?" The negative motivator is godly doubt, similar to Piaget's terms *dissonance* or *disequilibrium*. The positive motivator is godly joy, encouraging him in troubled times.

How the Disciplines May Mature Us

When it comes to the Christian disciplines, most evangelicals agree on six concepts, based on the representative writings of the two leading evangelicals in this field, Richard Foster and Dallas Willard:

1. There is *no agreement on the exact number* of the disciplines. For example, Foster lists twelve, and Willard suggests fifteen.[7]
2. There is *no agreement as to the disciplines' organization*. Foster gives three categories: Inward, Outward, and Corporate. Willard uses only two: Abstinence and Engagement.
3. There is *no agreement as to what should be called a discipline*. Foster has two entries that Willard does not include: meditation and guidance. Willard's five entries are silence, chastity, secrecy, sacrifice, and fellowship.
4. There is full agreement that no discipline is a goal or end in itself.
5. There is agreement that the completion of a discipline *does not automatically guarantee God's blessing*. Disciplines are not sacraments.
6. A helpful way to think about the disciplines is to see them as *spiritual exercises* that create, sustain, and utilize skills to enable the believer in his faith walk.

Luke 21:14 – 15 well defines the essence of the Christian disciplines: "*But make up your mind not to worry beforehand* how you will defend yourselves. For I will give you words and wisdom that none of your adversaries will be able to resist or contradict." First, this passage indicates that commitment to the disciplines is largely a commitment "beforehand," prior to life involvement — like most exercises. Second, the disciplines begin with a focused mind, will, and choice, because the most effective disciplines start with deliberation. And third, disciplines frequently take aim at a related vice; in the case of Luke 21:14 – 15, the disciplined mind battles the vice of worry.

Jesus' Modeling of the Disciplines

It is useful to picture Jesus in at least three seasons of life when it comes to his total human development and maturation: (1) infancy; (2) childhood to twelve years of age (or young adulthood in the Jewish culture); and (3) middle adulthood (the last three years of his life).

Season One: Infancy — Luke 2:1 – 40 feature several examples of Jesus' nurturing spiritual background: (1) obeying God's command, the parents of Jesus have him circumcised on the eighth day (v. 21); (2) also following the "Law of Moses," Jesus' parents carefully observe the purifications laws and the Jewish consecration of the "firstborn male" to God, including a sacrifice (vv. 22 – 24); and (3) Jesus' family meets and are blessed by Simeon and Anna, "when the parents brought in the child Jesus to do for him what the custom of the Law required" (vv. 27 – 38). In sum, Joseph and Mary do "everything required by the Law" for Jesus in his early days (v. 39).

Among other disciplines of faith, we see Jesus' parents — partially on his behalf — participate in worship, sacrifice, submission, and probably prayer.

Season Two: Childhood to Young Adulthood (starting at age 12) — Luke 2:41 – 52 summarizes the disciplined life for Jesus in this second season. Similar to the first, Jesus is the beneficiary of his parents' disciplines. Unlike the first, Jesus (by age 12) now makes some of his own decisions about the disciplines of faith.

The passage shows us that: (1) "every year his parents went to ... Passover" (v. 41); (2) when Jesus was twelve, they observed Passover "according to the custom" (v. 42); (3) when Jesus' parents eventually found him in the temple, Jesus "amazed" everyone by "his understanding and his answers," as he also listened and asked questions of the temple teachers (vv. 46 – 47); (4) Jesus told his parents he had to be doing his Father's business (v. 49); and (5) even though they did not understand his reply, Jesus obeyed his parents, returning to Nazareth with them (vv. 50 – 51).

This Scripture indicates that Jesus was the beneficiary of these disciplines: worship, study, meditation, and submission (to parents). Additional disciplines evident in his formation are routine observance of annual holy days, Scripture memory, and passion to do God's will.[8]

Season Three: Middle Adulthood (starting at age 30) — In the last three years of his life, Jesus experienced all the disciplines that are normally given in such lists. The only exceptions are categories like confession, which indicate sinfulness.

Two concepts about Jesus' adult maturation need attention before continuing, and both come from Luke 4:16: "He [Jesus] went to Nazareth, where he had been brought up, and on the Sabbath day he went into the synagogue, as was his custom."

First, the phrase "had been brought up" is the Greek word for "nourish" and "nurture." It's the same root for "feeds" (Eph. 5:29), "training" (Eph. 6:4), and "caring" (1 Thess. 2:7). Nurture is a potent blessing almost any caregiver can pass on to the next generation. The investment will always be rewarded, now or in heaven.

Second, it's worthy to note that Jesus' discipline of Sabbath attendance in the synagogue is somewhat comparable to our faithful Sunday church observance (see Heb. 10:25). This is yet another discipline that needs to be added to the standard lists of disciplines. Luke describes Jesus, now an adult, with faithful synagogue attendance "as was his custom." It's not coincidental that the last time that exact phrase was used by this same gospel writer is Luke 2:42, to explain to Jesus' parents' custom of annual Passover observation. That is, Jesus' parents' customs have become his. Humanly speaking, Jesus can never pay back his parents who nurture him so well. As godly Jewish parents, they do not do anything fancy or unusual. They simply do their job.

How Obeying God's Will May Mature Us

One of the main components of the "Final Hurdle" passage in Hebrews 5 is that Jesus *"learned obedience* from what he *suffered"* (v. 8).

Sometimes, after a particularly difficult experience, we receive even more blessings than we first imagined. That's often true about suffering — all kinds of suffering. It's not uncommon to hear people say, for example, after they recover from their sufferings, "I never knew I had it so good before those troubles started," or "I really took things for granted back then," or "I won't ever overlook God's hand in my life again — even for the little things."

Suffering is just one part of God's will for us, as chapter 12 of this book later explains.[9] Hebrews 5:7 – 10 reveals that suffering is the actual *source* of Jesus' "learned obedience." If for no other reason, this topic of suffering commands our respect. When we study Scripture, we might be surprised by the multiple instances when Jesus suffers or may have suffered.

How Did Jesus Suffer? If asked, most people — many without any ties to Christianity — will recall the times of Christ's suffering on the cross, which is by far the most familiar of all Jesus' painful experiences.[10] Conversely, only a small percentage might name half of these remaining categories:

- Christ suffered various types of pain in his early childhood years.[11]
- Christ suffered from his temptations with the devil.[12]
- Christ suffered from various threats to his life.[13]
- Christ suffered from rude attacks on his personal background and heritage.[14]
- Christ suffered from the hard-heartedness of his enemies.[15]
- Christ suffered from the rejection of his beloved Israel.[16]
- Christ suffered from his own followers' "slowness of heart."[17]
- Christ suffered from the religious leaders' entrapments and tests.[18]
- Christ suffered from his thirst, hunger, and exhaustion.[19]
- Christ suffered from his family's rejection of him and his ministry.[20]
- Christ suffered from his sharing of others' pain, even that of strangers.[21]
- Christ suffered from the shared pain of close friends, including personal loss.[22]
- Christ suffered from insults, taunts, and scoffing.[23]
- Christ suffered from physical pain "in his body."[24]
- Christ suffered from his experience that the Father was forsaking him.[25]

Besides these numerous references to Jesus' sufferings, there are an astonishing number of additional references to his sufferings.[26]

How Did Jesus Trust God While Suffering? Jesus' trust in the Father during crises is highlighted in 1 Peter 2:23: "When they hurled insults at him, he did not retaliate; when he suffered, he made no threats. Instead, he entrusted himself to him who judges justly." Crucial about this passage is its context. Just two verses earlier we are commanded to "follow in [Jesus'] steps." And Jesus' primary trust was in God as *Just Judge.* So when Jesus directs us disciples to continue the work of the Father and the Son with the Holy Spirit living inside us, he also means we can trust in the Father, the Spirit, and God's Word, just as Jesus did.[27]

There are at least two more ways to dependently lean on God when we suffer. First, guidelines for trusting God during suffering come from the inspired instruction of 1 Peter 4:19: "So then, those who suffer according to God's will should commit themselves to their *faithful Creator* and continue to do good."[28]

Second, in Mark 14:36 Jesus trusts the intimate side of God's loving personality.[29] Only in that gospel does Scripture record Jesus' invocation to *"Abba"* in his Gethsemane prayer. Jesus also concludes that prayer with his need to submit to God ("Yet not what I will, but what you will").

It is noteworthy, in contrast, that three of the main criticisms from suffering believers include these accusations about God:

- He is *not there*, because God seems absent in suffering.
- He does *not care*, because suffering camouflages signs of God's concern.
- He is *not fair*, because injustice arises from suffering.

To counter these criticisms, Chart 4.1 summarizes the key points about God and suffering, and indicates the ways that suffering may mature us.

CHART 4.1 — How Suffering May Mature Us as We Face Criticisms about God

Three Major Criticisms of God from Suffering Saints	God's Primary Role — Which Suffering Saints Must Trust	Related Scriptures	Additional Tasks That Suffering Saints Should Accomplish
He is not THERE	God as "Faithful Creator"	1 Peter 4:19	Commit yourself to the "faithful Creator."
God is Alpha — he has always "been there" — even before time; he can be trusted.			
He does not CARE	God as "Abba" Father	Mark 14:36	God is our intimate "Daddy."
We need to submit our will to his will and trust his plans for us.			
He is not FAIR	God as "Just Judge"	1 Peter 2:21 – 23	We don't need to retaliate.
Trust that God will eventually show justice (1 Tim. 5:24 – 25). God is Omega — he is faithful to the end.			

How Doubt May Mature Us

Jean Piaget's theory of cognitive development contends that people are motivated to learn and to mature because they need to interact with — and desire to master — their environment.[30]

A young child, whom I'll call Brad, begins this lifelong process by using whatever cognitive abilities are at his disposal to make sense of his surroundings. This procedure is technically called *assimilation*. For instance, for months young Brad regularly observes a four-legged, furry animal with a tail that runs around the house. The young child eventually learns to say "cat" upon subsequent encounters. Brad also uses the same word for other cats he sees in the neighborhood. And the "big people" in Brad's life all smile and nod approvingly.

But one day Brad experiences confusion — technically known as *dissonance* — when "big people" in his life shake their heads sideways and laugh every time he says "cat" to a new and larger animal that has recently moved next door with its family of big people. Brad's confusion is this: Cats have four legs; they're furry and have a tail. This new animal — even through it's bigger — has all those same parts too. So isn't this a cat?

After several days, Brad's dissonance turns to *disequilibrium* because he still doesn't have any answer to his problem of small and big cats.

Then it comes to him! Brad remembers that small cats talk differently than this big new one. In fact, this big one — when he barks — can really be loud! What young Brad has just done is technically called *accommodation*, because the youngster now learns to differentiate between two kinds of "cats," calling the larger ones "dogs." And that newfound place of serenity, called *equilibrium*, satisfies Brad — until, when he gets older, he sees a horse!

Piaget concludes that all people constantly move between disequilibrium and equilibrium. Because the latter is so uncomfortable (we all know what it's like to listen to dissonant music for any length of time), most of us are motivated to resolve unsettling conditions and to seek equilibrium as soon as possible.

As painful as disequilibrium is, here's the important lesson: *Nobody can grow cognitively without disequilibrium.* Disequilibrium causes us to think in more refined, precise, and accurate categories. It enables us to discern, compare, and contrast; to be creative; and to reorganize our previous field of learning. Without disequilibrium, in other words, there would be no need to think that cats are different than dogs.

Dissonance and Faith

Generally speaking, other terms used for dissonance include confusion, uncertainty, hesitation, skepticism, and suspicion. In theological circles, one word for dissonance is *doubt*.

In Scripture, there are two kinds of doubt or unbelief. The first type refers to honest, seeking, painful, sincere, and humble forms of belief mixed with confusion. It often emerges from major question marks of faith — normally based on difficult personal experiences, especially crises. This doubter is teachable and seeks truth. Consequently, for all these reasons and more, these are seen as *acceptable doubters* in Scripture.

The second category of doubters is actually better described by terms like *stubborn* and *proud*. People in this second category lack a malleable, teachable spirit because biblical synonyms label these individuals as "hard-hearted" and "stiff-necked." It is no small wonder that the religious leaders of Jesus' day are regularly compared to their belligerent ancestors who wandered in the desert for forty years. Both embody the personality of the *unacceptable doubter*.

Even though both categories contain the word "doubter," they are radically different. Unacceptable doubters represent some of the worst biblical examples of humanity because of their cynical, single-minded skepticism. They're totally unwilling to change for the good, because they advertise a "don't-confuse-me-with-the-facts-my-mind-is-made-up" attitude. Consequently, these people are rarely, if ever, found among the heaven-bound.

Doubting and Bicycle-Riding

Acceptable doubters, similar to Piaget's earlier concepts of dissonance and disequilibrium, cannot grow in their faith unless they regularly experience their brand of spiritual unrest. Much like the process of successful bicycle riding, these doubters lean to one side of their faith — then to the other side — for both balance and momentum that carries them forward. Unless that side-to-side motion (of alternating disequilibrium phases) is consistently performed — while also experiencing moments of equilibrium, as the rider passes over the center of the bike's frame — neither rider nor bike advances.

Contrary to the spiritual status of their counterparts, acceptable doubters often find blessings within their turbulence and pain, as each of the following three cases from the life of Jesus indicates. Most significantly, a primary blessing that each shares is personal maturation. The slogan "no pain, no gain" fairly summarizes the maturity that often emerges from acceptable doubt.

Doubts from Jesus Himself

It's impossible to address the topic of biblically acceptable doubts without mentioning Jesus' doubt on the cross.

Matthew 27:46 and Mark 15:34 fulfill the striking words of prophecy from Psalm 22:1, "My God, my God, why have you forsaken me?" How can God the Father leave God the Son? This is a very serious statement of personal doubt. We'll never fully resolve that troublesome text, but here are two points to contemplate. First, *Jesus' doubt was very real and agonizing.* Here we witness one more illustration of how he experiences all essential human experiences that we do, yet without sinning.

Second, *Jesus' doubt was uncompromisingly torturous.* Sometimes we grow concerned that Mary's son did not, or could not, feel all the struggles we do. But when we reflect on that view, it looks pretty selfish! Reverse that picture for a moment. Yes, Jesus felt the spiritual pain of our human doubts, but none of us can *ever* experience the abandonment of the Father like he did. We certainly cannot comprehend being part of the Trinity, nor can we know, on earth, what sinlessness is like.

All that is to say that Jesus' full-blown doubts were both *sin-free* and *tormenting.*

Even though the Man of Sorrows never seems to fully resolve his doubts, he does come to closure with his Father. In fact, that's the last thing he does. Luke 23:46 records that "Jesus called out with a loud voice, 'Father, into your hands I commit my spirit.' When he had said this, he breathed his last" (see also John 19:30).

In the end, it is not too difficult to see how acceptable doubting is quite distinct from the don't-confuse-me-with-the-facts skepticism. Honesty, humility, teachability, and desire for truth are difficult virtues to criticize in any setting, let alone when serious questions provoke our faith.

Let's review some of the ties that acceptable doubt shares with Piaget's theory of cognitive development: question marks of faith are necessary for maturation to occur; doubts frequently help us come to grips with confusion and inconsistency in our belief system; the disequilibrium that doubt causes often motivates us to seek answers, to reestablish order and balance; and finally, as we desire a healthy mastery of our personal world, acceptable doubts eventually bring equilibrium, along with a stronger faith. That's a more precise, more balanced faith — one that has more answers to questions, brings greater personal confidence, and provides a heightened appreciation for emerging character qualities.

How Joy (and the Holy Spirit) May Mature Us

Augustine concludes, "Everywhere a greater joy is preceded by a greater suffering."

Scripture's references to suffering frequently have their share of correlating joy. The early church displays this combination through persecution and subsequent praise in Acts 4:23 – 31. The same thing happens in Acts 13:46 – 52, where filling of both joy and the Holy Spirit occurs.

The apostle Peter takes joy to new heights when he exhorts, "But rejoice that you participate in the sufferings of Christ, so that you may be overjoyed when his glory is revealed" (1 Peter 4:13).

The apostle Paul commends the believers at Thessalonica, who "became imitators of us and of the Lord; in spite of severe suffering, you welcomed the message with the joy given by the Holy Spirit" (1 Thess. 1:6). He further ties together the trio of suffering, joy, and the Holy Spirit as it pertains to the believers at Thessalonica. Then he adds that these saints imitated his own ministry team as well as the Lord.

We know that joy is associated with the Holy Spirit as one of nine "fruits of the Spirit" in Galatians 5:22. And the earlier reference to Acts 13:46 – 52 identifies some "fruit" from the combined ministry of Paul and Barnabas at Pisidian Antioch. So those facts acknowledge Paul's reference that the Thessalonian church "became imitators of us."

But what about Jesus? Where is that same trio of suffering, joy, and Spirit found in his life, for the Thessalonians to imitate? Two possibilities come to mind: The first instance is Luke 10:1 – 21, where the seventy-two ministers are sent out by our Lord (vv. 1 – 16). Were they to expect opposition? Absolutely. Jesus describes the people they will meet as "wolves" (v. 3), as unwelcoming (v. 10), as more opposing than Sodom (vv. 11 – 12), and as those who will reject them as they reject Jesus (v. 16b). As those thirty-six ministry pairs returned from their service to give their report to the Son, they were elated "with joy" because the demons "submit to us in your name."

But what about Jesus himself? What experience with suffering, joy, and the Holy Spirit did he personally have that the Thessalonian believers imitated? He has just referred to his suffering by rejection (v. 16b), and the other two parts of that question are answered by verse 21: "At that time Jesus, *full of joy through the Holy Spirit*," praised the Father for his plan of restoration.

The second illustration of Jesus' tie with this trio shows even more relevance to personal maturation. Hebrews 12:2 might unlock an earlier-noted problem, how Jesus comes to closure with his Father following severe spiritual affliction and doubt: "Let us fix our eyes on Jesus, the author and perfecter of our faith, who *for the joy set before him* endured the cross, scorning its shame, and sat down at the right hand of the throne of God."

Now, the Holy Spirit is not explicitly cited in Hebrews 12:2, but the second person and the third person of the Trinity are normally found in many of the most significant events of Jesus' life, including:

- Jesus' birth (Luke 1:34 – 35)
- Jesus' baptism (Matt. 3:16)
- Jesus' leading into the wilderness (Luke 4:1)
- Jesus' leading to begin his ministry (Luke 4:14)
- Jesus' guidance to preach his first sermon in Nazareth (Luke 4:16 – 18)
- Jesus' exorcism miracles (Matt. 12:38)
- Jesus' predictions of the Holy Spirit's coming at Pentecost (John 14:26; 15:26; 16:13 – 15)
- Jesus' temporary gift of the Holy Spirit — given to his followers — in the transition time before Pentecost (John 20:22)

If those illustrations aren't enough, then Peter's Acts 10:38 testimony provides the necessary evidence of the Holy Spirit's presence in Jesus' life at key moments. Peter summarizes his Lord's ministry: "You know ... how God anointed Jesus of Nazareth with the Holy Spirit and power, and how he went around doing good and healing all who were under the power of the devil, because God was with him."

In other words, *the Holy Spirit's anointing of the Son always empowered Jesus to perform good while he was on earth.*

Conclusion

How do we grow holistically? How do we enable others to likewise grow? These simple concepts are as pervasive and as elementary as any in the Bible. Yet their answers are among some of the most illusive and complex in all of Scripture.

Wisdom tells us to start with the basics, to never take things for granted. We need to see, for instance, that because people learn all the time, students are probably *not* learning everything we think they are. And they *are* learning things we never dreamed they would. Thus, as they grow, there may be times when we don't recognize them.

John Dewey put it like this: "Perhaps the greatest of all pedagogical fallacies is the notion that a person learns only the particular thing he is studying at the time. Collateral learning in the way of formation of enduring attitudes, of likes and dislikes, may be and often is much more important that the spelling lesson or lesson in geography or history that is learned. For these attitudes are fundamentally what count in the future."[31]

Consider this example from C. S. Lewis. The very first time Aslan's name is mentioned in the Narnia series doesn't surface until well into the first book. Mr. Beaver does the honors. As he tells the children about what is to come, the reader notes that every child's reaction to Aslan is completely different. Each one hears the identical *objective words*, yet in their responses we detect elements of difference based on subjectivity, gender, personality, age, and preference:

> "They say Aslan is on the move — perhaps has already landed."
> And now a very curious thing happened. None of the children knew who Aslan was any more than you do; but the moment the Beaver had spoken these words everyone felt quite different.... At the name of Aslan each one of the children felt something jump in his inside. Edmund felt a sensation of mysterious horror. Peter felt suddenly brave and adventurous. Susan felt as if some delicious smell or some delightful strain of music had just floated by her. And Lucy got the feeling you have when you wake up in the morning and realise that it is the beginning of the holidays or the beginning of summer.[32]

What strategies of mentoring would you employ with these four children, based on your first impressions of these brief descriptions? How would you attempt to encourage each of their spiritual journeys?

NOTES

1. John Dewey, *Education and Experience* (New York: Macmillan, 1938), 25.
2. Ibid., 47, my emphasis in the second quote.
3. See chapter 12 for pertinent details surrounding Jesus' plea to the Father — including an imperative (command) word in the Greek from Mark 14:36. It was as though Jesus cried out, "I *beg* you, Daddy, stop this plan for me to go to the cross!"
4. The Septuagint takes the Greek term (later used here in Heb. 5:7 as "reverent submission") and selects it for use in Joshua 22:24 and Proverbs 28:14. Both times it is translated into English as "fear."
5. The foundational Greek root of this term comes from *telos*, which represents various English words such as "finish," "complete," and "mature." This particular Greek word is specifically found in Philippians 3:12 (meaning "to reach a goal") and in 2 Corinthians 12:9 (meaning "fully developed"). A better word than "perfect" is "totally mature."
6. In Hebrews 5:7 – 10, two disciplines cited are prayer and submission.
7. See the table of contents in *Celebration of Discipline* by Richard J. Foster (HarperSanFrancisco, 1998), and *The Spirit of the Disciplines* by Dallas Willard (HarperSanFrancisco, 1988), 158, respectively.
8. Passion deserves consideration as a discipline if for no other reason than how we Christ-followers need to passionately *love* what he loves and passionately *hate* what he hates.
9. Apart from those passages that may exclusively pertain to the twelve disciples (perhaps like Luke 10:19 and John 15:20b – 21), at least three Scriptures are intended for all Christ-followers. The first concept comes from 2 Timothy 2:12, which states that if someone wants to live a godly life, he will be persecuted. The second support, from 1 Peter 4:1 – 2, indicates that those who suffer physically, like Christ and for Christ, tend to focus more on doing God's will than on satisfying human desires. And the third point is the original "What Would Jesus Do?" passage from 1 Peter 2:21. However, most people have not noticed that in that verse the specific "example" Jesus left us to "follow in his steps" is the example of suffering.

   In addition to these three, there is a broader principle of suffering in the Christian life — based on Jesus' life — that emerges from *loving* what Jesus loves and *hating* what Jesus hates. Luke 7:11 – 17, where the Lord raises the widow's son in Nain, records that Jesus' "heart went out to her" (v. 13). That identical pain is an example of what mature believers should experience as they "participate in the sufferings of Christ" (1 Peter 4:13).

   Another form of suffering is hating what Jesus hates — like people who creatively rationalize how they can save their money but refuse to help the financial needs of their own struggling parents, thus breaking the Ten Commandments (Matt. 15:1 – 9).
10. See Isaiah 54:3 – 6, 10 – 11; Romans 4:25; 1 Corinthians 15:3; 2 Corinthians 5:21; and Hebrews 9:28.
11. Jesus lived through a range of painful issues like infanticide, a refugee flight to Egypt, and his family's return to Nazareth out of fear. Certainly, Jesus later heard about and retained these tragic stories of his childhood.

12. The wilderness temptations from Luke's account (4:1 – 13), especially the last verse, imply that there was more than this solitary encounter: "When the devil had finished all this tempting, he left him until an opportune time." Regarding Jesus' personal torment in these situations, note the concise and insightful truth of Hebrews 2:18a: "[Christ] himself suffered when he was tempted."

13. Matthew 12:14; John 5:18; 6:15; 7:1, 19; 8:59; 10:31; 11:8; 11:53; and 12:9 – 10. Especially see John 10:39 regarding Jesus' full "experiential" escape from his enemies at the very last second. Contrast John 8:20b: "No one seized him, because his time had not yet come."

14. In John 8, the Pharisees began a methodical argument with Jesus about religious heritage. They first asked, "Where is your father?" (v. 19). Then they crudely said, *"We are not illegitimate children,"* possibly implying that Christ *was illegitimate* (v. 41b). Finally, they speculated that Jesus was a demon-possessed "Samaritan" (v. 48).

15. Mark 3:5 records the only explicit reference to Jesus' anger, based upon the fact that he was "deeply distressed" at the "stubborn hearts" of the religious leaders.

16. Luke 13:34 – 35.

17. See Mark 7:18 and 8:21 along with Luke 24:25 – 27 and 45 – 47.

18. Mark 12:15 and Matthew 22:34 – 36.

19. All three of these physical needs are noted in John 4:6 – 8.

20. See Mark 3:20 – 35 and John 7:1 – 5.

21. See Jesus' immediate response of total empathy to the widow of Nain, who appears in this text as a virtual stranger (Luke 7:11 – 17).

22. Within minutes after writing this section on suffering, I was informed by my wife that a mature, godly fifteen-year-old member of our church had just accidentally drowned during a family outing. Believers, like nonbelievers, experience the same grief from loss and also cry out "Why?!" By God's grace, however, we also have hope and peace, though the pain of lost fellowship remains. Jesus experiences this very physical decay with taunting.

23. Matthew 27:39 and 44. Also see Psalm 22:7 and 42:10, which tie physical decay with taunting.

24. Matthew 26:67 – 68; 27:27 – 31; and 1 Peter 4:1.

25. Matthew 27:46; see Psalm 22:1.

26. Notice the consistent reminders of our Savior's suffering: Mark 8:31; 9:12; Luke 9:22; 17:25; 22:15; 24:46; Acts 3:18; 17:3; 26:23; Romans 8:17; 2 Corinthians 1:5; Hebrews 2:9 – 10; 2:18; 5:8; 13:12; 1 Peter 1:11; 2:21, 23; 4:1; and 4:13.

27. Jesus' high view of Scripture (John 10:34 – 35; 17:17) as God's unbreakable truth helps lead him to conclude that by accurately knowing Scripture one can also experience the power of God (Matt. 22:29).

28. This verse affirms that a certain kind of suffering *is* "God's will." Specifically, the context indicates that "legitimate" forms of suffering include being insulted because we belong to Christ (1 Peter 4:13 – 14 and 16). Then legitimate suffering is contrasted with suffering that comes from breaking the law (1 Peter 4:15).

29. Chapter 12 provides commentary on the uniqueness and richness of Mark 14:36.

30. This universal motivation to desire mastery of one's environment parallels our Maker's original directive for people to "rule over" creation.

31. Dewey, *Experience and Education*, 48.

32. C. S. Lewis, *The Lion, the Witch and the Wardrobe* (New York: Macmillan, 1950), 64 – 65.

Chapter 5

THE DEVELOPING PERSON: CONTEMPLATING THEORIES OF MAJOR SCULPTORS

John M. Dettoni

Remember when you reached the fifth grade — on top of the food chain at your elementary school? You finally made it! You were part of the biggest, fastest, strongest group around. All others looked up to you — literally. Then, just as you were getting comfortable with everybody serving you, the "angry gods of adolescence" turned the tables! Sixth grade plummeted you to a new low. It was a humbling, if not humiliating, time.

Without any formal invitation listing an RSVP, you were summoned to appear at the institution known as "Middle School," where the first nine months stretched into what seemed like a life sentence without parole. The clock s-l-o-w-l-y made its way around enough times so that you may have surfaced once again on the top of the heap: eighth grade.

Much older and wiser, you now braced yourself for the next cycle of humiliation. It didn't do much good though, because nobody could have prepared you for the lowest-rung-on-the-ladder of ninth grade. Nobody could have warned you enough about the "Extreme Hormonal Games," a.k.a. high school. . . .

Then, just when time once again brought you to the top of the heap and you thought you had it all figured out by your senior year, you attended your first day of class at the university. . . .

The ebb and flow of human life is constant, scary, and exhilarating. It's one thing to *read* about that constancy of change; it's quite another to *experience* it. So, as you reflect on your subsequent insights into how people mature, keep all your mental files of personal experience close at hand. Every one of them is priceless, because collectively they transform the following developmental theories into practical realities you may recall when you most need them.

This chapter analyzes key contributions from major theorists who have sculpted hypotheses on the most common ways people mature. *Not everyone proceeds at the same rate, nor do we all attain full maturity in every part of our lives.* However, through these theories, we can view some significant movements of people from lesser to greater maturity. Sculpting is an apt metaphor for the process that takes a "lump" of human clay and shapes it into something quite different. Actually, *our Creator is the sole Sculptor,* so technically, these theorists *discovered* prominent ideas within specific areas of human life that correlate with the Creator's earlier portfolio.

I refer to these theorists as "sculptors" also in the sense that the sovereign Lord enabled them to make their valuable discoveries, shape those findings from their own words and backgrounds, and exhibit their work to others. Each set of ideas has proven useful in anticipating and describing human growth, even though no one ever achieves complete maturity in this life.

Seven insights at the end of this chapter will help parents and instructors of Christian education and formation become more effective in their roles as teachers, mentors, equippers, and encouragers. This is *not* the same as saying that the ideas from these theorists are inspired — not by a long shot. That's why each is called a "theory" — an idea that starts out as an educated hunch and tends to get stronger and more credible as further tests affirm it over time. No theory ever loses its status as a sophisticated idea that requires constant testing.

Sculptor One: Jean Piaget and Cognitive Development

Piaget identifies four major stages of cognitive development — the process by which humans "come to know" through assimilation of information and accommodation — from infancy to the teenage years (and presumably into adulthood). Stage One, called *Sensorimotor,* begins with birth and goes through about age two. In this first stage, little ones begin their intellectual growth through increasing reflexive behavior, which refers to the child's intentional movement. At the start of this stage, few deliberate actions are evident, but at the end, a considerable amount of purposeful behavior appears. For instance, young children know how to suck and to grasp a finger placed in their hands, but these actions are still relatively passive, since they do not proactively seek external stimuli.

Stage Two is called *Pre-operational* (ages two to seven). Conceptual behavior, memory, imagination, and language develop. But cognition is limited, since at that stage, a youngster's thinking centers on that which is perceived. This pre-logical thought is specifically limited by: (1) *Egocentrism* — the inability to differentiate between one's own thoughts and those of others. For instance, when an object appears and then is taken out of the infant's sight, this young one believes the object actually disappears and *nobody* can see it; (2) *Irreversibility* — the inability to follow a line of reasoning back to where it started. For example, a youngster knows that $1 + 1 = 2$ but can't comprehend that $2 - 1 = 1$; (3) *Centering* — Attention is limited because it is fixed on only one major set of perceptual stimuli; and (4) *Non-transformations* — The child's focus is locked exclusively on elements in their sequence, not on the possibilities of how things might be altered. The pre-operational child's thinking is limited because he perceives the world in separate and unrelated pieces. He cannot yet process life in any logically related way.

Piaget labels the third stage *Concrete Operational* (ages seven to eleven) because although this stage contains logical thought, the child's cognitive processes are restricted to literal thinking. These children are unable to apply abstract, formal logic to their problems, so they cannot think hypothetically. They can only handle issues that they have experienced, not things that require speculation. But reversibility and conservation are now attained. This means that a child is able to conceptualize that the amount of matter stays the same despite changes in an irrelevant dimension: a cup of water poured into a short, fat container does not become "more" when that same amount of water is poured into a tall, thin container. Problems are solved in their heads, but they can only deal with literal problems and realities they have personally experienced.

Piaget names the fourth stage *Formal Operational* (over eleven years). Not all people mature to this stage. In fact, probably the majority of the world's adult population operate within Stage Three, not Stage Four thinking. Stage Four individuals apply logical operations to all classes of problems: verbal and hypothetical problems, and problems that deal with the future. That is, for the first time, many young teens think about possibilities and potentials — hypothetical issues they don't need to have personally experienced. They can grasp the concept of consequences. People at this stage deal with problems, questions, and arguments, regardless of the content, because they now deal with the *form* of the problem and not just the content.

There are great difficulties in teaching adults certain scriptural lessons that require this last level (e.g., teaching from the books of Romans, Hebrews, or Revelation). Abstract theological concepts such as justification, righteousness, sanctification, or the Trinity all require Formal Operational thinking. People still in Stage Three, Concrete Operations, must have literal examples and illustrations of such theological ideas, but often literal explanations cannot do justice to a concept's full meaning. Hence, people at Stage Three (or lower) are able to understand only a portion of theology's abstract ideas — and sometimes they misunderstand certain theological concepts altogether.

Sculptor Two: Lawrence Kohlberg and Moral Development

Lawrence Kohlberg, influenced by Piagetian tradition, identifies three levels (containing six total stages) of moral development. According to his definition, moral development is the process by which a person makes moral judgments, which may or may not manifest themselves in actual behavior. The emphasis is on the way an individual *thinks* about moral and ethical issues, and not necessarily the way he or she *acts*. Moral development answers the question, "How *should* a person act?"[1]

Kohlberg's first level is titled *Preconventional Morality* (ages four to ten). This level is characterized by children who are egocentric, not in terms of selfishness, but in the sense that the world (as far as they know) revolves around them and their responses to life. They are motivated to think about moral issues through punishment and reward — anticipated physical consequences they will receive from their choices. People at Level One therefore make moral decisions based on the consequences they expect. They avoid punishment and seek rewards. They defer to others who are more powerful. People who are slightly more mature than those who just think of physical rewards and punishments (the first stage of Level One) can function as an "instrumental relativists" (the second stage). That is, good is now seen as a relative notion, based upon what satisfies the person. If it feels good and the person likes it, it must be good. In either of these two stages of Level One, *external rewards* (or lack thereof) provide the necessary stimuli for making moral judgments. It is important to note that such stimuli are separate from the person's making these moral judgments.

Kohlberg names Level Two *Conventional Morality* (ages ten to thirteen). Moral judgments at this level are based on *external interpersonal ties and laws*, all of which are "outside" the person. Rewards and punishments from Level One are no longer the focus. Rather, moral judgments are made according to what will please the others in one's life (e.g., peers, parents, teachers, pastors, special relatives, special adult friends, and so on). The peer group is a strong factor, which also influences the stereotypical behavior of being a "good" boy or girl (Stage 3). People will obey rules either for the rules' sake or because the rules are linked to obeying authorities (who are perceived as synonymous with those laws). Relationships and laws are viewed as fixed rules for the good of all, so people must respect authority, rules, and social order (Stage 4). On Level Two, relationships and society take precedence over individuals. People maintain rules because they understand that society needs rules. Level Two is a more advanced than Level One because individuals don't function on the basis of private rewards and punishments, but on broader relationships dealing with people, law, and society.

Kohlberg's Level Three is called *Formal Operations* (ages over thirteen years) and is characterized by abstract thinking that balances the individual with society. All people are in harmony with one another. The primary instrument for harmony among people is *justice*, which Kohlberg defines from within a Platonic worldview. "Right" has been critically examined and agreed upon by society. Laws are made for people, not people for laws. So laws can be changed in order to make society and people more just for all. Laws are rationally considered and based on the principled thought of equal justice for everyone. National constitutions and international laws are examples of Level Three *Formal Operations*. A person should therefore consider the broad application of equal justice for everyone — which is not concerned with rewards, punishment, or pleasing others or merely following the law because it is the law. The universal base of justice is the crux of moral decision making for Level Three people.

Beyond Kohlberg's three levels, it would be helpful to revisit a fourth level that he suggests in some of his lesser-known writings. Kohlberg quickly rejects this new level as not being a moral judgment because it is based on supererogation (performing more than what is required by obligation) and not based on more mature moral development. However, all of Kohlberg's attempts to make justice the universal capstone of moral development require a constant weighing of people's rights against each other and against an individual's self-interest. This procedure results in nothing more than a sophisticated legalism, with more weighing and deciding based upon more moral calculations.

I want to amplify that which Kohlberg only suggests and then rejects, especially as it pertains to Christian interests. Kohlberg's Level Four is a final level that allows a person to act justly for other than legalistic reasons. Level Four is grounded in God's agape love for the world — his unconditional love — and the compassionate sacrifice of the Lord Jesus Christ for his people. Moral and ethical judgments don't need to be based on externals or even on principles of justice. Level Four, therefore, seeks loving decisions and actions. It is set upon nothing except God's foundational affection. For if God used only the rule of justice in making moral decisions regarding humanity, then we would all be condemned.[2] Instead, in both the Old Testament (through the concept of loving-kindness and steadfast mercy) and in the New Testament (through agape love), God does not merely treat people with calculated justice. Rather, God extends unconditional forgiveness to individuals in both the Old and New Covenants. And that forgiveness was never based on the impossible demand for human obedience to his just law. God's forgiveness emerges through his offer of agape, mercy, grace, and loving-kindness to all who truly believe.

Jesus Christ, then, is the ultimate demonstration of the agapic level of moral judgment. When people are fully mature in their moral development, they consistently and habitually make moral decisions based on agape. The person who is supernaturally strengthened by agape love will be challenged to ask this two-part question: What does the other person need *and* what can I do to help them satisfy that need? The highest level of moral decisions, therefore, is not grounded in some complex moral calculus system, but in the divine revelation of agape, the undeserved and unreserved love for the other person.

Sculptor Three: James Fowler and Faith Development

To begin, there are significant differences between the Christian meaning of "faith" and Fowler's use of the word. Fowler defines faith development as a *verb*, "to faith."

Like a verb, faith means to know, to construe, and to interpret (cognitively and affectively) one's own definition of ultimate reality, which exists within a relational-covenantal triad composed of one's self, one's community, and whatever a person understands of the Transcendent. By application, "to faith" is the action that people take to make sense out of their understanding of ultimate reality.

Consequently, Fowler's faith developmental theory applies equally well to any and all religious, non-religious, and philosophical systems. It doesn't matter if an individual espouses Christianity, New Age, atheism, or agnosticism. Every person gives ultimate allegiance to some idea, ideal, or deity. All people have faith development, then, since they all potentially give their ultimate allegiance to something or someone.

Fowler calls Stage One the *Intuitive-Projective Stage* (early childhood). A person at this stage primarily holds the faith of his or her parents or first caregiver. Thus, if someone is born into a Hindu family, this first faith stage is some form of Hinduism. The same principle applies to those born into any other religious or non-religious family. Faith is based on family authority. Primary adults determine ultimate reality and truth for young ones, who uncritically and unquestioningly imitate their elders.

Fowler labels Stage Two the *Mythic-Literal Stage* (childhood). This second category shifts the authoritative focus to the larger faith community. Ultimate reality and truth are what the predominant local religious (or non-religious) organization teaches.

Stage Three is the *Synthetic-Conventional Stage* (adolescence). At this juncture, people move beyond identifying with and internalizing the beliefs of people from their own immediate group. They still maintain those views, but they begin to synthesize the beliefs of "my group" with beliefs from others similar to, but beyond "my group." These larger group norms become the guiding factors for their faith development. Ultimate reality and truth are found in the creeds of that larger religious group. Thus, people at this stage identify with their larger denomination, where they can be heard to say, "We Presbyterians believe … or we Methodists believe … or we Baptists believe … or we Hindus believe.…" Third-stage people readily accept the faith that they are taught because they are still without skills of critical reflection to assess parents, respected religious leaders, and other heroes.[3]

Stage Four is called *Individuative-Reflective* (young adulthood). People in this stage take their commitments, beliefs, and attitudes to a deeper level as they face several tensions: between themselves and their community, between subjectivity and objectivity, between self-fulfillment and serving others, and between relativity and absolutes. Ultimate reality and truth exist within the boundaries that individuals themselves have developed internally. This includes personal construction of their own theology, philosophy of life, and worldview (*Weltanschauung*). In one sense, this fourth stage is the first time that a full internalization of faith occurs in Fowler's theory, because beliefs are personally owned, and individuals are no longer dependent on others to tell them what "to faith."

Stage Five is the *Conjunctive Stage* (adulthood). People at this phase recognize the validity of others' beliefs as they continue to internalize their own beliefs without discounting either point of view. A valuable perspective is gained by being part of a faith community that exists independent of diverse belief systems. Ultimate truth and reality go beyond clearly defined boundaries of standardized theological statements. People in Stage Five probe all facets of faith and faithing.

Fowler labels Stage Six the *Universalizing Faith Stage*. This is a very rare stage and one that is usually achieved only by those older than forty. These individuals realize that they are in the world and have oneness with God/god. Fowler describes this as a stage where participants have a "mystical experience" of unity with the Ultimate Reality. God directly communicates with them. In this stage, to know the truth is to know God. There is oneness with all of creation and the universe. This oneness causes a person to act in a radically different manner, espousing righteousness and justice and relationship with Ultimate Reality. All relationships are synthesized into one grand, complex, reflective scheme. People at this stage say, "God is on the throne and all is well with the universe, and I know that without doubt." Interestingly, Fowler's description of Stage Six suggests that all people at this stage recognize the God of the universe whom Christians worship.

Sculptor Four: Erik H. Erikson and Psychosocial Development

Erik Erikson identifies eight stages of psychosocial development from infancy through older adulthood. In each stage people face a crisis of choice between two alternatives — positive versus negative. If the crisis is not resolved positively, then a weakness appears in the psychosocial development of that person.

Stage One: *Basic Trust versus Basic Mistrust* (birth to one year old). Infants must determine if their environment is trustworthy and whether or not they can trust themselves. If parents are loving and nurture and care for the infant adequately, then the child senses basic trust in both the environment and in himself. Hope and trust are internally valued.

Stage Two: *Autonomy versus Shame and Doubt* (ages one to three years). Children seek to establish themselves as autonomous selves. The child's first "no" in response to an adult's command suggests that child is beginning to see himself as independent, not totally under the control of others. Control of body functions (e.g., toilet training) gives children more of a sense of self-control. If they do not properly develop autonomy, children will feel shame and self-doubt.

Stage Three: *Initiative versus Guilt* (ages four and five). Children seek to extend their relationships beyond their immediate environment to include people outside their homes. Children establish connections with playmates and others. If they are too aggressive in this task, they can be socially rejected and reap a sense of guilt because they are unable to make these connections. If they can positively establish relationships with others, they will develop a sense of purpose.

Stage Four: *Industry*[4] *versus Inferiority* (ages six to eleven). Children at this stage focus on skills that help them feel useful. If the skills are mastered, they feel competent and industrious. If few or no basic skills are developed, then a sense of inferiority and low self-esteem develop, along with a sense of worthlessness. Sports, academic accomplishments, music, and drama are some of the ways for children to become industrious and to attain a healthy sense of self-worth.

Stage Five: *Identity versus Role Confusion* (ages twelve to eighteen). Teenagers live in the middle of major developmental progress that seeks self-identification. Philosophical questions of life lie at the core of this stage: Who am I? What do I value? Whose am I? And who are my friends? If adolescents satisfactorily navigate these questions, they demonstrate that they possess a respected self-identity, which provides a foundation for them to establish their lives. Failure at this stage causes confusion in self-understanding, so that youth are unable to commit themselves to others. They cannot be "true to themselves" because they don't know who they are.

Stage Six: *Intimacy versus Isolation* (ages eighteen to thirty-five). Post-adolescents face the challenge of giving themselves to others in loving, caring, and intimate relationships. Without intimacy, teens become disengaged — severed from those who would provide fullness. The emotional growth is stunted as adults. With intimacy, teens are strengthened from being able to love and be loved with mature personal development.

Stage Seven: *Generativity versus Stagnation* (ages thirty-five to sixty-five). Adults must regularly choose between continuing to give themselves away (e.g., by encouraging others to learn, grow, and develop) or not (e.g., by conserving whatever they have accomplished). Failure to be generative causes self-absorption and selfishness. For example, business people who are near retirement may continue to encourage their business associates to take more responsibility, or they may seek to isolate themselves from associates through attempts to control everything. Choosing the first option generates an ongoing legacy with colleagues, while choosing the second shackles one's legacy to selfish outcomes. The former produces generativity, whereas the latter produces stagnation of all people involved (including the organization where this occurs).

Stage Eight: *Ego Integrity versus Despair* (ages over sixty-five). Older adults turn their attention to assessing their entire lives. As they make these reflective evaluations, they examine the contributions they have made to others. They ascertain whether their lives made sense and whether they made a difference. Everyone will recall both positive and negative occurrences, but the overarching hope is that one's life — as a whole — was positive. Without this conclusion, older adults experience despair regarding both their past and their future. They are left with a sense of boredom and purposelessness.

Practical Insights for Christian Ministry

Based on these major developmental theories, several guidelines can be drawn to promote the ongoing restoration of the image of God within believers (2 Cor. 3:18). The following seven specific suggestions are aimed to restore:

Insight #1: People are more alike than dissimilar. Christian education and formation are more effective when we understand how people, at various life stages, process their view of their particular reality.

Insight #2: Maturity is an anticipated process for all people; it is an inner process with which teachers and parents engage. The developmental issue is not *whether* a person will grow — but *how* and *in what direction*. Every Christian leader must know how to help people learn, grow, and mature. Although teachers, parents, pastors, and bosses can't control growth, each person assists (either positively or negatively) as an external influence. John Dewey, when talking about educational objectives, once cautioned his readers that without clear goals even a bank robber might "grow" to become a better bank robber!

Insight #3: Environment either enables growth or hinders it. Christian teachers and parents are responsible for helping to create and maintain settings that promote holistic restoration toward Christlikeness.

Insight #4: *Patterns* (or outcomes) of development can't be altered significantly or even accelerated. The *processes* (or procedures leading to outcomes) can be hindered but cannot be accelerated very much. All caregivers should work along with acceptable processes, not against them.

Insight #5: Development is rarely represented by a straight and smooth line on a chart. Growth is often uneven, almost random. It can be charted as slowing down, speeding up, or plateauing.

Insight #6: Development is an internal reorganization and construction of how people process their experiences. As individuals mature, they reorganize these inner categories of personal experience and construct new categories. The task of teachers and parents is to provide stimuli and guidance for these times of internal readjustment, which prompts growth toward ever-maturing levels. We Christian leaders must teach, nurture, and challenge — then we need to observe how individuals develop. If they don't, we must locate any possible disconnections: Was our teaching counterproductive, or was there some negative factor within the environment? Was there a certain internal factor out of sync within that individual that we love and serve, or was there a principle of human development forged by our Maker that we violated or overlooked?

Insight #7: When someone does not develop as they should or at all, dysfunction occurs. Some people, for whatever reason, refuse to change, yielding stagnation. Some are thwarted by environment or because they lack capable teachers and encouragers. In any case, failure to develop frustrates the will of God. Our loving Father desires total restoration for each believer. Jesus Christ is the very best example of this full human maturity (Eph. 4:13).

Conclusion

There are obviously more developmental theorists than the ones featured here, but these particular sculptors will always land within everyone's "Top Ten Theories List." It is important for Christian leaders who desire holistic restoration to be aware of ongoing research in the social sciences like these developmental theories. God's comprehensive truth often shines through such sources of general revelation. But even when it doesn't, we believers must still keep apprised of diverse current issues related to the ministries we serve. And that alone is why pertinent human development theories are worth both our attention and our input.

NOTES

1. This focus on a *hypothetical* situation — "How *should* a person act?" — as opposed to real behavior has always been one of the predominant criticisms of Kohlberg's research and theory.
2. This is the apostle Paul's persistent appeal, especially in books like Romans (see Rom. 2:5 – 10; 3:9 – 23; 6:23a; and 7:7 – 13).
3. For some teens, these larger "religious" groups might be defined as groups that are anything but religious. These adolescents may gravitate toward groups within subcultures like art, music, drama, sports, or technology.
4. "Industry," in this developmental stage, might be better known in its adjective form, rather than as a noun. In this way, a person who works and develops skills is called "industrious."

Part 2

INCARNATION FOR RESTORATION

How to Emulate Christ's Example

How to Emulate Christ's Example

Chapter 6

THE ROLE OF MASTER TEACHER: FOLLOWING JESUS' ANSWER TO *WHERE?*

A boy and his father are in a car accident. The youngster is rushed to the nearest hospital ER and requires surgery. In the operating room, the surgeon takes one look at the boy and exclaims, "I can't operate on him. He's my son!" How is that possible?

The answer, of course, is that the surgeon is the boy's mother.

Jesus' Five Life Roles

This riddle is a reminder of an important lesson from Jesus' life: he is much more than our precious Savior. He assumes many roles. But his are not arbitrary roles. Each is calculatingly deliberate. In particular, Jesus takes on five roles to answer the five questions of life (analyzed in chapter 3). These questions are inquiries we all raise at one time or another. They are universal. A *review* of those five universal questions, coupled with a *preview* of the next five chapters, follows in chart 6.1. Then Jesus' first role of Master Teacher is analyzed.

CHART 6.1 — Five Life Questions and Jesus' Answers

Five Life Questions	Jesus' Answers (chapters 6 – 10)
Q#1 — "*Where* did I come from?"	Jesus is the *Master Teacher* who begins his instruction by focusing on our creation significance, made in the image of God. *Chapter 6*
Q#2 — "*What* is my background and culture?"	Jesus is the *Faithful Learner* who, as a human himself, purposefully studies history and culture, while remaining holy. *Chapter 7*
Q#3 — "*Who* am I?"	Jesus is the *Son of Man* (his favorite title for himself), which means "totally human." *Chapter 8*
Q#4 — "*What* should I do with my life?"	Jesus is the *Great Physician* who follows his Father's restoration plan for all creation while displaying servant leadership to other people. *Chapter 9*
Q#5 — "*How* do I get to where I must go?"	Jesus is the *Submissive Servant*, submitting his personal will to the Father's will, which makes him completely mature. *Chapter 10*

Each of the five "hats" Jesus wears is backed by intentional thought and purpose. Our Lord is not just our generic life example; he pinpoints roles that precisely match our major life inquiries and needs. When all roles merge, we get something of an "aha" insight, like what happens when we fit together the last sections of a jigsaw puzzle. Consequently, Church Father Athanasius correctly claims, *"He became what we are that he might make us what he is."*[1]

The three sections of this chapter provide solid support for the Father's restoration plan for his people. The first section highlights "how we became what we are," and the last two sections feature how Jesus begins to "make us what he is." The Father's corresponding role in this chapter is "faithful Creator" (1 Peter 4:19b).

Prelude to Following the Master Teacher: Returning to Eden

Answering the first universal life question, *"Where* did I come from?" Jesus grounds his instruction in pre-fall creation three times. This curriculum pattern is not random. It is a pointed reply to the challenges of human origin and related issues. The Master Teacher consciously establishes a creditable starting point — both historically in Adam and Eve, and literally in our own birth — since every person ponders his or her beginning. It's only natural (and supernatural) that this first question stirs inside us.

Christ's three creation examples supply a threefold strategy: (1) to return to Eden to understand what we once had; (2) to emphasize God's image in all people; and (3) to stress the task of holistic human restoration — especially that full health comes by adhering to God's holy standards. Here's a quick summary of those three pro-creation passages:

+ In Matthew 19:1 – 4 the Master Teacher responds to his enemies' challenge to describe his own view of divorce by quoting Genesis 1:27, which highlights humanity's special creation in God's image.
+ Mark 2:23 – 3:6 features the Master Teacher's instruction on two separate yet consecutive Sabbaths. On the first Saturday, Jesus reviews the original Seventh Day and concludes with two potent truths: "The Sabbath was made for man, not man for the Sabbath. So the Son of Man is Lord even of the Sabbath" (2:27 – 28). On the next Saturday, Jesus proclaims that people should "do good" — even on the Sabbath. Then he demonstrates what that "good" looks like, as he fully restores a man's withered hand (3:4 – 5; also see Matt. 12:13).
+ Matthew 25:31 – 40 refers to the Lord's eternal blessing for the righteous "sheep," expressly noting the "time" their gift was issued: it has always been prepared "since the creation of the world" (v. 34). Verses 37 – 40 add the "why" of their gift: the righteous are given eternal life because they genuinely serve the needy as true Christians should serve — without expecting payback — which

actually means they are serving the Lord. A foundational link is now forged: How we treat people EQUALS how we treat God (see Jer. 22:15 – 16 and James 3:9).

Two of these three references to Eden also inject Jesus' scathing critique of his well-educated opponents: "Haven't you read?" In essence, Jesus says, "You aren't reading the Bible the way you should. You have to begin at Eden. Start where it all started." The Master Teacher then offers them an alternate, *comprehensive* plan of instruction for godly living. It is a plan that must start in Genesis 1.

Jesus' Eden focus is so strong in these three passages that I label them the "New Eden Standard" (see figure 6.1). In the creation account, we begin a refreshingly biblical understanding of people. The three creation passages cited above examine three complementary topics:

+ Our Origin
+ Our Responsibilities
+ Our Relationships

Origin is discussed below; Relationships are addressed in chapter 8 and Responsibilities in chapter 9.

FIGURE 6.1 — The New Eden Standard

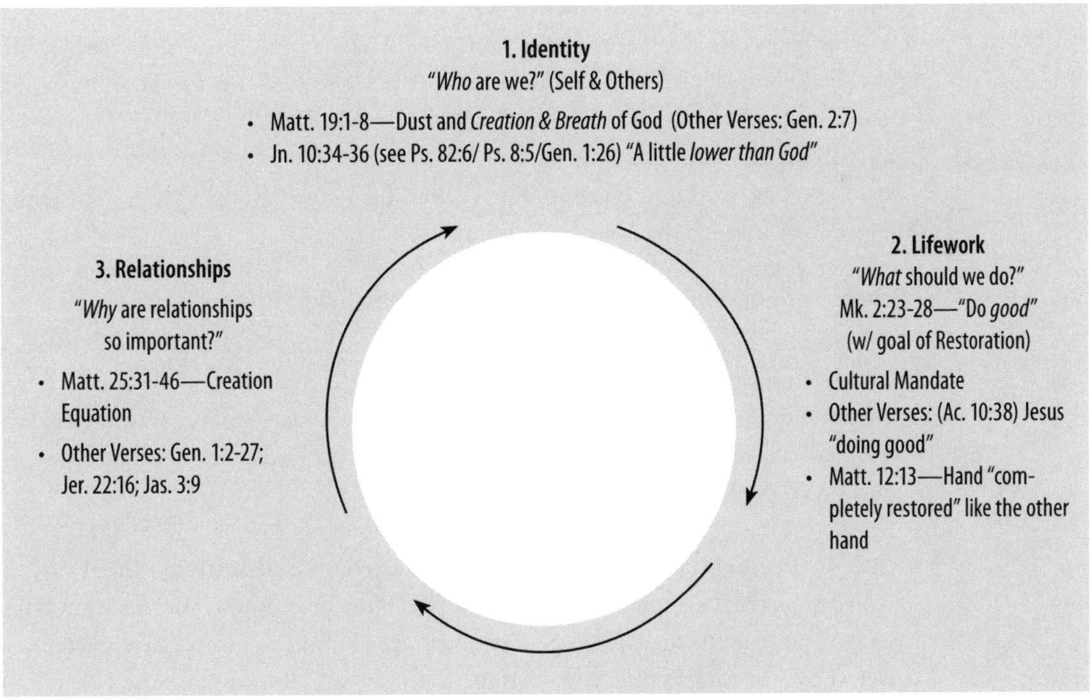

1. Identity
"Who are we?" (Self & Others)
- Matt. 19:1-8—Dust and *Creation & Breath* of God (Other Verses: Gen. 2:7)
- Jn. 10:34-36 (see Ps. 82:6/ Ps. 8:5/Gen. 1:26) "A little *lower than God*"

3. Relationships
"Why are relationships so important?"
- Matt. 25:31-46—Creation Equation
- Other Verses: Gen. 1:2-27; Jer. 22:16; Jas. 3:9

2. Lifework
"What should we do?"
Mk. 2:23-28—"Do *good*"
(w/ goal of Restoration)
- Cultural Mandate
- Other Verses: (Ac. 10:38) Jesus "doing good"
- Matt. 12:13—Hand "completely restored" like the other hand

Our Origin: More on Matthew 19:1 – 8

Centuries after the Holy Way of God is announced in Isaiah, Jesus reintroduces it and its relevance for both his day *and* ours. Christ's bold recall of the sinless garden days supports the Creator's plans for righteousness, which he has always had for his people. Matthew 19:1 – 8 begins with Jesus being verbally attacked by Pharisees, who push him to validate Moses' extremely lenient divorce policy — "to divorce ... for *any and every* reason" (v. 3b). Instead of placating the Pharisees by compromising God's Word, the Master Teacher deliberately communicates a half-dozen concepts, each of which upholds the New Eden Standard.[2]

What Jesus teaches is neither an unrealistic look at the past nor some nostalgic "good ol' days" pep talk. Jesus' flashback is not merely descriptive. The Great Physician issues a *prescription* for all humankind, the way we must live if we desire complete health.

> The Bible tells us who we are.... We do not need to be confused, as is much of modern mankind, about people's distinction from both animal life and ... complicated machines.... Suddenly people have unique value.
>
> — FRANCIS SCHAEFFER,
> *WHATEVER HAPPENED TO THE HUMAN RACE?*

Correspondingly, we can also lean on the Father's character of goodness as faithful Creator. Why? Because that title means God not only creates everything, but graciously sustains it. James 1:17 says it best: "Every good and perfect gift is from above, coming down from the Father of the heavenly lights, who does not change like shifting shadows." We can count on those two incredible promises: the Father is the source of every good gift and he is changeless.

The "way from the beginning" (Matt. 19:8b), Jesus prescribes, is the path of life that obedient disciples need to always pursue. It is the standard for all saints for all time. The Son essentially instructs, "Don't undo what the Creator did! Don't even think about messing with it!"

In response to Life Question #1: "*Where* did I come from?" then, Jesus sufficiently answers with the New Eden Standard.

Process of Following the Master Teacher: Restoring Image Traits

Nine education-formation insights arise from Jesus' three years of public instruction.[3] Each insight identifies a *specific human trait that represents God's image*. Each trait potentially indicates God's character, yet each ultimately needs restoration. All nine insights are as relevant and transferable as those found in the latest textbook of educational psychology.

#1 — The Trait of Ability: Honor Your Learner's Self-Initiated Input

Every person, because of being made in God's image, possesses the awesome abilities to contribute to the church's educational opportunities. From Eden, people are given the command to rule over creation and a special blessing from the Creator to

PART 2: Incarnation for Restoration—*How to Emulate Christ's Example* actually accomplish that task (Gen. 1:28). Humans are endowed with the talents to both learn and teach (Gen. 2:15 – 23), and they are given a range of communicative skills to express both reason and emotion (Gen. 2:20b – 23).

Robert Radcliffe's research reveals that, of the 125 teaching situations in the Gospels, approximately 60 percent are initiated by the people Jesus encountered. Given what has been identified in this trait of *ability*, we shouldn't be awed by this percentage. But Radcliffe probes deeper when he asks, "Why would Jesus wait for people with limited knowledge to raise the issues he knew needed to be discussed? Waiting for people to initiate, even if he knew they would, just doesn't seem to be a wise use of our Lord's time." Then Radcliffe offers this application: "If the Lord of the universe allowed and even encouraged his pupils to raise questions, comment on what he said, and in effect, participate in guiding the direction of the teaching episode, how much more should we?"[4]

> People are special and human life is sacred, whether or not we admit it.... Every person is worth fighting for, regardless of whether he is young or old, sick or well, child or adult, born or unborn, or brown, red, yellow, black or white.
>
> — FRANCIS SCHAEFFER,
> *WHATEVER HAPPENED TO THE HUMAN RACE?*

In light of this seemingly inefficient plan, there must be something important about patiently waiting for and encouraging learner response. By creating a student-sensitive approach, teachers are empowered to understand their students' concerns. That benefit alone is worth the wait time, thinking time for students and teachers alike. But such a change from teacher- to student-centered focus is both radical and fundamental. Many teachers, who like to hear the sound of their own voices, are threatened by more student talk. They perceive this as a loss of control.

Perhaps the most comprehensive, positive alterations to the traditional learning experience come when a teacher simply values the learner *as a person*, not *for what he or she can do*. This approach lies at the heart of Christian education and formation.

#2 — The Trait of Personality: Know Your Students as Individuals

Personality is the collective sum of distinctive and private qualities in an individual. In a related yet different sense, groups of people also possess a certain type of personality. A few times in Scripture, Jesus' enemies tried to stone him. We often describe these groups as having a "mob mentality."

From the creation account, the theme of personality arises through God's gifts to Adam and Eve (the abilities to learn, teach, solve problems, to rule over creation, to work and to care for the garden, and to communicate). Perhaps the most important gift (which tends to ignite the other gifts) is the *individual* blessing of human will, enabling us to choose, to obey or disobey, and to serve (Gen. 2:16 – 17). Since this latter gift is individual (everybody chooses for him- or herself), it's more than likely that the Creator customized the former gifts, too — at least, in terms of gender differences — so that Adam and Eve learned, taught, and solved problems each in their own way, their own style.

Prudent teachers know that circumstances in the classroom constantly change. Effective leaders "read" these circumstances, processing both proactively and reactively, just as Jesus did.

First, our Lord Jesus intentionally studies the situation, accessing learners individually and collectively, before he responds. The gospel of Mark records that Jesus purposefully "sat down opposite the place where the offerings were put and watched the crowd putting their money into the temple treasury" (Mark 12:41). He carefully observed that many wealthy people tossed in "large amounts" of money; meanwhile, a poor widow gave only two insignificant copper coins. Calling his disciples over to him, Jesus concluded: "I tell you the truth, this poor widow has put more into the treasury than all the others. They all gave out of their wealth; but she, out of her poverty, put in everything — all she had to live on" (Mark 12:43 – 44). Jesus' careful observation of an individual person (among several others) produces significant findings regarding our responsibility to participate in offerings.

By proactively reading their own students, classrooms, and larger culture, contemporary instructors emulate Jesus. Patient observation like his can bring a wealth of insight into students' motives, values, aims, and behaviors.

Besides *proactive* skills, *reactive* abilities are also critical for the skillful teacher. Christ demonstrates both skills in Luke 13:1 – 5. Some people told Jesus about "the Galileans whose blood Pilate had mixed with their sacrifices." Upon hearing this gory report, Jesus turned the gruesome news into a relevant lesson by quizzing the listening crowd. "Do you think that these Galileans were worse sinners that all the other Galileans because they suffered this way? I tell you, no!" Jesus knew how to take a familiar local news item and link it to his listeners' misunderstandings about that particular event.

This is analogous to today's teacher who, upon inferring how his or her students might be processing some disaster like Hurricane Katrina, tells the class: "Don't think of this awful event as necessarily God's judgment. Those victims were no more evil than those who were spared. Be careful what you tell yourself about such tragedies."

Good Christian educators know their students as individuals, whether it's before, during, or after an educational encounter.

#3 — The Trait of Boundary: Know Your Learner's Limits

Perhaps the most underrated characteristic of God's image is that it contains *limits*. Because this chapter's discussion of image is largely framed within the days before the fall, we know that the Creator's own restrictions (Gen. 2:16 – 17) still exist within Eden's parameters to be assessed as "very good" (Gen. 1:31). That is, humans — even perfect humans — need limits and boundaries. We are made to function best and to experience our fullest, most satisfying lives within God's boundaries. This particular principle needs extensive exposure in today's church.

Besides those bedrock theological boundaries, the less substantial borders in Christian education-formation must be heeded. For instance, effective teaching often boils down to balance and moderation. Extreme positions overlook substantive and complementary sides of biblical education. This wisdom is particularly needed in cases involving the teacher's basic question: How far do I push my students? What represents "too little" and "too much"?

Jesus accommodates his followers. He demonstrates the need for all teachers to precisely know "where the student is." Jesus knew how to locate an instructional starting point. Mark 4:33 records: "With many similar parables Jesus spoke the word to them, as much as they could understand." Implicit in this pivotal verse is the fact that he realizes exactly how much his disciples can understand before he tries to teach them something new.

How did Jesus determine their comprehension level? He "reads" their nonverbal cues, from puzzled looks to enlightened countenances. He listens to their feedback, from questions to commentary. He observes how they respond to each other regarding what he says. He thoroughly knows each disciple's idiosyncrasies, abilities, and weaknesses.

At least twice, Jesus is prevented from discussing certain issues because his audience is not ready. For example, he states, "I have spoken to you of earthly things and you do not believe; how then will you believe if I speak of heavenly things?" (John 3:12). Likewise, John 16:12 notes Jesus' confession that, "I have much more to say to you, more than you can now bear."

Translated into modern teaching-learning settings, Jesus encourages instructors to admit to their hearers: "We've got to stop here. We can't finish the complete lesson I prepared. We'll need to spend more time on this material we've already discussed before we move on."[5]

On the other hand, Jesus doesn't always allow his listeners' limited personal experience and understanding to restrict his teaching. At times he challenges them to move beyond their present state — sort of a "Let's get with the program, guys!" type of challenge.

#4 — The (Twisted) Trait of Deformity: Dare to Confront Ignorance, Stubbornness, and Prejudice

At some point we need to acknowledge the distorted realities of God's image that we face and not just focus on our sinless beginnings. This shift reflects one applied "boundary of balance" that alternates between the *ideal* of the first Adam and the *real* culture of the last Adam, Jesus, which was fallen. So for the sake of equilibrium, the next insights locate some of our educational challenges on this side of Eden. The trick is to maintain balance: not to overlook our sinfulness, while at the same time remembering our priceless God-breathed origin.

When godly instruction and nurture are conducted properly in a fallen world, all types of broken human bridges hold out hope for repair. Jesus is the ultimate model for how to rebuild those human bridges. This is best expressed by his enemies, who criticized him by calling him, ironically, the "friend of sinners." The Son of God serves both the down-and-outers and the up-and-outers by extending dignity to all people. Furthermore, since most people are receptive to what he says, our Lord is empowered to minister freely to those who admit their need for him.

Consider the converse perspective, which reflects ignorance: *In the minds of some, Jesus isn't the "successful" educator everybody thinks he is.* These cynics revisit the time Christ tells the rich young ruler what he has to do to gain eternal life. As the man turns sorrowfully and walks away, Jesus doesn't pursue him. On a harsher note, some refer to instances when Jesus finds no time for those who attempt to entrap him. When plotting religious leaders verbally challenge Jesus with the demand to know where he gets his authority, Jesus promises to satisfy their inquiry if they first answer his question about the authority of John's baptism (Matt. 21:23 – 27). The religious leaders know their trap has been sprung on them, so they stubbornly refuse to answer Jesus' return question. He stops talking with that small group. There are examples of prejudice too, including representative biases (just in John's gospel) against women (4:27), Samaritans (8:48), and a blind man (9:34).

Jesus has little time for those who think they know it all. *He doesn't teach the unteachable.* In fact, that's impossible to do. In such cases where he *does* get heard, however, the wide range of societal castaways who participate seems endless. He consciously and consistently serves the unlovely. In so doing, he attacks every form of human bias known, from sexism to racism and from ageism to sheer snobbery. We too quickly forget the blatant ignorance and prejudice in the historical period of time that Jesus lived. Or maybe our own ignorance, stubbornness, and prejudice blind us to our own problems.

It is within this hostile milieu that Jesus radically revolutionizes the social order. Once again, he sees people for *who* they are, not for *what* they are, or what they will become or produce. It's a sobering lesson for twenty-first-century Christian education, which often emphasizes outcomes and not the student.

#5 — The Trait of Sentimentality: Appeal to Their Basic Human Emotions

Another example of Jesus' educative-formative skills is his ability to address the emotional conditions of his hearers. In the Sermon on the Mount alone (Matthew 5 – 7), a broad spectrum of topics deal with various emotions, mostly damaged and distorted ones:

- Mourning (5:4)
- Anger (5:21 – 26)
- Lust (5:27 – 30)
- Retaliation (5:38 – 42)
- Love for enemies (5:43 – 48)
- Giving to the needy (6:1 – 4)
- Lure of materialism (6:19 – 24)
- Worry (6:25 – 34)
- Criticism of others (7:1 – 6)

Today we speak of emotional intelligence, but centuries ago Jesus likewise promoted relevant learning from knowing his hearers' emotional states. He capably addressed human needs by pinpointing virtually every inner drive.

#6 — The Trait of Inclusivity: Involve Your Learners in Their Own Learning

From the beginning in Eden, Adam is invited to "problem solve." The first identified assignment that comes from ruling over creation is to name the animals. But God does not sit by idly. First, at creation he provides Adam with all the necessary human tools he will need. Second, God models a task similar to the task of naming the animals when he earlier gives names to every star (Ps. 147:4). And third, the Creator gets even more directly involved as he rounds up all the creatures and brings them to the man "to see what he would name them" (Gen. 2:19b).

Repeatedly, the Son of God follows his Father's lead on earth. He seeks active involvement from his pupils as they confront life's problems. Contrary to the superficial version of this strategy, which values "activity for the sake of activity," Jesus' participatory strategies are purposeful, even from the very beginning of his work. To show his control over nature, Jesus commands Peter, who is fishing on the lake, "Put out into deep water, and let down the nets for a catch" (Luke 5:4). Peter's obedient, albeit reluctant, response yields a large catch. This participatory lesson prompts Peter to leave his nets, follow Jesus, and become one of the "fishers of men."

#7 — The Trait of Rationality: Be Sure Your Learners Use Their Heads

Several times God's image links up with skills of reasoning. The earlier example of Adam naming the animals represents both a right-brain and a left-brain phenomenon. By creating new names, the artistic, right-sided abilities of Adam are employed, and by distinguishing livestock from birds and from wild animals, Adam connects with the scientific left hemisphere of his brain.

Luke 14:25 – 33 exemplifies the imperative to think. In verses 28 – 32, Jesus sets the stage with two potent illustrations. First, Jesus asks what a person does who wants to build a tower. Answering with more rhetorical questions, he then asks: Won't this builder initially sit down and estimate the cost? Then won't he see if he's got enough money to finish, even before he begins? In fact if he does otherwise, won't he barely get started and then have to declare bankruptcy? Second, Jesus raises the topic of a king who is contemplating war with another ruler. Won't he, likewise, sit down and initially determine whether he (with 10,000 soldiers) can defeat an approaching army of 20,000? If he decides he can't, wouldn't it be far better — before the battle starts — to send a delegation to draft terms of peace? Both of the Lord's illustrations could not be more straightforward: We *use our heads* before important decisions are made. We're logical. We're rational. We plan accordingly or we might lose everything.

The very next verse (v. 33) commands, "*In the same way*, any of you who does not give up everything he has cannot be my disciple." What "way"? The way of thinking. Jesus pleads for followers to "count the cost." This process begins by consciously and literally counting by using our heads — yet I have *never* heard that challenge employed by Christians who extend an "altar call" to hearers concerning discipleship! They usually refer to something like, "What is your *heart* telling you?" They never ask the same question about our *heads*.

#8 — The Trait of Teachability: Mainly Serve Hungry Learners

"God helps those who help themselves" is an often-quoted phrase, erroneously attributed to the Bible. A fairer representation of Scripture is that Jesus *never* assists anybody who *doesn't* want assistance. Frequently Jesus asks "unusual" questions of those he meets, raising inquiries that seem to have really obvious answers. Or do they?

For instance, Jesus hears about a lame man who has lain by the pool of Bethesda for thirty-eight years. Upon meeting him, Jesus' first words are: "Do you want to get well?" (John 5:6). In a related manner, upon encountering two blind men, Jesus' initial response to their plea for mercy is: "Do you believe that I am able to do this?" To which they answered, "Yes, Lord" (Matt. 9:28).

Why did Jesus take what appears to be a reticent posture? A don't-get-involved-too-quickly attitude? In the first case, the "student" has to publicly identify, for himself, a particular need in his life. Every teacher is thoroughly frustrated by pupils who fail to admit what help they need. Nothing of substance happens between a teacher and a student until that student identifies his own personal need.

In the second case, the "students" Jesus meets need to publicly state that they believe that Christ (versus someone else) can help them. Admitting a personal need is one thing, but acknowledging that someone could actually help is another matter altogether.

Most contemporary instructors find that their hands are figuratively tied by learners who dismiss their teachers' assistance, expertise, or counsel. Students can only be helped once they decide they want to be helped. Jesus effectively models this fundamental premise of effective education.

Paralleling the principle to serve the hungry is the companion concept of readiness. In schools we speak of reading readiness, writing readiness, readiness for various physical activities based upon psychomotor development. In the example of the lame man (John 5:6) and the two blind men (Matt. 9:28), personal desire is virtually synonymous with readiness. Do they acknowledge they are ready for Christ's healing? Christ does not provide healing until they are ready.

Formal teaching and learning are no different. Covering material before students are ready is a waste of instructional time and teacher/student energy. What good teachers do is to continually set the stage for the introduction of new information. It's much like laying a foundation for a building. Any building without proper underpinnings is analogous to teaching lessons based on inadequate readiness.

#9 — The Trait of Identity: Press for Personal Ownership of Ideas

The most awesome privilege-responsibility combination that God gives people is the human will, which lets us choose. We choose to obey or not, and we choose who we will serve. Personal choice is not an inherent sign of rebellion, for the gift of choice first appears in pre-fall Eden as an implicit part of the Creator's one and only prohibition to "not eat from the tree of the knowledge of good and evil" (Gen. 2:16 – 17). Choice helps define our identity, who we are and who we are becoming. It ultimately provides the backdrop necessary for ownership (what we *really* value) as it asks each of us: What is it that you genuinely believe for yourself?

In teaching teens and some adults, there's nothing quite so aggravating as the learner who never claims personal ownership of an idea. Instead, that learner often cites authorities, "So and so said …" or traditions, "We've always done it this way." But for exceptional biblical education to occur, learners must personalize truth for themselves.

Jesus demonstrates his insights into these concepts when he takes the time to poll his followers. "Who do people say the Son of Man is?" (Matt. 16:13). It isn't like Jesus didn't know what others were calling him; rather, he is attempting to tabulate a list of public sentiments and opinions. No personal ownership is required of Jesus' followers to answer the first inquiry. There was no need to incorporate what they were about to say and their identity — who they were. They replied, "Some say John the Baptist; others say Elijah; and still others, Jeremiah or one of the prophets" (v. 14).

Jesus' follow-up question, however, quickly moves the discussion to the heart of the matter; it takes the conversation to the level of ownership: "But what about you?" Jesus asks. "Who do *you* say I am?" (v. 15).

Peter answers: "You are the Christ, the Son of the living God" (v. 16). Not only is Peter's insight correct and profound, but most Bible experts say that this personal testimony marks the watershed of Jesus' life and ministry. With Peter's words — a verbal extension of his personal identity — Christ's work suddenly shifts from public service to a private focus on his close disciples. The power of ownership instigates this dramatic shift.

Summary

The biblical commands for disciples to emulate Jesus as Master Teacher never demand our perfect completion of that task. But all grace-substantiated achievements of that task go a long way in satisfying humankind's question of origin. Christ-centered restoration, as odd as it might sound, begins at Eden's beginning. From a human perspective, that's where Life and Truth start. We are indebted to our faithful Creator, who makes all this possible. Subsequently, like Christ, we value the sanctity of each person's existence (based on God's image) and we honor all of the Word through our teaching and practice. As obedient disciples, we take active steps toward holistic restoration. We understand what we initially possessed as humans, what we lost in sin, and how — in Christ — we continue to renew all creation.

NOTES

1. Several years earlier, Irenaeus stated that same idea: "Jesus Christ, in his infinite love, has become what we are, in order that he may make us entirely what he is."
2. From Jesus' response in Matthew 19:1 – 8, six concepts are derived that support the New Eden Standard:

   + Jesus begins by sarcastically asking his verbal attackers if they had ever read Genesis 1 and 2 (Matt. 19:4a). This accusation might not sound too alarming until we realize that in Jesus' day everybody knew the Pharisees had actually memorized these chapters. We're certain that the Son now has his hearers' attention!
   + Jesus proceeds to quote the second half of Genesis 1:27 (how God made "male and female"). The first half of verse 27, which Jesus also revered, features the truth that every person was made in God's image (Matt. 19:4b).
   + Jesus next quotes Genesis 2:24, the "leaving and cleaving" guidelines found within the Creator's institution of marriage (Matt. 19:5).
   + Jesus then pronounces a personal blessing on the New Eden Standard by inserting his own commentary in Matthew 19:6, so don't look for those words in the Genesis account. Jesus' conscious words of blessing are that the husband and wife are no longer two people, but one. And because God joined these two together, they are not to be separated by anyone.
   + After one last attempt by the Pharisees to trick and persuade Jesus (Matt. 19:7), Jesus says that Moses' lenient interpretations of divorce are established only because of Israel's extreme hard-heartedness (v. 8).
   + Finally, Jesus concludes that Moses' divorce policies are not what God first intended — which was *not this way from the beginning* (Matt. 19:8).

3. These nine insights are modified from a similar list in Joyce Armstrong Carroll and Ron Habermas, *Jesus Didn't Use Worksheets: A 2000-Year-Old Model for Good Teaching* (Houston, TX: Absey & Co., 1996), 42–51.

4. Robert Radcliffe, "Jesus — The Teacher Revisited," *Christian Education Journal* 16 (Fall 1995): 85–97.

5. The human limitations of the twelve disciples prohibited Jesus' full instructional plans. Was this a sign of failure on our Lord's part? No, it's a sign of his moral virtues of sensitivity and accommodation. It's a realistic dimension of every teaching experience. All instructors are limited by their students' maturity (or immaturity). As do all good teachers, Jesus rejects two other options: speaking "over their heads" and manipulation.

Chapter 7

THE ROLE OF FAITHFUL LEARNER: FOLLOWING JESUS' ANSWER TO *WHAT?*

Scripture's greatest indictment of those who disconnect themselves — and their learning — from their past is Judges 2:10 – 11: "After that whole generation had been gathered to their fathers, another generation grew up, who knew neither the LORD nor what he had done for Israel. Then the Israelites did evil in the eyes of the LORD and served the Baals."

The disgraceful testimony of verse 10 reveals two serious transgressions: (1) Israel's ignorance of the Lord at a *personal* level, and (2) Israel's ignorance of the Lord's faithful work within their nation at a *historical* level. The consequence of that two-part neglect, from verse 11 on, begins a devastating cycle for several centuries: Israel rebels through idolatry; after several years, God turns his people over to an oppressive enemy; following a judgmental period in captivity, the Jewish nation repents; and this ushers in God's human judge, who rules until Israel lapses back into her rebellion. The entire book of Judges repeats that depraved cycle time and again. The anarchy and chaos are best described in that book's last verse (21:25): "In those days Israel had no king; everyone did as he saw fit."

By contrast, one of the best and most concise passages that links Israel's learning with their culture and faith is 1 Chronicles 12:32: "Men of Issachar, who understood the times and knew what Israel should do." Issachar was one of the twelve tribes, settling west of the Jordan River and just south of the Sea of Galilee (called the Sea of Kinnereth in ancient Israel). Jesus' hometown of Nazareth was later established close by Issachar's northernmost border.

This tribe's priceless testimony produces two specific types of knowledge that are difficult to master yet are critical for today's mature Christ-follower: (1) *descriptive understanding* to know "the times" — to comprehend what was happening in their particular culture; and (2) *prescriptive understanding* to know "what Israel should do." In biblical history, this second knowledge was always accompanied by faithful obedience to the Lord God.

Two Image Traits

In these two extreme cases, a pair of human characteristics emerges: the ability to *learn* and to *worship*. Both characteristics are permanently fixed to God's image in all people. Both require individual choice to exercise. And both are identified by the following questions, which everybody asks themselves throughout life:

- What will I learn (including personal values)?
- Whom (or what) will I worship?

Notice these questions don't say, *Will* I learn? or *Will* I worship? for that's like asking Will I breathe? and Will I eat? Learning and worship are givens — everybody participates — for good or for evil. What is important is *how* we regularly answer those two inquiries, based on personal decisions. The rebellious generation after Joshua, along with the tribe of Issachar, answer the same questions about learning and worship — but they end up at opposite ends.

What is your present answer to that universal inquiry of worship?

Behind the Scene of Jesus' Second Role

The second universal life question for every human being is "What is my background — my history and my culture?" As we saw in the previous chapter, this book necessarily modifies that universal question slightly to reflect our Christian faith: "What is my Christian heritage, and what are my values and my perspectives?" There also we saw that Jesus' answer to "Where did I come from?" features the comprehensive instruction of God's Word, starting where life and truth began — in Eden. The Father's main role is Faithful Creator. The Master Teacher models two traits of God's image from Eden: the characteristics of teaching and of mastery (doing things well). Both of these traits are detected in Adam's task of naming the animals, for he finishes his assignment competently (mastery) and communicates his selected animal names to future generations (teaching).

In this chapter we see how Jesus embodies the complementary side of teaching through his second role of Faithful Learner. Jesus is not only a dedicated "learner," but his witness as "faithful" speaks of his intentional holy living. Correspondingly, the Father's role is Holy One. The word for holiness is found at least eighty-four times in the Old Testament, counting only the references to the Father's nature and how he makes his people holy. The book of Isaiah alone reaffirms that theme thirty times (see especially Isa. 6:3).

In Eden, our God-given traits reflect both learning and holiness. Learning is described by Adam's careful observation of the animals before he names them. Two extensive categories are recognized (Gen. 2:20) through the terms "livestock" and "beasts of the field." Faithfulness centers in the spiritual devotion that Adam initially demonstrates toward his Maker.

Jesus is also a tenacious and consecrated learner. Luke 2:40 and 52 signal his holistic growth — both as a few-days-old infant and as a twelve-year-old. But his learning didn't stop there. Several subsequent passages speak of his active lifelong learning pattern. Jesus is also devotedly obedient to his Father. Regarding sin, Jesus is spotless. He is without sin because he is God. Yet we also see Jesus actively confronting temptations in order to stay holy.

Jesus was a devoted student, one who learned in essentially the same ways that all people do, while he maintained holiness. He predominantly learned from two wide-ranging sources — natural and supernatural — that are available to us today. We can become more like our Faithful Learner every time we emulate Jesus' routines of learning and righteous living while trusting in the Holy One.

Natural Sources of Jesus' Learning

Let us look at the five sources (from what is known as "general revelation") selected from Jesus' personal life.

#1 — Diverse Settings

Sometimes we forget that Jesus lived a fairly ordinary Jewish life up to age thirty. His avenues of understanding were like those of all Jewish boys:

+ Learning through formal dialogue with teachers in the temple courts (Luke 2:46 – 48), which parallels the rabbinical school structure of "listening to them and asking them questions"
+ Learning through the informal education in the home.

What was Jesus' home life like? Although few verses reveal direct answers, several biblical statements indirectly address that topic. Matthew 1:19 describes Joseph as a righteous man who was kind to Mary. He was obedient to God's revelation through his angel (Matt. 1:24), and he exhibited realistic human fear (Matt. 2:22). Mary is described as "highly favored" (Luke 1:28), as "the Lord's servant," and also as obedient (Luke 1:38).

Together, Jesus' parents abide by the Jewish laws that especially nurture the family (Luke 2:21 – 39, esp. 39; and 2:41 – 42). Both indicate concern for their twelve-year-old's disappearance following the Passover (Luke 2:43 – 50). And even though neither understood Jesus' explanation for being in the temple, the fact that Jesus still obeys his parents illustrates the positive learning atmosphere in Jesus' home (Luke 2:50).

Jesus' learning also occurred through his apprentice work as a carpenter — and, ultimately, from being a full-fledged carpenter himself (Matt. 13:55; Mark 6:3a). The Faithful Learner's attendance at annual Jewish holidays (both as a child and as an adult) indicates the consistency within his healthy upbringing and learning (Luke 2:21 – 41).

#2 — Past Knowledge

Previous insights also launch Jesus into routines of lifelong learning. First, as a student of humanity, Jesus knows the evil nature of people (John 2:24 – 25), the evil thoughts we have (Matt. 9:4), and our evil deeds (John 3:19b). The Son of Man also knows people's basic needs, such as the need for physical nourishment (Matt. 15:32; Luke 8:53 – 55).

Second, Jesus is able to learn from erroneous ideas within his culture. He comprehends a popular *mis*understanding of his day, that a blind person is handicapped because of somebody's sin, usually his or his parents. The Twelve hold that belief, for their inquiry implies it (John 9:1 – 2). The Pharisees also buy into it (v. 34). But Jesus' earlier reply indicates that he wants nothing to do with that faulty thinking. Instead, he states that the reason for blindness in this particular case is so that "the work of God might be displayed in his life" (John 9:3).

Third, Jesus' specific knowledge of Peter's unrelenting love for fishing provides a helpful learning source. From that insight Jesus designs a hands-on learning activity for Peter that requires him to fish for tax money (Matt. 17:24 – 27)!

Three divergent sources of information — one in anthropology, one in theology, and one in ichthyology (the study of fish) — assist the Messiah, our Faithful Learner, to effectively modify his diverse ministries to needy people.

#3 — Current Experiences

The Master Teacher consciously shifts back to the vital role of Faithful Learner when he attends to his present-day understandings. Three helpful sources of knowledge are modeled by our Faithful Learner for every disciple:

+ Learning through human senses (Mark 5:32 – 34)
+ Learning through purposeful observation (Mark 12:41 – 44)
+ Learning through active listening (Luke 13:1 – 5)

In the first case, after somebody touches him in a crowd in order to be healed, Jesus attempts to locate that person. The disciples tell Jesus his search is futile because crowds of people press in on him. But Jesus doesn't heed their advice as he continues "looking around," relying on his sense of sight, which matches his earlier sense of touch.

In the second example, Jesus intentionally "sat down opposite the place where the offerings were put and watched the crowd putting their money into the temple treasury. Many rich people threw in large amounts. But a poor widow came and put in two very small copper coins." This behavior officially represents the study of subcultures, but informally it's called people-watching. What is so fascinating is how intentional the Faithful Learner is: deliberate as to where he sits, whom he watches, and how he distinguishes between types of givers. This second category of learning, in my opinion, is particularly underrated by Christian learners today.

In the third case, because Jesus is an excellent listener, the Faithful Learner hears the conversation about a well-known regional tragedy. Once again, this public knowledge is tied to a popular but false theological idea: that people who tragically perish are being judged by God for their personal sins. In our own day, religious leaders' comments about recent tragedies tell us that not all Christians have grown beyond this display of ignorance.

#4 — Dialogue

The simple give-and-take of conversation prompts many learning experiences for Jesus. I list five settings where this type of dialogue occurs. The new information the Messiah actually learns — just the way we can learn — includes (1) what "great faith" is (Matt. 8:5 – 10); (2) what are the publicly stated needs of the blind (Matt. 20:29 – 34); (3) how many loaves and fish Jesus has on hand (Matt. 15:34; Mark 6:38); (4) what happens in a couple of separate "mission trips" (Luke 9:10; 10:17); and (5) who the crowds claim Jesus to be, according to the polling of his disciples (Matt. 16:13 – 15).

#5 — Broader Culture

From the very widest range possible — across the entire culture — the Faithful Learner continues growing in his knowledge.

For example, three Scripture passages identify folklore or popular sayings. The first saying, "Physician, heal yourself," is linked to Jesus' hometown acquaintances attempting to force him to do miracles, which he refuses (Luke 4:23). The second (Luke 4:24) reminds us that a prophet is not accepted in his hometown. And the third passage (Matt. 16:1 – 4) notes that the religious leaders accurately "read" impending weather from the colors in the sky, but they cannot interpret "the signs" of their own wicked generation.

Two other passages announce unhealthy cultural practices, like that of the religious hypocrites' prayer life (Matt. 6:1 – 18) and their inadequate adult curriculum, which has been "standardized" for their culture (Matt. 5:21 – 48).

Lastly, Jesus proclaims that the sly but ungodly tradition of the Pharisees (involving "Corban," or gifts to God) actually breaks the commandment to honor parents (Matt. 15:1 – 11).

Each of these half-dozen citations recognizes a well-known cultural tradition in Jesus' day. Unfortunately, each of them also indicates something that is twisted. Yet precisely these types of illustrations provide excellent examples for how to ascertain specific cultural needs. All of these sources arm Jesus with a wealth of information as Faithful Learner. And every source remains relevant and available for us.

Supernatural Sources of Jesus' Learning

As the God-Man for thirty-three years, *Jesus is always God*. Nothing ever changes that status. However, because of the truth of *kenosis* (his voluntary commitment not to independently use any of his powers for thirty-three years), Jesus depends on the first and the third persons of the Trinity as well as on the Word of God. This last source, which is often called "special revelation," provides Jesus with substantial learning and holiness.

Many of the Son's blessings from these Supernatural Sources are "transferable benefits," meaning that *the Father or the Holy Spirit or God's Word may also direct those same blessings our way* as we similarly seek divine assistance the way Jesus did. The discussion in this section gives readers the opportunity to study several instances where Jesus receives aid from the Father, the Holy Spirit, and the Scriptures. Keep in mind that some of Jesus' blessings are intended only for him (e.g., the Holy Spirit's power to bring about his Virgin Birth).

Assistance from the Father

The Scriptures show that God the Father at times initiates necessary strength for his Son. Two particular events note the Father's outspoken encouragement toward Jesus. At Jesus' baptism he explicitly supports "my Son, whom I love; with him I well pleased" (Matt. 3:17). Then, at the Mount of Transfiguration, similar praise is heard: "This is my Son, whom I love; with him I well pleased. Listen to him!" (Matt. 17:5).

Following a plot to kill Jesus, Matthew records that the Messiah withdrew from that place. Continuing to heal, Jesus warns the crowd "not to tell who he was" (12:16). Matthew adds that this event fulfills Isaiah 42:1 – 4, including the prediction that the Father would "put my Spirit on him, and he will proclaim justice to the nations" (v. 18). That is, God was affirming his Son, in this life-threatening struggle, by anointing Jesus with the Holy Spirit.

The Father offers explicit help when it come to miracles, such as exorcisms (Luke 11:20). Other passages pinpoint Jesus' own initiative when it comes to receiving assistance from the Father. One indirect example is found in 1 Peter 2:23. This apostle testifies that when Jesus was insulted by his enemies, "he did not retaliate.... Instead, he entrusted himself to him who judges justly." Our Lord, then, drew straight from his commitment to God as faithful Judge.

More directly, perhaps the clearest accounts of explicit intervention are when Jesus intentionally goes off to pray and seek God's will (Luke 5:16; 6:12 – 16).

It is significant to remember here that this Father to Jesus is also called "our Father" (Matt. 5:16, 45, 48; 6:4, 6 – 8, 9, 14 – 25, 26, 32; 7:11 and so forth).

Assistance from the Holy Spirit

Multiple occasions note the ties between the Second Person of the Trinity and the Third Person. The Spirit plays an intricate role in Jesus' virgin birth — which is both "through the Holy Spirit" (Matt. 1:18) and "from the Holy Spirit" (v. 20).

The Holy Spirit is also present at Jesus' baptism, descending "on him in bodily form like a dove" (Luke 3:22; cf. Matt. 3:16 – 17). Then the Holy Spirit leads Jesus into the desert to be tempted (Luke 4:1) as well as back to Galilee (v. 14). The Spirit specifically strengthens Jesus to do ministry: teaching (v. 15), advocating justice (Matt. 12:15 – 21), and exorcising demons (v. 28).

One of the most remarkable evidences of the Holy Spirit's power in Christ is found in Luke 10:21, where the Son is uniquely described as being "full of joy through the Holy Spirit" immediately following the joy expressed by his seventy-two disciples-missionaries (v. 17).

Assistance from the Word of God

God's Word is called "the sword of the Spirit" by the apostle Paul in Ephesians 6:17, and that powerful metaphor is apparent in Jesus' life. For example, it is the only weapon the Son uses in his threefold temptation (Matt. 4:1 – 11; Luke 4:1 – 13). In his first recorded reading of Scripture (Luke 4:16 – 30) Jesus shows his familiarity with God's Word, and he specifically links its prophecy with his fulfillment of Isaiah 61:1 – 2 at that time.

Speaking of prophecies, there are numerous predictions that Jesus fulfills. Furthermore, he goes out of way at times to be sure that Scripture is fulfilled (Matt. 26:31, 54). Just as important, Jesus equates God's Word with "truth" (John 17:17). Finally, reversing the critique that came from his opponents, it is fair to assess that Jesus personally knew "the Scriptures" (Matt. 22:29).

Conclusion

An Illustration from *Pilgrim's Progress*

In John Bunyan's classic allegory of the Christian life, the main character spends several dark days in a dreary site known as Doubting Castle. Giant Despair captures Christian (the hero) and his friend Hopeful. In the dungeon the two men are beaten mercilessly by the giant. It gets so bad that the giant tries to convince the believers to take their own lives, showing them the bones and skulls of previously incarcerated pilgrims. Hopeful almost turns hopeless.

Giant Despair promises to tear the two believers into pieces at the end of ten days. Despair's wife, Diffidence (meaning "Distrust" in older English), warns the giant that his captives may have tools to pick the lock on their cell. Despair promises to search both in the morning.

Christian and Hopeful spend that same night in prayer, from midnight until almost daybreak. Just before the sun comes up, Christian speaks — half-amazed, but quite passionate: "What a fool am I, to lie in a stinking dungeon, when I may walk at liberty! I have a key ... called Promise, that will, I am persuaded, open any lock in Doubting Castle."[1]

Sure enough, with the key of Promise, every door they try opens with ease. The believers exit the dungeon and make it back to the King's Highway, where they are safe once again, because they are out of Giant Despair's jurisdiction.

We modern-day pilgrims need to similarly take inventory of what we already possess: the awareness of Jesus' example as Faithful Learner, our own access to the Father and the Holy Spirit, and the power of God's Word — the key of Promise — to live the Christian life victoriously.

NOTE

1. John Bunyan, *Pilgrim's Progress* (Chicago: Moody Press, n.d.), 136.

Chapter 8

THE ROLE OF THE SON OF MAN: FOLLOWING JESUS' ANSWER TO *WHO?*

I f someone said to you, "So tell me — what is a Christ-follower? What do they stand for? What do they look like?" what would you say?

I list below seven traits from Scripture that some people believe are characteristics of a Christian disciple. Pretend this is a pop quiz and rank these traits from one to seven, with one as your top attribute. After you finish ranking, you may want to read the passages that are associated with each trait.

Serious students of the Bible (like studying prophecies about the Messiah) (John 7:41 – 44; 50 – 52)

Totally committed to constant public worship (Luke 11:43)

Thankful they are not living ungodly lifestyles (Luke 18:11)

Careful to obey all of Scripture (like fasting and being cautious of blasphemy) (Luke 5:33; 18:12a; John 10:33)

Not afraid to publicly denounce the devil's work (Mark 3:20 – 22)

Intentionally living their lives before others (Matt. 23:5)

Faithfully tithing (giving 10 percent) to God (Matt. 23:23a; Luke 11:42; 18:12b)

Actually, *none* of these seven traits are solid answers for biblical discipleship. Someone pointed out that these seven are actually more descriptive of Jesus' enemies — the religious leaders of his day![1] Probably the *best* answer to the question "What is a Christ-follower?" is someone who is consistently recognized as having "been with Jesus" (Acts 4:13b).

Okay, so this quiz is bogus!

Jesus' Role as Son of Man

The third universal human question, *"Who am I?"* is best resolved by studying the person of Christ. That's not a cliché. *Nothing helps us know ourselves better than first understanding the one who created us, the one who then voluntarily became totally like us.*

I am not speaking about investigating an irrelevant theological treatise or an esoteric archaeological discovery. I refer to three practical aspects of Jesus' life that directly influence our lives in those same categories:

+ Who Jesus is
+ What Jesus believes about people
+ Whom and how God loves

One of my students prudently framed this perspective: For the most part, the better I understand Jesus' nature, the better I know my own. Hebrews 2:17 and 4:15 declare Jesus is "made like his brothers [us] in every way" and he is "tempted in every way, just as we are." That's the place to begin.

It is also valuable, in this light, to realize that Jesus' favorite name for himself is Son of Man, which simply means "totally human."[2] Whatever name Jesus selects as his all-time favorite must convey significance. And it does.[3] As the perfect Son of Man, Jesus fulfills all requirements for God's perfect sacrifice for our sins. That title also connects the sinless God-Man — as the Last Adam — to the First Adam (1 Cor. 15:45 – 49). Using that comparison, Scripture tells us who we are and who we will become in Christ.[4]

Who Is Jesus: Both Negative and Positive

It is often useful, when describing what you are talking about, to first discuss what you *don't* mean. The apostle Paul did this by initially identifying Israel as what *un*godly people look like. They are the kind of example we're *not* to follow.

FIGURE 8.1 — Heresies Concerning Jesus (Bible views in parentheses)

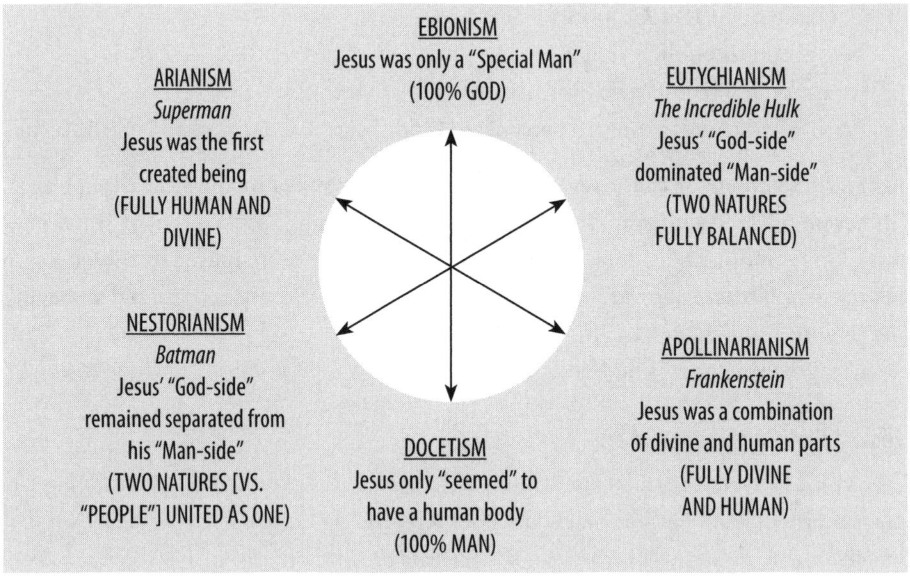

EBIONISM
Jesus was only a "Special Man"
(100% GOD)

ARIANISM
Superman
Jesus was the first
created being
(FULLY HUMAN AND
DIVINE)

EUTYCHIANISM
The Incredible Hulk
Jesus' "God-side"
dominated "Man-side"
(TWO NATURES
FULLY BALANCED)

NESTORIANISM
Batman
Jesus' "God-side"
remained separated from
his "Man-side"
(TWO NATURES [VS.
"PEOPLE"] UNITED AS ONE)

DOCETISM
Jesus only "seemed" to
have a human body
(100% MAN)

APOLLINARIANISM
Frankenstein
Jesus was a combination
of divine and human parts
(FULLY DIVINE
AND HUMAN)

Who Jesus Is Not

Six heretical views of Jesus are outlined in figure 8.1.[5] The following discussion identifies those six falsehoods as well as Scripture's correctives. These faulty views are grouped into three major categories: (1) whether or not Christ is actually God or man or both (technically known as the subject of *reality*); (2) whether Christ is fully divine and human (*integrity*); and (3) whether Christ remains God or man after the incarnation, when his two natures merge (*union*).[6] Figure 8.1 summarizes these heresies along with the evangelical response (parenthesized words in bold capital letters).

So, Who Is Jesus?

Again, Jesus is totally human — designated by the title Son of Man. He is our model for life. He is fully God and fully man.

One of the simplest, most useful illustrations of Jesus' total humanity (and ours) is shown in figure 8.2, the Hand Model.[7] From the thumb to the pinky finger, five distinct domains are represented. The palm stands for the human spirit, our spiritual dimension. The human soul is symbolized by the complete hand.

FIGURE 8.2 — The Hand Model of Humanity — Christ's and Ours

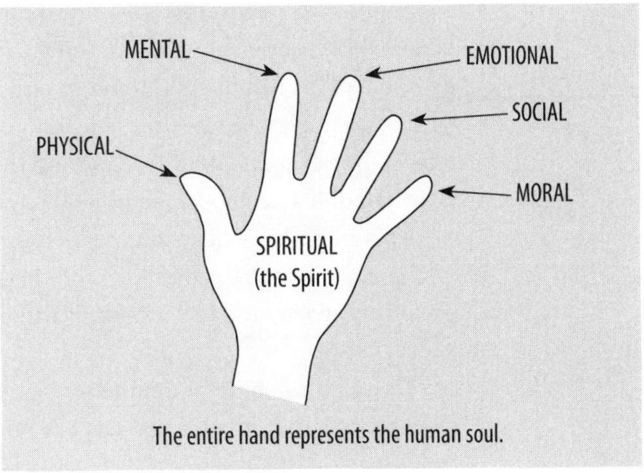

MENTAL · EMOTIONAL · SOCIAL · PHYSICAL · MORAL · SPIRITUAL (the Spirit)

The entire hand represents the human soul.

Space limits further details of Jesus' humanity. However, two additional resources are available for study.[8]

What Jesus Believes about People

In your mind, create sentences out of the following paragraph the way you normally would: Add commas, periods, capital letters, etc. Work fairly quickly, and *do not go back to make corrections.*

he is an old man and experienced in vice and wickedness he is never found in opposing the works of iniquity he takes delight in the downfall of his neighbors he never rejoices in the prosperity of his fellow creatures he is always ready to assist in destroying the peace of our society he takes no pleasure in serving the Lord he is uncommonly diligent in sowing discord among his friends and acquaintances he takes no pride in laboring to promote the cause of christianity he has not been negligent in endeavoring to stigmatize all public teachers he makes no effort to subdue his evil passions he strives hard to build up satan a kingdom he lends no aid to the support of the gospel among heathen he contributes largely to the devil he will never go to heaven he must go where he will receive the just recompense of reward

Regardless of how you punctuate that paragraph, if you are consistent, there is a second approach you could take. In other words, there are two solutions to this challenge.

Rethink that same assignment and discover that second solution.

(Don't read any farther if you don't want to know the two-part solution just yet.)

Solution #1 begins like this: "He is an old man and experienced in vice and wickedness. He is never found in opposing the works of iniquity. He takes delight in the downfall of his neighbors ... (and so on)."

Solution #2 goes like this: "He is an old man and experienced. In vice and wickedness, he is never found. In opposing the work of iniquity, he takes delight. In the downfall of his neighbors, he never rejoices ... (and so on)."

Amazing what a little punctuation can do, don't you think?

Spin a few commas this way, and the guy turns out to be an evil man. Spin a few periods that way, and he's an elderly saint!

Through a couple of parallels, what Jesus believes about people is reflected in this exercise. In fact, our Lord actually selects *both* solutions to express his views. For Solution #1, Jesus believes people are evil. That statement probably doesn't surprise most readers, because many are familiar with these passages:

- "Knowing their thoughts, Jesus said, 'Why do you entertain *evil thoughts* in your hearts?'" (Matt. 9:4).
- Jesus tells Nicodemus, "But *men loved darkness* instead of light because *their deeds were evil*" (John 3:19).
- "But Jesus would *not entrust* himself to them, for he knew *all* men. He did not need man's testimony about man, for he knew what was *in a man*" (John 2:24–25).

Jesus sides with the fact that all people are evil, and his view of sin was not superficial either. He makes it clear that unless an individual turns to him for salvation, because of his thorough depravity, he is "condemned already" for not believing in the Son (John 3:18). Christ also draws some implications of this evil human nature, like the limited knowledge of the religious leaders: "Why is my language not clear to you? Because you are unable to hear what I say. You belong to your father, the devil, and you want to carry out your father's desire" (John 8:43–44a).

There is no doubt that Jesus "punctuates" his view of all people with a Solution #1 approach. The Son of Man does not need to be persuaded about the devastation that sin makes inside every individual.

But Jesus also applies a Solution #2 perspective to humans who have been born again. He sees us believers as saintly because of what he has done.

Somebody once harmonized the ability to hold these two solution perspectives in tension by saying something like this: The balance of Scripture shows that people are both *in need of saving* and *worth saving*. The second phrase does not praise people but praises their Maker. The psalmist states this same truth in Psalm 8.

Reflect upon the wilderness temptations once more. In two of the three challenges the tempter begins with, *"If you are the Son of God ..."* (Luke 4:3, 9). He cruelly questions Christ's identity. And we might ask, "How could he?!"

Yet every time we view Christians — including ourselves — differently than the view God holds of us, we do exactly what the tempter did!

We question who saints really are, following the devil's example, because we settle for an inferior résumé of Christ-followers. And since we choose that perverted list of qualities over our Creator's list, we also create an idol.

How does God actually see us believers? Chart 8.1 provides ten assurances.

CHART 8.1 — Ten Out-of-This-World Assurances for All Believers

I am born again in Christ.	(John 3:3, 7; 1 Peter 1:23)
I am forgiven of all my sins.	(Ephesians 1:7; 1 John 1:9; 2:12)
I am free from the power of darkness and welcomed into God's Kingdom.	(Colossians 1:13)
I am victorious through God.	(Revelation 21:7; 1 Corinthians 15:57; 1 John 5:4; 2 Corinthians 2:14 – 16)
I am strong in the Lord.	(Ephesians 6:10)
I am safe from the Evil One.	(1 John 5:18; 2 Thessalonians 3:3; 2 Timothy 4:18)
I am being changed to become more like Christ.	(2 Corinthians 3:18; Philippians 1:6)
I am loved by God and called to be a saint.	(Romans 1:7; 1 Thessalonians 1:4)
I am blessed because I now have eternal life.	(John 5:24; Matthew 19:29; John 6:47)
I can do all things through Christ.	(Philippians 4:13)

Whom and How God Loves: Background Information

The third and final subtopic to the universal question, "Who am I?" centers on whom and how God (the Father and the Son) loves. The quick-fix answer is that God loves everybody — "all the children of the world," as the song goes. He even loves his enemies.

For some that's enough said, so they say, "Let's move on."

I disagree — not with the first part on God's love, but the last sentence.

I'm now going to do something I've never done before: I want to restrict my reading audience — well, sort of.

If you have *any* of the following characteristics, you will especially benefit from what you read next. Are you:

+ A sensitive and caring personality?
+ One who rarely says "no" to a friend's personal request?
+ An empathetic, feeling-type individual?
+ Someone who's intuitive and spontaneous (especially to needy people)?
+ One who desires mentoring for themselves and wants to mentor others?
+ Personality-wise (from Bible characters), one who is like a Barnabas?[9]

If these are not your personality traits (perhaps yours are more like the personality of the apostle Paul), you will also benefit, but more indirectly.

Why do I limit the focus of my audience? Because readers who identify with these traits — like Barnabas — *must* understand the content of this section: whom and how God loves. It is essentially meant for you and your particular approach to Christian growth.

I particularly base my personality comparisons of Barnabas and Paul on Acts 15:36 – 41. Barnabas's personality favors "people," as he decides to mentor John Mark and discontinue his missionary focus with Paul. The apostle Paul shows more of a "task" personality, since he returns, with Silas, to strengthen the churches that were earlier visited in Asia Minor.

The Pure Focus of God's Love

The Father and Son love the world, and they love their enemies. At a foundational level, furthermore (in the purest and best biblical sense), Jesus also loves himself with a thoroughly godly love. If he did not, the Son would not love himself the exact same way his Heavenly Father loves Him — God's Love Standard.

In light of this, there are two general statements I make about people who are more like Barnabas:

+ Empathetic Barnabas-people give so much of themselves to others that they often don't have a lot left to give the same care to themselves.
+ Barnabas-types are such caring people that they especially need to follow Jesus' example of loving one's self exactly as God does.

Because of these tendencies, many Barnabas-types suffer the consequences of low spiritual nurture and nourishment within the body of Christ.

A Practical and Necessary Curriculum

Four vital lessons about biblical, godly self-love need to be taught to the church — to every person and to every personality. Included in these lessons is the reality that *all* Christians really *do* believe in (and actually live by) godly self-love, whether they know it or not.

Lesson 1: Explain What Godly Self-Love Means. Godly self-love is "the biblical way to love ourselves *exactly* as God loves us — nothing more, nothing less, and nothing other than that."

Return to chart 8.1, which provides too-good-to-be-true blessings from our compassionate Father. In your mind, add to each entry: "God loves me so much that …" For instance, "God loves me so much that I am forgiven." In other words, that's how high into the heavens God sets the bar of his love for you! That's God's Love Standard for you as a Christ-follower, as his beloved daughter or son.

The question you must now ask yourself is: "Do I *really believe* God loves me *this much?*"

Anytime anyone loves you at a level that is different than that specific mark our Maker has set (whether too high,[10] too low,[11] or just "different"[12]), God's Love Standard is ignored, abused, or rejected.

The "anyone" in that sentence may be the person in your mirror. I knew a female disciple of Jesus who said to herself, "I don't think I've been forgiven of my sins, because God could not love me when I keep repeating the same sin" — even though she genuinely confessed her sins to God. First, she is not believing the Truth of 1 John 1:9, which promises us that God "is faithful and just and will forgive us our sins," subsequent to sincere confession. Second, she is not accepting the complete world our Father created — a world that includes divine forgiveness — which is just as real as other parts of his creation, like trees and butterflies, and fish. None of it is up for discussion. It simply exists. It's real. Period.

Finally, if this Christian woman refuses to accept God's forgiveness, she *also* refuses to accept the Father's love behind that wonderful promise to forgive. In short, one consequence is that *she is not loving herself as God loves her.* Her level of self-love is far too low. It is much lower than God's Love Standard for her.

Lesson 2: Explain What Godly Self-Love Does *Not* Mean. Based on the above definition, anything "more, less, or other" than God's biblical love for us equals what godly self-love *cannot* be.

The best passage that describes *ungodly* love is 2 Timothy 3:1 – 5: "But mark this: There will be terrible times in the last days. People will be lovers of themselves, lovers of money, boastful, proud, abusive, disobedient to their parents, ungrateful, unholy, without love, unforgiving, slanderous, without self-control, brutal, not lovers of the good, treacherous, rash, conceited, lovers of pleasure rather than lovers of God — having a form of godliness but denying its power. Have nothing to do with them."

The primary reason this passage illustrates *ungodly* love is that all six words for "love" or "lovers" come from the Greek root *phileo*, meaning "brotherly love." Contrariwise, godly self-love is described in terms of God's unconditional love, *agape*. That linguistic contrast also provides one example of why godly self-love never conflicts with the other duties of mature Christians, such as self-denial.

Lesson 3: Provide Biblical Examples of Godly Self-Love. Ephesians 5:22 – 33 features practical expressions of God's love for us. Then, it simultaneously expresses two related concepts: how husbands *should love wives* and how husbands *are already loving themselves* in godly ways. The best part of this familiar passage is that these biblical guidelines are God's ideas, not anything that a human being designed.

Ephesians 5 should humble every Christian husband, because we are each commanded to love our wife "just as Christ loved the church and gave himself up for her …" (v. 25). In contrast to 2 Timothy 3:1 – 5, every reference to love in this section of Paul's letter to believers at Ephesus springs from *agape*-type love in the Greek.

Did you ever teach a group of adults where, for whatever reason, the participants' maturity range was enormous? The spectrum might include brand-new believers as well as experienced and knowledgeable saints. That's never an easy group in which to teach every person, let alone to teach everyone well. Yet Ephesians 5 is a passage that has no problem addressing such a range of believers, those who are both immature and mature. All husbands ponder, for instance, how they will ever come close to Jesus' extraordinary sacrificial model. But that's the ideal command we must teach if we want to be true to all Scripture. Even though it is a perfect model of love, it's there in the Bible for a reason, and it will always challenge mature husbands in the body of Christ.

But God's grace also holds up husbands at the other end of the spectrum. Ephesians 5 identifies baby steps that any husband may take in obedience, moving them in the proper direction toward greater biblical challenges. Consider how Ephesians 5:28 – 33 commands every husband to love his wife, by citing the fact that he already loves his own body, which is God's Standard ("as") he should now use to love his wife. By loving his wife, the last half of verse 28 says he *is actually* loving his own body. Verse 29 adds these related truths: No one hates himself because, by feeding and caring for his own body, each husband also demonstrates godly self-love — loving himself in the practical ways that the Creator first loves him *and* wants him to love himself.

As it pertains to my spousal duties, then, when I provide food and nurture for my wife, I am both loving her and myself. I am also following Christ's example of practical love, which comes from nurturing the Church — "his body" — the Body of Christ (v. 29b – 30).

In sum, one could ask: "Do you feed and care for yourself?" *Any* positive response whatsoever indicates biblical, godly self-love based upon Ephesians 5.

Lesson 4: Provide Examples of Jesus' Godly Self-Love. Several illustrations could be cited here but the space limits of this book force me to discuss only one application of Ephesians 5:28 – 29 *from* Jesus' life and one application *for* our lives. Recall the biblical principle: Anytime Jesus — or anybody else — feeds or cares for himself, godly self-love occurs.

This daily behavior is nothing more or nothing less or nothing different than how the heavenly Father wants all people to mirror his love for them. It is yet another illustration of God's Love Standard. Several passages portray Jesus' feeding and caring for himself. But my limited focus settles in on a handful of passages where the Son of Man withdraws from the world. Why does he withdraw? For various reasons, including protection, relaxation, prayer, rest, restoration, and just to get away.

In each incident, Jesus is properly motivated by — and he experiences — godly self-love. There are two powerful categories of his self-love:

- Jesus exhibits godly self-love by his withdrawals from public ministry, accompanied by his disciples (Mark 3:7a; 4:34b; 6:31; 9:2 – 13; 14:32 – 34)
- Jesus exhibits godly self-love by private withdrawals, purposefully heading off alone (Mark 1:35; Matt. 14:13 – 15; Mark 14:35a; Luke 22:41)

Two of these most extreme cases are when our Lord completely gets away. Today we would say he turns off his cell phone and leaves behind the company car along with all company credit cards — even his personal identification.

The Son of Man goes beyond what most of us ever imagine he does: *Christ desires — he longs for — absolute secrecy!* In the first case, Mark 7:24 says Jesus takes off for Tyre, far off the beaten path, all the way to the Mediterranean coast — to a non-Jewish seaport town, of all places.[13] His motive? "He entered a house and *did not want anyone to know it.*" In the second case, John 12:36 concludes: "When he had finished speaking, Jesus left and *hid himself from them.*"

How many sermons have you heard on these two "incognito Jesus" passages? How many lessons have you been taught from these two verses? For instance, were you ever taught, from Mark 7:24, that Jesus did not want to be known as Jesus in Tyre? It's really a shame that the Church doesn't proclaim this message, because its truth lies at the heart of how our Creator wants every Christ-follower to see Jesus' proper self-love and to emulate him by similarly loving ourselves.

These two deliberate behaviors in Mark 7:24 and John 12:36 are pure expressions of the Son's godly self-love. Jesus needs to get away — totally away so he will not be known. It is not only a natural, human, and sin-free behavior, but also precisely what the Father wants him to do.[14] Specifically, the Father wants his Son to experience godly love through self-care. So when we have the same needs, and we do, we have our Brother's model in Scripture. His example is not only biblical; it is independent of unrighteousness.[15] Our escapes hold that potential as well.

Life Application Suggestions

There are an endless number of ways, then, we can love and care for ourselves as God does. The topic of sleep is one excellent illustration. How long has it been since you had a good night's sleep? How long has it been since you also read Psalm 127:2b, "he [God] grants sleep to those he loves"? Now combine those last two sentences. Also note how this love-gift of sleep promotes our Maker's ultimate purpose of holistic restoration.

God's love for us is unreservedly tied to his foundational blessings of personal care. [16] Every saint should have a "theology of sleep," because it pertains to such vital truths as God's conscious love for us, holistic restoration, and our biblical responsibility for self-care.[17]

Each of us needs to brainstorm more holistic strategies to care for ourselves — and to care for those we love. Fifteen rudimentary strategies are listed below to get started. But don't be tempted to speed-read through that list. Treat each item in the same manner we have just discussed sleep. Treat each entry for what it is: the dignified expressions of our Maker's love for you personally. Endnotes are added to three of the strategies because many of us might not readily notice their connection to practical self-care. Be sure to study those particular verses.

- Maintain a balanced diet
- Give thanks — to God and to others
- Laugh a lot[18]
- Think virtuous thoughts
- Study God's Word (and other truth)
- Pray for others (praise and supplications)
- Learn to receive — not just give[19]
- Be ready to help the needy
- Live simply
- Stay out of debt
- Worship with your whole heart and mind
- Value leisure time; don't think about the clock
- Give freely to the poor[20]
- Have a plan of exercise and sleep
- Maintain healthy relationships

What are other practical ways you experience God's love for you?

In chapter 6, human Origin was analyzed via God's image, and an important conclusion was drawn: How we treat people equals how we treat God. Now take that truth to the next level of human Relationships: *You cannot love another person any more than you properly love yourself.*[21]

God's Love Standard is both the standard we personally aim at and the standard we use to love all people. Recall the second half of the Great Commandment: "Love your neighbor *as yourself*" (Matt. 19:19; Lev. 19:18b). A simple reading of that command pinpoints these realities (even if some are only implied):

1. People already love themselves (or Scripture would not note that given truth);
2. The godly self-love referred to in this command is both acceptable and good (or Scripture would not cite in such a favorable way); and
3. This acceptable and good love of self is, in fact, the standard (based on the word "as") by which we are supposed to love others.

Closing Prayer

"Father, help me know what you think of me — how much you love to love me,
Even in the blessings I take for granted, like sleep.
Help me love myself in the very same ways you love me — no more, no less, and
no other way — focusing on the same areas of your love and employing the
same Love Standard.
Father, help me know what you think of me — how much you love to love me,
Even if your thoughts toward me are Too-Good-to-be-True Thoughts — which
they always are!
Father, help me know what you think of me — how much you love to love me,
Even if I don't deserve it — any of it!
And, Father, help me know what you think of me — how much you love to love
me,
That others might see and say, 'He (or she) has been with Jesus!'
And so that others might also see how great your love is for them.
Amen."

NOTES

1. This quiz is inspired by a similar test from Duffy Robbins, *The Ministry of Nurture* (Grand Rapids: Zondervan, 1990), 53 – 54.
2. See "Son of Man" in *Interpreter's Dictionary of the Bible* (Nashville: Abingdon, 1962), 414 – 15.
3. There's at least one more reason for Jesus' selection of Son of Man as his favorite. The apostle Paul (in 1 Cor. 10 and 11) brings up the vital subject of mentoring by human examples and the part that exemplars play in our lives.

4. First Corinthians 10:1 – 12 first identifies the *negative* example of Israel as she wanders in the desert, commits idolatry and sexual immorality, tests God, and is severely punished. Twice Paul cautions believers to avoid that kind of lifestyle: (1) "Now these things occurred *as examples* to keep us from setting our hearts on evil things as they did" (v. 6); and (2) "These things happened to them *as examples* and were written down as warnings for us" (v. 11).

   Then chapter 11 begins with an upbeat statement about *positive* examples: "Follow *my example*, as I follow the *example of Christ*." A handful of potent truths emerge from that simple sentence, as the last two items particularly tie to the Son of Man as "totally human":

   • Truth #1: Christ-followers are supposed to emulate godly examples.
   • Truth #2: Sometimes it is helpful to follow godly *human* lives, which reflect Christ's life.
   • Truth #3: The life Jesus lives is "imitatable" — it contains realistic human qualities that permit saints to actually replicate the Son of Man.
   • Truth #4: Beyond the theoretical idea of Truth #3, some saints actually emulate Jesus, as Paul implies. For that matter, Peter and John also emulate Jesus in Acts 4, when the Sanhedrin recognizes they had "been with Jesus." So it's possible to really follow Jesus.

5. Figure 8.1 is also found in Ronald T. Habermas, *The Complete Disciple: A Model for Cultivating God's Image in Us* (Colorado Springs: Chariot Victor, 2003), 123.
6. This organizational scheme was implied a hundred years ago in Augustus H. Strong, *Systematic Theology* (Valley Forge, PA: Judson Press, 1907), 2:672.
7. Figure 8.2 originates, with slight alterations here, from Ted Ward, *Values Begin at Home*, 2nd ed. (Wheaton, IL: Scripture Press, 1989), 18.
8. See appendices 8.1 and 8.2.
9. When I refer to Barnabas's personality, I also think of:

   • One who gives (financially and otherwise)
   • One who doesn't mind not being the leader
   • One who's very loyal to family and to close friends
   • One who nurtures people
   • One who's quite relational (in values and time commitments)
   • One who takes a public stand for all these values
   • One who risks to help someone, even risking his life

10. Too "high" includes, among other possibilities, self-conceit; or humanistic praises that completely neglect God and his work; or within a Christian context, dismissing (or playing down) the destructive effects that sin still has upon all people, including saints.
11. Too "low" includes, among other possibilities, various forms of verbal self-abuse; or permitting verbal abuse from others; or within a Christian context, it can start with an *in*appropriate selection of Scripture, subsequent *mis*interpretation, and a *non sequitur* application toward a believer. For instance, someone may cite Isaiah 64:6: "All our righteous acts are like filthy rags" and then conclude that there's nothing good about any person. Therefore, godly, biblical self-love is not biblical. That is not what Isaiah 64:6 teaches. That misunderstood verse says that any person's complete collection of "good" acts — which they hope will bring "righteousness" (or, salvation by works) — totally equals "filthy rags" in God's eyes. All evangelicals believe that truth.

12. "Different" may include a host of *unrelated* issues, for example, saying that the topic of godly self-love is nothing but more "psycho-babble." This a smokescreen and doesn't do anybody any good.

13. In fact, the one person Jesus meets is a Greek woman, to whom he first tells (in Mark 7:27) that he's not supposed to be serving her, figuratively calling her a "dog," compared to the Jewish children.

14. In John 14:31, Jesus evaluates his entire earthly ministry, saying, "*I do exactly* what my Father has commanded me."

15. Much more could be discussed on this topic but limited space prohibits this possibility. Suffice it to say that one passage frequently used to speak against any positive statement of "self" is Philippians 2:3 – 5. Yet just the opposite is true; certainly "selfish ambition or vain conceit" (v. 3) must always be rejected as ungodly. Indeed, verse 3 at first *sounds* like we're *supposed* to believe that "others [are] better than" us. But the context is how "humility" plays itself out, functionally. Two other facts influence and balance this passage: (a) verse 4 explains the balanced attitude toward others, by looking "*not only* to your own interests, *but also* to the interests of others"; and (b) verse 5 illustrates that Jesus' "attitude" is precisely the correct one to take toward others, as verses 6 – 11 detail his life of submissive sacrifice.

    Verse 4 (which Jesus essentially embodies, according to verse 5) shows a *both-and* attitude (no longer "only" your *own* interests) but "*also* ... others." That's nothing like the "either-or" argument often cited — which basically says *stop* thinking about self-interests, so you can *start* thinking about *only* others' interests.

16. Be careful not to believe that the reverse of Psalm 127:2 must always be true: "Because I did not get sleep, God must not love me." Not true!

17. *The World Book Encyclopedia*, S-Sn, Vol. 17 (Chicago: World Book, 1990), 507 – 8, has some fascinating information about sleep patterns, our need for sleep, etc.

    There are additional facts in the *Oxford English Dictionary Online* regarding the subject of rest: (http://dictionary.oed.com/cgi/entry_main/50204350?query_type=word&queryword=rest&first) on 12/05/2005, 1 – 9. In particular (on page 2), reference is made to one of the rare meanings for "rest" in the late sixteenth century. "Rest" is described by the phrase "*restored vigour or strength*" — paralleling this textbook's emphasis on holistic restoration.

18. Luke's version of the Beatitudes (Luke 6:17 – 22) reveals the hope of laughter (in verse 21b), which holds well-documented medical research regarding total health.

19. Luke 8:1 – 3 indicate the financial support that Jesus and the Twelve receive from several women.

20. We know that Jesus advocates support for the poor, but we might forget that he actually makes regular donations to the poor, as John 13:29 indicates (also see the implication in John 12:5).

21. This general principle is also true for other areas of life, like:
    + You can't teach more than you've learned (or been taught);
    + You can't model for others more than who you are; and
    + You can't lead more than the leader you've become.

    Also see Proverbs 14:31; 17:5; 19:17; Jeremiah 22:16; Matthew 25:31 – 46; James 3:9.

Chapter 9

THE ROLE OF GREAT PHYSICIAN: FOLLOWING JESUS' ANSWER TO *WHY?*

If you have ever stood in the middle of your life, looked around, and asked, "*What am I doing here?*" you are not alone.

There is hardly a person alive who hasn't asked questions like "What does God want from me? What is his plan for my life?" in some form. Life is multifaceted and complex. While it's easy to get swept up or mired down in the day-to-day challenges, it's often difficult to step back, to see the "big picture," to make sense of it, and to know for sure that your life has any real value. Clarity and assurance about your life's purpose can be maddeningly elusive.

Think it's *just you?* Check out these four "Help Wanted" ads, which tell you what you can do with your life:

- Three-year-old teacher needed for preschool. Experience preferred.
- Auto mechanic for elite garage. Folks try us once and never go anywhere again.
- Girl wanted to assist illusionist in cutting-off-head routine. Blue Cross and salary.
- Wanted: Haircutter. Excellent growth potential.

Well, let's not send out our resumes just yet! By the end of this chapter, you might be surprised to learn you are best positioned for God's most purposeful work right where you are.

The fourth of five universal life questions asks: "*Why* am I here?" or "What should I do with my life?"

I've heard more than one frustrated person complain that life is so confusing because it doesn't come with an instruction manual. This couldn't be more wrong. The Bible is that manual. *When you ask the question about what you are supposed to do with your life, you find the answers when you specifically take a fresh look at what Jesus did.*

Scripture reveals some things through the life of Christ that not only apply directly to you but will surprise you.

Jesus' Job Description

Jesus comes to earth to obey his heavenly Father's will. He *says exactly* what the Father wants him to say (John 12:49 – 50), and he *does exactly* what the Father asks him to do (John 14:31). Consequently, Jesus assesses that he fully satisfies the job description he receives from his Father. Just as important, our Lord claims that by finishing every detail, he is actually glorifying the Father (John 17:4), because he worships God through his *work*. The Hebrew word for "work" (*abed*) holds some fascinating meanings. David Bruce Hegeman explains that the word means *manual labor*, or *service*, or *worship*.[1] In sum, Jesus' work for and worship of God are one in the same.

Jesus is certainly a multitasker, so practically speaking, how do we define his total work? He preaches. He teaches. And he heals. Matthew 4:23 is one of several verses that highlights these three tasks in concert: "Jesus went throughout Galilee, teaching in their synagogues, preaching the good news of the kingdom, and healing every disease and sickness among the people."

Why preaching, teaching, and healing? Why those three? Because each is part of God's restorative plan: restoration of soul, mind, and body. Again, our Creator desires his children to be totally and holistically restored.

Out of curiosity, I conducted a semi-scientific study of these three tasks — preaching, teaching, and healing — in order to see how often Scripture records Jesus performing each. I counted every verse in the Gospels that mentions Jesus preaching (that is, specific topics related to the good news), teaching (on matters that were not tied to the gospel, like godly living and how to understand Scripture), and healing. Of the 3,779 verses comprising the four Gospels, a whopping 2,701 of them — 72 *percent* — mention Jesus doing one of these three tasks. Of this 72 percent, 48 percent feature Jesus' teaching. Healing and preaching are each represented in 12 percent. The remaining 28 percent includes passages like transition sentences, Jesus' travel patterns, or background information.

The Purpose of Restoration

In an effort to conceptualize Jesus' total work as a three-part effort, let's examine the details of one of his healings. Remember the remarkable Matthew 12:9 – 13 story of Jesus healing the man's shriveled hand in the temple? There is literally no other passage like it. By the way, if you remember that the Hebrew word *abed* overlaps "work" and "worship" as one single concept, it is much easier to understand why Jesus had no problem simultaneously working — and worshiping — on the Sabbath. On the seventh day in the temple, Jesus says to the man, "'Stretch out your hand.' So he stretched it out and it was completely restored, just as sound as the other." *The dis-*

torted hand is completely restored. It is made just like his healthy hand. It returns to the complete condition that the Creator originally intended — nothing more or less.

That Greek word for "restored" means, "returned to its former state." It's the same word used at the end of Acts 3:1 – 26, where Peter heals a crippled beggar, gives the astounded crowd a brief history lesson, and then tells them the good news: "It is Jesus' name and the faith that comes through him that has given this complete healing to him" (Acts 3:16b). Peter further tells the crowd to repent and be ready for Christ's return, explaining, "He [Jesus] must remain in heaven until the time comes for God to restore everything" (Acts 3:21).

Restore everything. That describes the Father's primary intention for his entire creation, because his role here is ultimate Restorer.

Let's talk a moment about biblical restoration. Through preaching, teaching, and healing — which the Great Physician performs in almost three-quarters of all verses in the Gospels — Jesus' earthly work always brings restoration. His work combines *redemption* for salvation and *rejuvenation* for all other forms of complete health, such as those of mind, body, and relationships. At the core of restoration is redemption — essential if we are to be reunited with God. Then God continues his work of rejuvenation in our lives and in the world.

We conclude that Jesus' job description was to provide "R and R." Normally "R and R" means "Rest and Relaxation." But Jesus compellingly upgrades that term, as he establishes a revolutionary version of R and R: "Redemption and Rejuvenation." Our Great Physician knows exactly what we all need. Furthermore, in turn, we believers can now offer *Christ-centered* "R and R" to the world through Jesus. That's why we are here — the answer to the "why" question. That's a huge reason why God's image is restored in Christ-followers.

Christ's disciples are so eager for the Bible's promise of complete restoration of all creation that they press him for it immediately prior to his ascension back to heaven: "Lord, are you at this time going to restore the kingdom to Israel?" (Acts 1:6). Their timetable is a little shortsighted, because our Maker's calendar calls for that event to occur closer to the end of time. But the disciples' understanding that the Father *does* have a Restorative Plan hits the bull's-eye! The Lord corrects them by saying that knowing "times and dates" is only the Father's privilege. By not challenging the actual topic of complete restoration, Jesus implicitly validates total renewal as a fact.

Ultimate restoration is yet to occur. But we are confident of its coming for two powerful reasons: Scripture promises it, and *daily* restoration toward that end perfectly describes Jesus' earthly work.

How "R and R" Compares to Our Task of the Great Commission

Again, Jesus' only work is to do the Father's will. At the core of that will is the message of *redemption* (John 6:38 – 40). The Great Physician's comprehensive work soon becomes the same work his disciples inherit. Carefully note the word "we" in John 9:4a: "As long as it is day, we must do the work of him who sent me." Just as they cooperatively labor with Jesus, we disciples today are given similar obligations — like the imperatives to love other believers (John 13:34 – 35); to teach and to practice all of the Bible (Matt. 5:17 – 20); to love our enemies (Matt. 5:43 – 48); to honor God and to obey government as much as it is possible (Matt. 22:15 – 22); to be a "Good Samaritan" to needy people (Luke 10:25 – 37); and to both love and fear God (Mark 12:18 – 34; Luke 12:4 – 7).

Those additional commands — and only a handful are listed here — indicate diverse *rejuvenation* ministries. Collectively, they add up to the *complete restoration* of all human domains: the physical, mental, emotional, social, moral, and spiritual areas of life. Just as in the example of redemption above (John 6:38 – 40), it is crucial to notice that Jesus did not simply *tell* us to do these rejuvenation ministries; he first *shows* us.

In chapter 2, I said: *redemption + rejuvenation = restoration*. We partner with the Restorer of all things, to help people become "holy whole" individuals.

Only this comprehensive job description does justice to the Great Physician's complete restoration design in the Scriptures. Repeating that phrase in reverse, anything less than this full job description discredits the Son's breadth of service and the fullness of God's Word. If we settle for anything less, the Great Commission of Matthew 28:18 – 20 turns superficial, because it reduces the totality of what Christ's disciples were commanded to do.

Our common Christian life "calling," then, is to continue Jesus' life purpose (except for his role as Messiah, of course) — to partner with the God of ultimate restoration so that we leave people, places, and things more complete than when we found them.

Allow me to massage a few clarifications into this simple interpretation of the Great Commission. First, although the temptation is great, you must never forget about your *own* need for regular restoration. The reference to "all nations" in Matthew 28:19a also includes the person you see in the mirror every day. Don't forget to nurture your own discipleship needs.[2] Second, you should value human choice. When any individual refuses your attempt to help him toward restoration, you should never manipulate.[3] Third, you never fully know our Father's mind, so your job is to be faithful in your restorative activities, and let him handle the outcomes.

In sum, every Christian's life work is to essentially replicate what Jesus does. Our Lord depends on the Father to proclaim the good news of redemption. And he performs a wide range of holistic rejuvenation ministries to make people, places, and things more complete. The Great Physician dispenses a comprehensive plan for total restoration. We can never do less.

Restoration Does *Not* Equal "Professional Ministry"

You might legitimately respond: "Okay, so the church's life purpose is to continue Jesus' life purpose, but how does his 'R and R' design specifically apply to me, as an individual Christian?"

You should be encouraged that Jesus indirectly supports all kinds of vocations and avocations as he champions the causes of people involved in building, gardening and farming, ruling and leading, educating, worshiping and playing musical instruments, banking and managing money, and judging. Jesus declares the value of work within the family, church, personal relationships, and business. We are assured that these important activities continue to find their place of significance in heaven as they do in our lives today.[4]

On a related, yet more specific topic of ministry, the church's diverse work and common worship do not require every believer to be educated for professional service. Christians who are not officially "in ministry" can restore God's creation just as saints who are called to professional service can. It is of paramount importance that Jesus represents *both* categories, modeling life as a carpenter for eighteen years and then as a "minister" for three.

But the key lesson is this: *Regardless of the job title he carries at any particular time, the Son obeys the Father by doing restorative work for all twenty-one of his adult years.*

Luke's account of Jesus' childhood is unique to the Gospels in several ways. It is providential that the only writer of Scripture who is also a physician (one charged with looking out for total human health) consciously includes Spirit-led details about Jesus from his birth to age twelve. Why did Dr. Luke bring these facts to our attention? Because the full scope of Jesus' total life and work were not confined to his last three years. Luke records that Jesus, from eight days old to twelve years old, increased in stature, grew in favor with God, and "grew in favor with ... man" (Luke 2:40, 52). Jesus' holistic human growth is so important that Dr. Luke is inspired by the Holy Spirit to express that significant truth *twice*, separated by only eleven verses.

Jesus begins his restorative work at least by age twelve, the traditional coming of age for a Jewish man, not age thirty. One surprising, fascinating side note on Luke 2:49 is when this twelve-year-old says to his parents, "I must be about my Father's *business*" or "in my Father's *house*," depending on the translation. The surprise is that neither of these two italicized words is the best English rendition of the Greek. That single word (which is actually a plural article) is more ambiguous in Greek, so the verse is better translated more broadly: "I must be part of my Father's activities, interests, and works — which necessarily includes activities in his House."

Again this means that, at least by the age of twelve, Jesus both *knew* his Father's work and was *doing* it. That correspondingly means that Jesus' first vocational calling — what his Father expressly plans for him to do — was carpentry work. Immediately following Luke 2:49 (and for eighteen years after age twelve), Jesus is continuously "about his Father's business" through his day-in-and-day-out service *as a carpenter.*

Between ages twelve and thirty, Jesus is known in Scripture as both "the carpenter's son" and "the carpenter."[5] For eighteen years of adulthood, the Son of God is totally obedient to his Father. Within his carpentry calling, Jesus fully restores the Father's world. How could he "restore" while planing doors and framing cabinets? Well, to start with, Mary's son is a skilled craftsman and an honest businessman, mastering the same abilities of competency, quality of product, and excellence associated with doing *any* job well. He most certainly extends kindness and fairness to customers and others alike. In short, by performing his calling (albeit a humble one) Jesus models work for all followers: *he always left the people, places, and things he encountered more restored than when he found them.*

This complex and admirable example of Jesus may mean that it is more important to God *what we do in our lives* than *what we choose for our livelihood* — the specific job we select. Don't misunderstand — the concept of biblical calling is very important. God's people might be called, for instance, to parenting, pastoring, or painting. But every saint is called, in a fuller sense, to total restoration.

Here's an analogy that is biblical in principle. It extends from chapter 2 of this book, which features the trio of purposes the Maker has for his entire creation. Sometimes it's helpful to distinguish two types of calling; calling that is *unique* versus Calling that is *uniform* for every child of God. The first category is more or less our defining title or role, our particular contribution of service to the kingdom. The second is our common task, including duties like those outlined in the Great Commission. To value the difference, the former category is put in lowercase terms and the latter in uppercase, because of their relative importance. For instance, if you are personally called to parenting and your friend is called to pastoring, both may have chosen God's best area to serve individually. But if neither person restores, both miss the uniform (and core) Calling for all saints — the non-negotiable duty for every Christian.

Your work for and worship of God, then, are not so much about your title; they're about doing what every believer is supposed to do. That's why the disciple Matthew (also known as Levi) and Zacchaeus, both tax collectors, have *unique* callings. One is supposed to join Jesus' band and the other is to serve as a typical tax collector. Neither, however, is exempt from the *uniform* Calling of restoration.

More Than People Are Restored

Besides "people," let's turn our attention to the two other categories of our restoration definition, both of which Jesus models: "places and things."

First, Jesus restores at least four prominent "places" of authority in his teachings:

1. The *place* of marriage and home
2. The *place* of government
3. The *place* of the Scripture
4. The *place* of Sabbath

The place of marriage and home. The restoration of marriage and the home is earlier noted in chapter 2, so little will be repeated here. In Matthew 19:1 – 8, Jesus is challenged as to why he does not support Moses' lenient rules of divorce. He verbally returns to the "New Eden Standard" of the Creator's original design and reverence for marriage. After directly quoting from two pre-fall Eden passages (Gen. 1:27 and 2:24) in Matthew 19, the Master Teacher summarizes that the reason for Moses' liberal divorce laws was based on Israel's hardened hearts. Then Jesus concludes, "But it was not this way [of liberal divorce laws] *from the beginning*" (v. 8b).

In other words, as harsh and irrelevant as Jesus' words may sound at first (within an extremely permissive culture), he is positive that *God's pre-fall design of marriage and home is still the best plan for everyone!* It's not coincidental, then, that the Son's inaugural miracle is at the wedding of Cana (in John 2:1 – 11), where he deliberately affirms the dignity of the wedding couple.

The place of government. Christ also upholds government authority more than once. This fact is particularly significant because of the masses' popular (albeit erroneous) perspective that the Messiah would soon establish political reign. Two illustrations arise from Matthew 17:24 – 28, where we find Jesus' general support of the foreign Roman government and a specific illustration of Jesus' habit of tax payments, even though he knows he is "exempt" as God's Son.

The place of Scripture. The whole of Scripture is reinforced repeatedly in Jesus' teachings, especially the significance of:

1. Teaching all that the Bible instructs (Matt. 5:17 – 19)
2. *Knowing the Bible accurately* (six times the phrase, "You've heard it said … but I say …" from Matt. 5:21ff., stresses proper interpretation)
3. Obeying all of God's Word (Matt. 5:19b)

The place of Sabbath. Sabbath-keeping receives special attention from Jesus' support of Scripture. Matthew 12:1 – 8 and Mark 2:27 – 28 first reinstate the original purpose of Seventh Day observance. Then Jesus makes it clear that this law was always meant to serve people, not vice versa. Finally, Christ stresses that he is the Lord of the Sabbath.

Similarly, at least three categories of "things" have their value restored by Jesus:

1. *Nature* — This topic includes the valued signs in the sky, which are often used to forecast weather (Matt. 16:1 – 3a).

2. *Food* — After the 5,000 are fed, Jesus issued an invaluable restorative principle of ecology: "Gather the pieces that are left over. Let nothing be wasted" (John 6:12).
3. *Living Things* — In Matthew 6:26 – 32 animal and plant kingdoms teach lessons of restoration through God's sovereignty for "the birds of the air" and for his created beauty in "the lilies of the field."

So Jesus daily exhibits *how we are to live on earth* — our lifelong work — through our never-ending duty of comprehensive restoration.

Power to Restore

The name of Jesus is extremely powerful. It was through the name of Jesus — and the names of the Father and the Holy Spirit — that our Lord issued the Great Commission in Matthew 28. It is so powerful, it might be compared (through a very weak human analogy) to *a supernatural charge card*. Or, simply, The Master's Card.

With that picture in mind, it's not too difficult to see how God's authoritative power could also be abused. Sure enough, the very first case of "identity theft" is recorded in Acts 19: 13 – 20. Seven sons of a Jewish chief priest — all non-Christians — were using the awesome power of The Master's Card to cast out demons. But it wasn't the police who busted this unauthorized exorcism ring — it was a demon!

Four outstanding promises come with every Master's Card, as the back of the card indicates. And there's no hidden charges for these promises!

- God's Power
- God's Protection
- God's Provision
- God's Presence

One notable point pertains to earlier portions of this *Restoration*

FIGURE 9.1 — The Master's Card

THE MASTER'S CARD

ALL Authority is Mine…Go make disciples, baptizing them in the Trinity's Name, teaching them to obey all I taught…and I am ALWAYS with you
—Jesus (Matthew 28:18-20)

Your Credit Line: <u>Unlimited—through Jesus' Name</u>

Your Name: _____
(Your signature is required to access Jesus' Power)

You wouldn't *dare* leave home without it!

(Front)

(Back)

Guaranteed Promises of The Master's Card

- **Power:** Acts 4:30—The early church's prayer to God: "Stretch out your hand to heal and perform miraculous signs and wonders *through the name* of your holy servant Jesus."
- **Protection:** John 17:11-12—"…Holy Father, *protect them by the power of your name*…I protected them and kept them safe…"
- **Provision:** Acts 3:16—"…*It is Jesus' name* and the faith that comes through him that has given this *complete healing* …"
- **Presence:** Acts 2:38—"Peter replied, 'Repent and be baptized, every one of you, *in the name of Jesus Christ* for the forgiveness of your sins. And you will receive *the gift of the Holy Spirit.*'"

resource: Acts 3:16 (in "Provision") links up with the main theme of this book, as it does to the restorative purpose of Jesus' ministry cited in this chapter. Peter is preaching in Acts 3:16, describing how the crippled beggar is earlier healed. Twice this apostle says that it was through "faith in the name of Jesus" that "complete healing" came to this man. So Peter was proclaiming *the total restoration of that man* — the primary task our Master passes on to the church. Note that this healing is more than physical, because Peter explicitly associates salvation with that miracle in Acts 3:14, 19, 23, and 26.

Just five verses later, *the total restoration of all creation* is featured as one of the outstanding benefits that will accompany Christ's return to earth (v. 21).

Conclusion

While we wait for the Son's return, the Father uses every willing believer to restore his creation. The Father's grace will usher in eternity in his perfect timing, but until that moment, he wants us to continue Jesus' work of total restoration through the Holy Spirit.

No, it's not because we earn favor from him. And no, it's not because he needs us, but because of the pleasure and fulfillment he wants us to enjoy in these acts of simple obedience. Initially, think of our task as God's helping us to inch creation back to something like Eden before the fall. I use that illustration because Eden is the only reality we have in our past that shows us what God originally envisioned for all life. And Eden is a beautiful preview of heaven's perfection.[6]

Within this concept of full restoration (redemption and rejuvenation), we each locate our common lifelong purpose. Obeying this purpose both honors our heavenly Father and yields exquisite joy — now — just as Jesus and his seventy-two disciples demonstrate when they review the results of their missionary campaign in Luke 10:1 – 24. The disciples' blend of teaching, healing, and preaching (commanded in verses 5 – 11) brings them overwhelming joy as they unanimously focus on their particular rejuvenation ministry of exorcism (v. 17).

Jesus steps in at this juncture to make a singular, but significant, readjustment in verse 20. This is another Habermas paraphrase: "Yes!" the Son says, "you have every reason to rejoice. But be sure to upgrade the focus for your celebration. Don't center on exorcisms or miracles; don't settle for those *rejuvenation* ministries. Rather, celebrate *redemption* — the core of all God's grace — illustrated by the fact that your names are now written down in heaven! That should bring you out-of-this-world joy!"

"*Why* are we here?" the fourth life question asks. The biblical answer is to emulate Jesus, the Great Physician. The universal query about our lifework is only satisfied by what *all* saints must do, regardless of their individual callings. This biblical answer demonstrates God's strong desire that people regain their complete health.

Our Creator-Savior-Lord wants us totally well. As God's junior partner — his interns — we need to daily attempt, through his power, to leave all people, places, and things more restored than we found them.

As if God wants to make the job description of our lifework abundantly clear, he goes one step farther in his Word and comprehensively summarizes the Christian life as *a life that does good*. This "good" is not the same as similar terms from humanistic philosophies or religions. This is a pronounced expression of God's good. Listen to how simply and purely Peter describes Jesus' entire life of ministry to Cornelius: "He went around *doing good* and healing all who were under the power of the devil, because God was with him" (Acts 10:38b). What makes this version of goodness unique to God's goodness is that God is singled out as the source. We Christ-followers honor him when we do the same. "Doing good" by God's strength is an easy enough concept for even a young Christian child to understand and to help him know what he's supposed to do every day.[7]

In time, each obedient believer becomes more Christlike in his lifework, as God's image is daily renewed in him.

NOTES

1. David Bruce Hegeman, *Plowing in Hope* (Moscow, Ida.: Canon Press, 1999), 43 – 47, 95.
2. Chapter 8 discusses this subject more fully.
3. Chapter 10 further describes this responsibility.
4. See Isaiah 65:17 – 25; Matthew 5:17 – 19; 25:14 – 23; Luke 19:11 – 27; 1 Corinthians 6:1 – 6; and Revelation 7:9 – 12; 15:1 – 4; 22:3 – 5.
5. See Matthew 13:55a and Mark 6:3a, respectively.
6. A wonderful blend of earth, Eden, and heaven is found in the prophecies of Isaiah 51:1 – 3 and Ezekiel 36:33 – 35.
7. Do a Bible study of some or all of these helpful passages that summarize the Christian life as doing good by God's strength. Even Jesus refers to this life goal as it pertains to what we are to do on the Sabbath (Mark 3:4), which implies what is also acceptable to do *every* day. Further note the summative testimony of Tabitha (Dorcas) in Acts 9:36. And consider these multiple affirmations to do good from Titus 1:8; 2:7; 3:1, 8, 14; Luke 6:27; 2 Corinthians 9:8; Galatians 6:9 – 10; Ephesians 2:10; Philippians 1:6; 1 Timothy 6:18; 2 Timothy 3:17; and 1 Peter 4:19.

Chapter 10

THE ROLE OF SUBMISSIVE SERVANT: FOLLOWING JESUS' ANSWER TO *HOW?*

In a world that increasingly offers fewer meaningful cultural traditions, especially those that lead youth into their future, one encouraging rite of passage from the Internet is a Cherokee legend,[1] whether true or urban:

> His dad takes him into the forest blindfolded and leaves him alone. He is required to sit on a stump the whole night and not take off the blindfold until the sun's rays shine through.
>
> He is all by himself.
>
> He cannot cry out for help. But once he survives the night, he is a man. It's the only way he can become a man.
>
> He cannot tell the other boys of this experience. Each must come into his own manhood.
>
> That night the boy is, naturally, terrified. He hears all kinds of noise. Beasts are all around him. Maybe even someone will try to hurt him. The wind blows the grass and earth and it shakes his stump. But he sits stoically, never removing the blindfold.
>
> It is the only way to become a man.
>
> Finally, after a horrific night, the sun appears and he removes his blindfold. It is then that he sees his father sitting on the stump next to him — at watch the entire night.

The fifth universal question all people ask is *How do I get to where I must go?* In the Cherokee legend, not one but two people answer that vital human inquiry. The boy obviously plays the necessary role of trusting son, as he believes in his people's tradition and leans heavily on his father's wisdom, goodness, and care.

The father also plays a significant part in his boy's quest for manhood. He capably embodies the goodness and care his boy trusts — but does so without being recognized. If the boy knew of his father's presence, it would undoubtedly have restricted his son's fullest character development.

Few modern stories concurrently portray our heavenly Father's relationship with his own Child, who raises similar questions about his earthly future. If *kenosis* means anything — and it must — we need to realize that the Son's excruciating pain during the last week of life is totally real and frightening. On the other end of the emotional spectrum, John 13:1 declares that just before his last Passover Feast, Jesus was about to wash his disciples' feet in order to show them "the full extent of his love." How much *more love* does Jesus exhibit later, as he purposefully suffers for the sins of the world?

These self-sacrificing moments of pain and compassion are only as good as we freely let Scripture speak, for God's truth vividly details Jesus' total humanity as he struggles with the fifth universal inquiry: How do I get to where I must go?

In theological terms, Christ's question is answered during the inaugural Holy Week between Palm Sunday and Easter. The Son's solution to this final question embraces total trust in and trusting submission to his heavenly Father, whose own complementary response features sovereign care.[2]

What Biblical Submission Does and Doesn't Mean

Submission is a nasty word for some individuals. I'm amazed, in this day of politically correct language, that this "s" word hasn't been altogether banned. For certain minds, this term smacks of everything from slave trade to inferior roles of women (especially wives) to doing stuff you don't want to do but your boss insists you must — all rolled into one!

Jesus, however, displays healthy and godly submission. Jesus submits to his Father and his Father's will. Consequently, Jesus also submits to the world as Suffering Servant.[3]

A pertinent fact from this book bears repeating: On the one hand, Jesus' life is totally unique, so nothing of his messiahship is intended for replication. On the other hand, the opposite is true: Jesus' humanity is precisely designed for his disciples' emulation, as the apostle Paul knows and commands: "Follow my example, as I follow the example of Christ" (1 Cor. 11:1).

What Godly Submission Does Not Mean

There are many topics we are not talking about when we discuss the biblical submission of Jesus' life. So let's get those out of the way:

- It's not being a "yes" man — or woman — where you're always agreeing with your superiors.
- It's not being a doormat, where you really think your ideas don't matter — so people figuratively walk all over you.

- It's not being hypocritical, claiming you are committed to an idea and then not following through on it.
- And, above all, biblical submission based on Jesus' life does not mean you never use your mind, emotions, or will in responsible — and even independent — ways.

What Godly Submission Means

Limited space in this book restricts my thoughts on Jesus' intense Gethsemane struggles, a model for submission to God. It is important to observe Jesus' submission of his *own will* (vs. the Father's will) and his subsequent need for (sinless) *self-denial*.[4]

Recall the Garden of Gethsemane's sober setting:

- Following his last Passover meal, Jesus and the Eleven head out to the Mount of Olives, as they often did (Matt. 26:30).
- Jesus requests that his followers pray (Luke 22:40).
- Jesus selects his three closest disciples to be "with" him (Matt. 26:37).
- Jesus retreats to a solitary place by himself "about a stone's throw beyond them" (Luke 22:41).
- An angel strengthens Jesus (Luke 22:43).
- Jesus experiences "anguish" (Luke 22:44a).
- Jesus is "overwhelmed with sorrow to the point of death" (Matt. 26:38).
- Jesus agonizes so intensely he possibly sweats blood (Luke 22:44).
- Jesus "fell with his face to the ground" to start praying (Matt. 26:39a).

All of this came before Jesus' turbulent Gethsemane dialogue with his Father!

Every Christ-follower does well to memorize Mark's version of this spiritual battle, particularly Mark 14:36, for it raises three points that the other two Gospel accounts don't (John doesn't record Jesus' Gethsemane prayers): "'*Abba*, Father,' he said, 'everything is possible for you. Take this cup from me. Yet not what I will but what you will.'"

Key Point #1 — Only Mark opens with, "*Abba*, Father." Though "*Abba*" means "Father" in Aramaic, Jesus' introduction is not redundant, but intimate.

Key Point #2 — Only Mark refers to one of God's attributes, omnipotence. As it is earlier acknowledged in 10:27, Mark repeats the Son's belief that the Father is able to do anything.

Key Point #3 — Don't miss this last vital fact. Only Mark is led by the Holy Spirit to select an *imperative* word within Jesus' prayer — a literal command. As the Son speaking to his Father, Jesus *begs*: "*Take* this all away!"

Jesus doesn't play games. He screams out with tears: "Please, take me out of the plan that involves the cross, which is why I came to earth!"[5] Have you ever heard Good Friday proclaimed from this biblical angle?

Again, here's the logical order for Jesus' prayer in Mark 14:36. Especially notice the direct link between the second and third points (in this Habermas paraphrase):

+ "Father, you are my intimate Daddy!"
+ "Daddy, you can do anything!"
+ "Father — Daddy — please, I beg you — because you are all-powerful — take this plan of suffering away!"

Can you see and feel Jesus' intense pain — for us? Do you hear what the Son is pleading for? Until you do, you cannot understand any more of this crucial and pivotal portion of Gethsemane or his death on the cross.

Yes, all three gospel writers add: "Yet not what I will, but what you will." And that's a fantastic ending. Thank God for it. But please — *don't* read that well-known ending too quickly, or you will miss Christ's plea: "*Take* it all away, Daddy!"

Restating these prayers from another angle, our Lord's struggles indicate:

+ Jesus knows the Father's "Plan A" (the cross);
+ Jesus also knows "Plan B," because any plan other than Plan A (even a plan to cancel Plan A) *is* Plan B; and
+ Jesus not only knows Plan B, in his mind, but he (1) articulates it, (2) prefers it initially, and (3) begs his Father for it.[6]

Based on Jesus' personal model for us, biblical submission means a daily and deliberate choice to totally trust God and his will, even though we may have been earlier contemplating other competing plans. I say "may" because we are not required to have these identical, intense doubts — but the potential is there.

All this said, this biblical approach to Jesus' submission to the Father's will is far more human (real to life), far more healthy (articulating his undeniable preference for Plan B, before his submission), and far more comprehensive than the explanations I have heard most preachers, teachers, and commentators take.

The church must do a better job of seeing the possibility of this bigger picture and applying this pivotal passage to spirituality and maturity.

In sum, each of Jesus' Gethsemane experiences is requisite for understanding how he comes to closure on his own fifth question, How do I get to where I must go? Furthermore, each of Jesus' personal experiences is helpful for possible use in our own journeys.[7]

What Submissive Trust throughout Life Looks Like

Appendix 10.2 provides a comprehensive and unique overview of Jesus' miracles. Seventeen categories of miracles are listed, along with all respective gospel accounts. But the last two columns make this chart unique: the third column identifies other people in Scripture who perform the same type of miracle that Jesus did in all seventeen categories. That is, every one of Jesus' miracles is found elsewhere in the Bible, when godly men and women similarly trusted God for assistance. Consequently, as the fourth column indicates, this chart is more about how each person, including Jesus, *matures through trust in God* throughout life.

Whether or not God chooses to replicate those miracles in our lives is not so much the issue. The challenge for us is to similarly trust God each day within this broad framework of faith in life.

A Patriarchal Example of Submission to God's Sovereignty

One of the most profound Old Testament accounts of human trust in and submission to God's will is Joseph's testimony from Genesis 50:18 – 21:

> His brothers then came and threw themselves down before him. "We are your slaves," they said.
>
> But Joseph said to them, "Don't be afraid. Am I in the place of God? You intended to harm me, but God intended it for good to accomplish what is now being done, the saving of many lives. So then, don't be afraid. I will provide for you and your children." And he reassured them and spoke kindly to them.

Joseph explains to his fearful brothers that three extravagant blessings come from Yahweh's sovereign intervention in his tempestuous life: God protects him, God provides for him, and God personalizes his care for him. Consequently, Joseph intends to pass on those same blessings to his brothers, in this manner:

- Joseph determines he is in *the exact place* the Sovereign Lord wants him. Even though his brothers desire harm for Joseph, God's power turns bad into good. There's no need for retaliation. As a result of God's efforts already, many people are saved from the famine (Gen. 50:19 – 21a).
- Joseph holds *the exact position* the Sovereign Lord provides him. As a top leader in Egypt, Joseph plans to provide for his family the same way God provides for him — undeservedly and mercifully (Gen. 50:21b).
- Joseph takes *the exact perspective* toward his brothers the Sovereign Lord wants for him. Joseph graciously exhibits God's kindnesses so much that, at the end of his benevolent message, Scripture records that Joseph "reassured them and spoke kindly to them" (Gen. 50:21c).

In the end, Joseph's brothers have no need to fear, to worry, or to doubt either God's power or Joseph's generosity. Chart 10.1 recaps Joseph's God-honoring witness.

How does this story from the ancient world of Genesis translate to the twenty-first-century need to prepare for the future? Quite well, actually. The transferable benefits, in fact, are much greater than most believers stop to consider.

CHART 10.1 — Joseph's Trust in and Submission to God's Sovereignty

Scripture: Genesis 50			
God's Roles in His Plan	God's Blessings to Joseph	Joseph's Subsequent Message to His Brothers	Joseph's Desired Reactions from His Brothers
Verses 19 – 21a The Protecting God	Joseph determines he is in *the exact place* God intends for him.	No need to be afraid of retaliation. Almighty God turns bad into good.	No Fears
Verse 21b The Providing God	Joseph holds *the exact position* God wants for him.	No need to be concerned about food shortage. Almighty God provides for all Egypt and he will for them too.	No Worries
Verse 21c The Personal God	Joseph takes *the exact perspective* God desires for him.	No need to question Joseph's promises. Almighty God is not only powerful but kind.	No Doubts

Blessing #1 — Don't Fear, for We Are Virtually Invincible

When we speak of God's sovereignty, our talk is dominated with words like "omnipotent," "supreme," "totally in charge," and "only true God." With such overwhelming first reactions, there is often no room left for second reactions. But we should never overlook how extremely practical God's sovereignty is in the Bible.[8]

Do you recall, for instance, Jesus' reference to the Father's authoritative care for his creation? In Matthew 10:29 the Lord initially notes the low cost of sparrows, then adds, "Yet not one of them will fall on the ground apart from the will of your Father." The Father's *knowledge* is not the primary subject. The Son's attention mainly centers on God's mighty *will* — his caring plan for what most of us see as relatively meaningless birds. How many of us ever take the time to contemplate God's will for the sparrows?

Now we have been reminded by the Son of the Father's concern and care.

In John 19:11 the Son makes a more sophisticated, yet still practical, reference to God's providence. Hours before his death, Jesus tells Pilate, "You would have no power over me if it were not given to you from above."

One angle from which to view our grace-backed invincibility is Luke 12:4 – 7, a one-of-a-kind Scripture. Several phrases are repeated from the earlier Matthew 10:29 reference to sparrows and God's will, but there are a few unique parts in Luke 12:4 – 7. Five times Jesus uses the word *phobos* (fear). The first time, the Master Teacher says don't fear Satan (who can only kill the human body); and the fifth time, Jesus says don't be afraid of death because people are "worth more than many sparrows." In between, *our Lord commands us to fear* — three times — specifically, to fear God, who can kill the human body then send people to hell.

Jesus reminds us what is really important — eternal life, not temporal life. John 5:24 says we are now living eternal life. And nobody can take that away. What's the worst that can happen? Our bodies die — but our spirits (with new resurrected bodies) live forever.

We, like Joseph's brothers, have no need to fear.

Consider this true story of someone who put Luke 12 to practice and experienced outstanding results: Dr. Josef Tson, faithful leader of the evangelical voice in Romania for decades, once confronted the tough topic of death as someone who personally encountered serious persecutions. From the pulpit at the Thomas Road Baptist Church in Lynchburg, Virginia, during the early 1980s, Dr. Tson recounted several instances of his own beatings and imprisonments. On one occasion he came to this conclusion: "I began to ask myself, 'How can a person remain sane, knowing that any day he might die?' to which I ultimately answered myself, '*The person who is not afraid to die is invincible.*'"

Our first blessing from Almighty God — extended from Joseph's message — is that he protects us, so much so that we are virtually invincible. We have no need to fear.

Blessing #2 — Don't Worry, Because We Have "Everything We Need"

What would you do if you randomly got a check for $1.5 million? The next day you got another check. And the day after brought the identical gift. The next three days follow suit. A note is attached to the final check that first week: "You will receive $1.5 million daily for the rest of your life. You only have to sign and cash each check every day. Otherwise it becomes worthless paper in twenty-four hours."

What would be your first response? Would you be skeptical or ecstatic? Would you try to investigate the source of the gift, asking, "Who's behind this?" Would you be leery of strings attached? Imagine what you would do with all that money. After all, in less than two years, you'd be a billionaire!

Something like this fantasy tale actually happens in the true story of Yates's Pool.[9] The story centers on an impoverished sheep rancher who, during the Depression, is close to losing his property. In desperation, Mr. Yates consents to a wildcat well drill on his West Texas property. Just below 1,000 feet, the drilling crew strikes an oil reserve that yields 80,000 barrels per day from only one well. Other drillings result in more than twice that yield. Three decades following the first drilling, reports still project a potential 125,000 barrels of oil per day — again from only one well!

In a matter of hours on one afternoon, Mr. Yates is radically transformed from a very poor sheep rancher on government subsidy to a multibillionaire.

But the notable part of this story is *not* Yates's rags-to-riches transformation. The remarkable part is that Mr. Yates was *always* outrageously rich — *he just never knew it until he investigated what he had!* Yates came within a whisker of losing everything, never suspecting his immense wealth. Yet he literally touches his countless riches every time he walks on his property.

Yates is clueless about what he owns, ignorant of his enormous fortune, until he tries the very first drilling.

There is a spiritual condition that strikes every Christian without exception — what I call Yates's Syndrome. Some disciples show this malady's effects only sporadically, while most of us battle it every single day. This illness is similar to Yates's condition before he struck it rich. The symptom of this universal Christian disorder is when which *every saint fails to tap all heavenly riches at his or her disposal.* This affliction also leads to a weakened spiritual immune system because we lose hope. We grow enfeebled, then totally worn out. And it's all because we, like the impoverished Yates, are clueless that we *now* possess God's unbelievable wealth to empower us in our Christian walk.

Don't dismiss this illustration as a cute little story. It's a real tragedy. God promises Christ-followers "everything we need for life and godliness" for our lifelong journey (2 Peter 1:3). But few of us seem to discover — or at least to exhibit — the blessings of that truth. Read the provocative passage 2 Peter 1:3 – 11 and list the eight or nine examples that illustrate "everything we need." The first gift is "divine power" in verse 3.

Second Peter 1:3 – 11 is compatible with another similar promise, Hebrews 13:20 – 21:

> May the God of peace, who through the blood of the eternal covenant brought back from the dead our Lord Jesus, that great Shepherd of the sheep, equip you with everything good for doing his will, and may he work in us what is pleasing to him, through Jesus Christ, to whom be glory for ever and ever. Amen.

In sum, there's no need for us to worry, because God's sovereignty always provides all we ever have to have "for life and godliness." Praise the Lord!

Blessing #3 — Don't Doubt That God Is Also Personal and Kind

As mentioned, sometimes at the start of a discussion on the doctrine of sovereignty we are figuratively knocked over by sheer force of its meaning. It's how disobedient Elijah wants to experience the Lord in 1 Kings 19:11 – 12 — first in a "great and powerful wind," then in an earthquake, and then in a fire. Yet God is not found in any of those natural forces. As a gentle whisper, by contrast, is how Yahweh confronts this wayward prophet.

There is a personal side of sovereignty that is just as secret and private as a gentle whisper. It is rooted in God's image, specifically in our human will to choose. The Sovereign Lord originally creates our trait of choice, and he is still the fiercest defender of that attribute.[10]

So the third blessing of sovereignty has two parts, two sides of the coin known as "personal will and choice."

Side One: God Never Coerces People (and Neither Should We)

It is amazing to see how Jesus is so persevering in his ministry, even when his own disciples often "didn't get it." At best, these moments show they are clueless; at worst, they are totally immature.[11] Christ's most pointed instruction on persistence comes from his parable of the persistent widow (Luke 18:1 – 8). The heroine of the story, after habitually disturbing a local judge (who had no respect for God or for people), finally persuades this magistrate. He confesses that he gives in just to keep his sanity. Jesus models that same tenaciousness when it comes to proclaiming the good news. But he never steps over the line. The virtue of persistence instantly tarnishes to vice if people are ever manipulated.

The best expression of Jesus' noncoercive method is modeled in Mark 6:1 – 6. As Jesus returns to his hometown of Nazareth, many people are initially "amazed" by his message. But scoffers eventually cry out, "Isn't this the carpenter … Mary's son?" (v. 3a). So Mark adds: "And they took offense at him" (v. 3b). After Jesus cites the proverb that says a prophet is not accepted in his hometown, the story concludes: "He could not do any miracles there, except [a few]. And he was amazed at their lack of faith" (vv. 5 – 6).

What starts out to be the entire town's amazement becomes his. Why? His hearers stubbornly refuse to believe. And it shocks the Lord. And it limits him too.

Consider the number of significant issues at stake in this passage: Jesus returns home for his first family reunion. Humanly speaking, if there is anybody he wants to save most, it is these people. His next of kin are everywhere. Also, the message Jesus proclaims is the most important truth of all time. Yet, figuratively, he allows his hands to be tied[12] by his listeners. Why? Because Jesus fiercely supports the freedom of choice given in God's image.[13]

In other words, if ever there is a time to manipulate — to coerce people, for the seemingly honorable "end justifies the means" reasoning — it is *now*. "One day they will thank me for interfering with their freedom to choose," Jesus could have legitimately thought. The "end" would be eternally worthwhile to those who are coerced.

But the Son of God did not manipulate. He never did.

Side Two: God Desires Us to "Own" What We Believe

The second implication of our Maker's personal kindness toward us is that he wants us to take ownership for what we claim we believe. He wants us to be sure that our beliefs are really ours. Real faith requires internalized faith. As a maturing saint, our beliefs are not supposed to be our best friends' beliefs or our pastor's theology or our parents' views. God wants us ultimately convinced by what we believe.[14]

Here is an overview of how ownership may progress in people, at increasing levels of maturation:

Level 1: Ownership of a *Personal Viewpoint* in friendly circumstances. (Jesus asks, in Matthew 16:15, "Who do *you* say I am?")

Level 2: Ownership that needs to be expressed within *Family Responsibilities.* (Children ask fathers, in Exodus 12:26, what does Israel's historical faith *mean to you?* Also see Exodus 13:8, 14 – 15.)

Level 3: Ownership *Regardless of Others' Decisions.* (Independent of what the entire nation of Israel decided, Joshua makes this claim about his own family: *"But … we will serve the* LORD" [Josh. 24:15]. Also see vv. 19 – 27.)

Level 4: Ownership *Within the Context of Temptations* to do evil and to compromise faith in God (Gen. 39:5 – 12).

Level 5: Ownership *Despite Mistreatment or Evil Pleasures.* (Hebrews 11:24 – 25 says Moses "chose to be mistreated … rather than to enjoy the pleasures of sin"; see also Mark 9:24.)

Level 6: Ownership *Even in the Face of Death* (Dan. 3:16 – 18, 28b; 6:10 – 23).

The purpose of ownership, then, is to know and to live by what we personally value, according to God's Word and will. Our Maker is glorified in this process, but there's more: he is also glorified because the specific traits of human will and choice are being restored to Christlikeness, just as our Father deeply desires.

Chart 10.2 reviews the past five chapters. Each of the universal questions is featured along with Jesus' life roles that match those five inquiries. One representative response for Christ-followers is also suggested for each category.

Conclusion

Master Teacher, Faithful Learner, Son of Man, Great Physician, and Submissive Servant — each role represents Jesus' heartfelt urge to know, to love, and to serve his

CHART 10.2 — Summary of Five Universal Questions and Jesus' Five Roles

Five Universal Human Questions	Jesus' Five Roles	The Father's Corresponding Titles	The Primary Focus	Our Response to Jesus' Roles
Where Did I Come From?	Master Teacher	Faithful Creator (1 Peter 4:19)	The *Word* of God	Praise
What Is My Background?	Faithful Learner	Holy One (Ps. 71:22)	The *Way* of God	Trust
Who Am I?	Son of Man	Heavenly Father (Matt. 6:9)	The *Witness* of God	Thanksgiving
Why Am I Here?	Great Physician	The One "to Restore Everything" (Acts 3:21)	The *Work* of God	Obedience
How Do I Get to Where I Must Go?	Submissive Servant	The Sovereign Lord (Acts 4:24 – 28)	The *Will* of God	Submission

people. All five roles reflect the spirit of the incarnation, for Christ came to earth as a full human being, ready to sacrifice himself. He is, undoubtedly, "God with us."

Someone told me the story of a young boy who, after being put to bed by his mother, got up and shouted from the top of the stairs, "Mom, I'm scared of the dark. Can you come back up till I fall asleep?"

"Go back to bed," the mother replied firmly. "Jesus is with you. He'll protect you."

The boy obeyed — at least for a minute or so.

"Mom!" he called again. "Could you send up Dad? I need someone with skin on them!"

Whether we teach our children the truths found in this chapter or not, the fact remains: There was never a person so thoroughly human as Jesus. Based on our Maker's original plans, in fact, *Jesus is even more human than we are.*

Jesus *is* someone with real skin on him. He shows us how to live. How to make the most of life. How to best answer life's most pressing questions.

In the end, as is often the case for Christ-followers, it comes down to a personal choice: "What will you do with what you now know? How will you live, now that you know the five roles Christ left for us to emulate?"

It's never a matter of *if* — if you choose — but *how*. Each of us regularly chooses whom we will serve.

God does not manipulate. That's not his way, because it directly conflicts with how he made us. And, since our Creator is the most ardent advocate for individual choice, he prefers a genuine "No" from his human creature over an insincere "Yes."

C. S. Lewis states it best in this familiar summary: "There are only two kinds of people in the end: those who say to God, 'Thy will be done,' and those to whom God says, in the end, '*Thy* will be done.' All that are in Hell, choose it."[15]

NOTES

1. This legend is slightly modified from an e-mail sent to me by www.mickeysfunnies.com.
2. The term "sovereign" is almost always used as an adjective to "Lord" (Sovereign Lord). In the NIV, the word "sovereign" appears 303 times — a whopping 217 times in the book of Ezekiel. Because the doctrine of sovereignty is much maligned — especially regarding issues related to election, heaven, and hell — one extremely pertinent verse is Ezekiel 18:23: "Do I take any pleasure in the death of the wicked? declares the Sovereign Lord. Rather, am I not pleased when they turn from their ways and live?" (see also v. 32). This is the biblically correct attitude we must take with regard to sovereignty.

   One of the most remarkable passages is found in a prayer from the early church in Acts 4:24 – 28. Both God's sovereignty and God's will are cited, which is most significant for this chapter on Jesus' fifth life role.
3. Mark 10:45 is a superb verse to memorize, in light of Jesus' wonderfully submissive gift of his life to us. Also read the foundational prophecy of this period of Jesus' life found in Isaiah 52:13 – 53:12, on the Suffering Servant.

4. Self-denial does not inherently require sin or sinful human nature — neither of which Jesus had. Self-denial has *everything* to do with "denying yourself — especially your own will and plans for yourself." As the next section shows, self-denial is essential for Jesus, before he submits to his Father's will. His life example shows a pattern for us to emulate.

5. It is important to realize, as later shown in this chapter, that Jesus (in Mark 14:36) pleads to have "this cup" removed — which essentially means to not follow through on the plan for Jesus to die on the cross. Jesus' prayer reflects his personal human will. Of course, saying "no" to the cup had to eventually be rejected — which it was — in order for Jesus to subsequently and voluntarily die on the cross. Also see Hebrews 5:7.

6. Matthew 26:36 – 46 indicates that Jesus prays his Gethsemane prayer (with certain variations) *three times*. That's persistency! Why do you think he prays three times?

7. I cannot reduce Jesus' Gethsemane experiences of trust and submission any less than these seven events within his prayers to his Father:

    a. Jesus is aware of God's primary plan for him (Plan A);
    b. Jesus is committed to God's Plan A (see John 4:34; 6:35 – 40);
    c. Jesus knows at least one Plan B — again, anything other than Plan A (even suggesting that Plan A be cancelled) *is* Plan B;
    d. Jesus is able to articulate Plan B;
    e. Jesus also articulates his preference for Plan B, initially;
    f. Jesus communicates total anguish, loud cries, tears (and possibly godly fear);
    g. Jesus finally trusts in and submits to his Father's Plan A.

8. For example, in Deuteronomy 7, Moses anticipates the fear of God's people as they enter the Promised Land. Verse 17 records, "You may say to yourselves, 'These nations are stronger than we are. How can we drive them out?'" That's an excellent and practical question. And why shouldn't that particular worry be on their minds? Just a few moments earlier (in verse 7), Moses reminds Israel how insignificant she really was in comparison to other nations: "The Lord did not set his affection on you and choose you because you were more numerous than other peoples, for you were the fewest of all peoples." Israel didn't need to bother with an "inferiority complex" — she *was* inferior!

    From within that context below, try to locate a subtle — and very practical — part of God's grace within Moses' prediction of Israel's entering Canaan's borders:

    > The Lord your God will drive out those nations before you, little by little. You will not be allowed to eliminate them all at once, or the wild animals will multiply around you. But the Lord your God will deliver them over to you, throwing them into great confusion until they are destroyed. He will give their kings into your hand, and you will wipe out their names from under heaven. No one will be able to stand up against you; you will destroy them. (Deut. 7:22 – 24).

    Did you see it? Did you locate God's grace folded into his omnipotence? The Sovereign Lord promises to drive out the pagan nations "little by little" not "all at once." Why? That sounds strange coming from One Who's All-Mighty, doesn't it? But God incorporates a wider — and — wiser picture of his invasion scheme: the need to control the wild animal population!

9. Bill Bright, *How You Can Be Filled with the Holy Spirit* (Orlando, FL: New Life Publications, 1971), 21 – 22.

10. It may sound cold or odd, but I am convinced the church needs to pursue a new reason (at least, new to me) for the most common criticism directed at Christianity: the problem of evil. C. S. Lewis refers to the door to hell being locked from the *inside*, and that, in essence, is what I have to say. But there's more. Certainly the nonbeliever's choice to say "No" to Jesus is a crucial part of why there is a hell. In fact, I believe 2 Thessalonians 2:10 is possibly the clearest cause-effect statement in Scripture regarding how people end up in hell: "They perish because they refused to love the truth and so be saved." *Love (or the lack of it) is the primary reason for hell.* Nonbelievers are not just people who "don't believe" in Jesus. They also "refuse to love" God's saving truth — the only antidote to redeem their lost lives.

    It's also God's love for who he made us, as his image-bearers, that gives hell its existence. In this day of tolerance as the supreme (and only?) virtue, we Christians need to announce that the Trinity is tolerance's greatest partner when it comes to personal choice. The Creator's total love, which prompts his absolute tolerance of humans to say "no," is why hell exists.

11. See passages like Matthew 16:6 – 11; Mark 6:5; 7:8; 9:16; and John 13:12.

12. Operating by the same principle, Psalm 78:40 – 41 similarly notes that, because the Jews who wandered in the wilderness regularly provoked and grieved Jehovah, they "*limited* the Holy One of Israel" (KJV).

13. Dallas Willard makes several useful points about human choice and God's image when he concludes:

    > Human creatures, like all living beings, have a life of their own. But though that life is mortal and short, it is still a life in which we alone among living beings can stand in opposition to God — in order that we may also choose to stand *with* God.
    >
    > If it were not for this ability, we could not fill our part in God's plan, because we would just be puppets. And no puppet could bear his likeness or be his child. The human body itself then is part of the *imago Dei*, for it is the vehicle through which we can effectively acquire the limited self-subsistent power we must have to be truly in the image and likeness of God.
    >
    > And herein lies the pivotal concept about our nature we need to understand when we begin talk of redemption. Let us try to make this point as clear as possible since everything turns upon it in practical theology.
    >
    > In creating human beings in his likeness so that we could govern in his manner, God gave us a measure of *independent* power. (*The Spirit of the Disciplines* [San Francisco: Harper and Row, 1988], 52 – 53)

14. A passage that affirms biblical ownership originally begins as "the faith of another person" — or *surrogate faith*. It is found in John 4:39 – 42. Listen to this marvelous contrast in verse 42, as the Samaritan crowd talks with the woman at the well, who was the first to tell them about Jesus: "We no longer believe just because of what you said; now we have heard for ourselves, and we know that this man really is the Savior of the world." Biblical salvation only occurs when personal ownership faith is placed in Jesus.

    Also study Romans 14 to see the value of ownership faith in the body of Christ.

15. C. S. Lewis, *The Great Divorce* (New York: Macmillan, 1946), 72.

APPLICATIONS OF RESTORATION

Applications of Ministry for Every Age

Applications of Global Tasks for Every Church

Applications in Daily Life for Every Believer

Applications of Ministry for Every Age

Chapter 11

RESTORING CHILDREN: SERVING BOYS AND GIRLS FOR CHRIST — BOTH NEAR AND FAR

Kevin E. Lawson

Hardly a week goes by that we don't hear more disturbing news reports of child abuse — locally, nationally, and internationally. When it's news of abandonment or kidnapping, we relearn painful lessons of a child's powerlessness, often as a helpless pawn in violent family disputes. When the news is about kids and malnutrition or obesity, we embarrassingly see the same societal reflection within contemporary Western life. When drugs, AIDS, or sex take center stage, we are reminded that these are worldwide trends.

In spite of seemingly overwhelming odds, those who serve children still have reason to hope. For starters — and finishers — *God sides with children*. Scripture leaves no doubt about this all-important fact.[1]

Ministry Motivations for Those Who Serve Children

The Bible specifically shows God's consistent love and care for children. Young ones have always been a sign of God's blessing and a cause for rejoicing.

> Sons are a heritage from the LORD,
> > children a reward from him.
> Like arrows in the hands of a warrior
> > are sons born in one's youth.
> Blessed is the man
> > whose quiver is full of them. (Ps. 127:3 – 5)

Time and again God declares the great value he places on the nurture of children. Often he commands both parents and the entire faith community to teach children so they will come to know God and follow him.

Hear, O Israel: The LORD our God, the LORD is one. Love the LORD your God with all your heart and with all your soul and with all your strength. These commandments that I give you today are to be upon your hearts. Impress them on your children. Talk about them when you sit at home and when you walk along the road, when you lie down and when you get up. (Deut. 6:4–7)

He decreed statutes for Jacob
    and established the law in Israel,
which he commanded our forefathers
    to teach their children,
so the next generation would know them,
    even the children yet to be born,
    and they in turn would tell their children. (Ps. 78: 5–6)

Fathers, do not exasperate your children; instead, bring them up in the training and instruction of the Lord. (Eph. 6:4)

Christian parents and congregational leaders throughout time and around the world have witnessed God's loving heart toward youngsters. In short, *our Maker models ministry to children.* Any corresponding church effort to help children to know God and to trust Jesus as their Savior will never go unnoticed. Yet because of this ministry's significance to the kingdom, its opposition is also never-ending.

Ministry Challenges for Those Who Serve Children

The church's goal is not simply for kids to know the Bible or to behave in "acceptable" ways. We want children to know, love, and walk with God. Meeting this goal is a complex, multifaceted endeavor that involves the care, acceptance, instruction, guidance, discipline, and modeling that children need to grow up into mature people of faith. In other words, young ones — like believers of any age — require the total restoration that their Creator-Savior-Lord provides. To that end, it's important that we recognize the challenges involved so that we may intentionally face them and find ways to overcome them.

Societal Devaluation of Children

Children are valued in some measure within all societies. However, in many cases, the way we actually treat them reveals an attitude of negligence and dismissal. For example, if children are viewed as a distraction from worship or as too noisy and immature for involvement in church life, we adults miss prime opportunities to help them know the Jesus who loves them and what it means to be his followers. The church is one place where children need to be valued, not marginalized. In this way, we follow Jesus' personal example from Matthew 18.

Media Manipulation of Children

In Western culture, even children are viewed as consumers to be shaped to support the economy. They are targets of marketing that seeks to build brand loyalty and to capitalize on the child's desire to belong and to be accepted. Youngsters too easily absorb consumerism. Thus children, like many of their elders, are distracted from kingdom values of compassion, sacrificial love, and contentment. The church needs a clear countercultural alternative to help children see how Christ's abundant life from John 10:10 truly satisfies.

Parental Disempowerment

Most societies have schools to which parents send their children for adequate education. Unfortunately, parents sometimes relate to their churches in the same way they relate to schools and have the same expectations: that their churches will provide the primary spiritual instruction their children need. This problem is compounded when parents believe that they don't have enough time to give instruction or don't feel equipped. Moreover, society and the church promote the trend that children should be handed over to "experts" who will do the important work of childrearing.

The church needs to find better ways to cooperate with parents. They must motivate and empower parents to do their part to nurture the faith of their children. The church's educational ministries are best viewed as complements to parents, not as replacements for them (see Eph. 6:4).

Professional Disinterest

Children sometimes find themselves on the bottom rung of the church's priority ladder. This is true both in the professional training of leaders and in the way some churches make decisions regarding ministry and finance. Because children are sometimes out of view in church life, their needs can be easy to overlook. Churches need reminders of the importance of childhood as a time for instruction and nurture of faith and faithfulness. Leaders would do well to welcome children as part of the church *today*, as Matthew 18 and 19 indicate, not just view them as "the church of tomorrow."

Investment

One hundred years from now,

it will not matter

… what your bank account was,

… the type of house you lived in,

… or the car you drove.

But this world — and the next —

may be changed for the better because

you made the difference

in the life of *one* child.

— Source Unknown

Ministry Objectives for Those Who Serve Children

Before examining some promising educational models, five overarching objectives need clarification. What do children require from parents and churches in order to learn and mature? What guidelines should a church follow as it develops effective ministries for children and their parents? Both parents and churches must wrestle with similar questions as they tag-team together to serve youngsters under their God-given care.[2] Consider this initial list of objectives as starting points for your personal reflection:

- *Children need to experience the love of God.* For children, the Christian faith is first experienced, and then their understanding grows. So kids must encounter divine compassion embodied in adults they know. This life expression of love (both in the family and church) just makes sense to youngsters.
- *Children need basic instruction in the faith.* Ideally, curricula for kids should include foundational truths set within age-appropriate structures and methods. Such topics might include the Trinity, human nature, salvation by faith in Christ, the work of the Holy Spirit in the believer's life, and the privileges and duties of God's children. Parents and church workers both benefit from coordinating this instructional design.
- *Children need to feel included.* Normal childhood development requires a sense of belonging to valued groups. People never outgrow that human need. With belonging comes the related need to make personal contributions to that group and thus to derive personal identity. Children require encounters of both quantity and quality with their gathered community of faith so that those exchanges may contribute to shaping their character fully.
- *Children need to experience gift development and service.* Children need opportunities to develop their own God-given talents and gifts, using them to glorify God and to serve others. This significant objective largely expresses one strategy to attain the previous point: making personal contributions to valued groups.
- *Children need capable and empowered parents.* Children need growing, maturing parents empowered to serve them. If children are to mature to their optimum, they require parents who have gone before them in their own adult journeys. A caregiver can never teach or nurture offspring beyond the maturity levels he or she has first attained.

Ministry Models for Those Who Serve Children

There are many effective approaches that address these five objectives. Four primary models are ministry to parents for the sake of their children, ministry of the church together with youngsters, ministry by the church to kids, and ministry by the children to others. As you study these four models and recall your own church's practices, contemplate ways to further strengthen those ministries in your church.

Model #1: Ministry to Parents *for* Children

If church leaders believe that parents play a critical role in the instruction and spiritual nurture of their children, they would do well to invest heavily in equipping parents.[3] This means that church leaders will strategically design the church's adult education to address these specific aims.

Pursue strong adult education-formation. At a foundational level, churches need to take adult discipleship seriously so that parents and other leaders know the faith, how to live it out, and how to explain it to others, including their children. Adult Bible studies (whether on Sunday morning or during the week) represent one dependable strategy for growing adult faith. Ministry involvement also shapes adult faith. Experience puts "shoe leather" to personal beliefs, encouraging greater reflection on those beliefs, which leads to more ownership of faith.

Propose practical parenting classes. Many parents want to pass their faith on to their children, but they don't know how. Churches that value the total needs of children will encourage training opportunities for parents themselves. These classes help parents understand basic issues of child development, the nature and nurture of faith, and insights for promoting faith at home. As God blesses these church classes, fruitful times of Bible study, prayer, and worship within the family will emerge.

Promote useful resources for the home. It's difficult for the average parent to keep up with the best available resources for instructing their children. Diversities in subject matter, personal interests, and age range further complicate this challenge. Churches that help parents in this effort offer their libraries as parenting resource centers. "Read-aloud" storybooks encourage parents to spend time and talk about God with young children. Books for older children encourage their own exploration of God's work in the world. Games, music CDs, DVDs, videos, and various activity books help caregivers share the story of God's love in Jesus Christ.

Plan church and parent collaboration. Parents need the encouragement of others as they begin nurturing their children's faith. Church leaders can organize parents' meetings, resource nights, and home strategies to help parents grow confident in their teachings. Advent and Lent are examples of special seasons of the year when churches can provide devotional materials and special activities for use at home. These materials help families experience meaningful celebrations during these "holy days."

For instance, Advent wreaths can be made at church, perhaps even as family projects. Then these wreaths can be taken home along with devotionals that include carols to sing, Scriptures to read, and family activities. Such collaborative efforts promote positive learning experiences between church and home. In fact, these seasonal activities may provide just the necessary affirmation of parents, so that nonseasonal learning experiences are also engaged as parents become more confident and intentional about their child's year-round instruction.

Model #2: Ministry Together *with* Children

As noted earlier, children want to be part of their church community so they can experience the reality of faith within the lives of others. Based on that foundation, children can then be challenged to embrace others' faith as their own. This firsthand experience also enhances children's growing sense of identity because kids learn best when they are actively involved in their own instruction. Here are a couple of suggestions for churches to help children grow in meaningful, personal faith.

Permit children to participate in corporate worship celebrations. It can be a challenge to involve youngsters in corporate worship, but it's worth the effort. Many churches find it beneficial to have young ones present at least up to the point of the sermon, when leaders may then dismiss children for their own worship or Bible study. When children join corporate worship where God is praised, Scripture is read, and prayers are lifted to heaven, they see a total faith community living its life together. They begin to understand the nature of worship and are encouraged to participate. Because of the numerous variables involved, plans for such worship must be formed sensitively, and pastors and worship leaders must consider children's various needs and abilities, along with ways of engaging them in worship. Instructional activity sheets, special stories just for children, and permitting children to help lead songs are a few methods that help children feel at home within the gathered church.

Provide intergenerational learning and fellowship. When children are included in intergenerational experiences, they increasingly perceive themselves as part of the church. Such experiences include fellowship dinners, church picnics, family-cluster gatherings, intergenerational Sunday school classes, prayer, or group events at Christmas or sunrise Easter services. Children who experience opportunities that include people of all ages are prompted to ask more pertinent questions, to see diverse role models outside their families, and to witness multiple sides of church life. When they are given the chance to actively participate in these events, the impact can be even greater.

Our church organizes December evenings for church members — children and adults together — to go caroling in the community near the church building. We share songs, cookies, and candy with our neighbors and then return to the church for hot chocolate and Christmas cookies. These simple activities bring children together with people of other ages as participants in the body of Christ. These early experiences within an intergenerational community can provide a powerful instructional design for a lifetime.

Model #3: Ministry by the Church *to* Children

As a community of believers called to share life together, it's appropriate for churches to provide ministries that nurture their children. Children benefit most from services that attend to their particular abilities and needs. These ministries should supplement what parents provide at home as well as offer outreach to children without Christian parents.

Prepare effective educational designs. The biggest investment most churches make is in providing kids with diverse and relevant forms of instruction. The evangelical church has a long and strong history of offering Sunday school classes, vacation Bible schools, and various kids' club programs during the week. We do this because we believe in the importance of individual children personally coming to know the Christian faith story and personally knowing God through Scripture. We believe in the importance of children being introduced to Jesus Christ and the gospel so that they can respond in faith as God works in their lives.

There are many creative and effective structures for these educational ministries,[4] including these five:

- The rotation pattern where instructional lessons appeal to different learning styles;
- The large group – small group design (like Promiseland), which uses dramatic presentations and a variety of creative activities to communicate a lesson to a large group, then employs small group interaction to discuss and apply what was learned;
- The contemplative-reflective structure (like Godly Play and Catechesis of the Good Shepherd), which encourages worship experiences through Bible stories and unhurried time for children to explore what they encountered through play;
- The instructional-analytic format (like AWANA clubs), including many Sunday school curricula that use Bible lessons, Scripture memorization, and group activities to promote the gospel message and demonstrate how God desires his people to follow him;
- Media-intensive structures that use high-quality video presentations along with caring adult relationships to reinforce teaching through active learning.

Propose a children's worship. Earlier I encouraged churches to include children in their corporate worship, at least up to the point of the sermon. In some cases, churches may want to provide specific times and places exclusively for children's worship, allowing kids to more fully praise their Maker according to their abilities. This is not a children's worship that excludes children from corporate church worship. Rather, it is a "both/and" ministry that complements corporate church worship. One great advantage of these distinct worship times is that many more children can actively participate than in corporate worship times. Specifically, more children can join in prayer, learning from Scripture, songs of praise, the sacraments, and liturgy. Many publishers of Christian curricula offer resources to aid in the planning of children's worship.

Model #4: Ministry *by* Children to Others

One mistake we sometimes make is thinking of children only as recipients of ministry, not as those who can minister. However, many active adult church members recall that their own involvement in ministry began when they were young, and it has been part of their lives ever since. Two suggestions that advance this fourth model include:

Plug children into regular church ministries. Children can participate in the church's mission projects, like raising funds for World Vision or putting together Samaritan's Purse gift boxes for needy children. They can join "work days" with adults, doing service projects like yard work in homes in the community. Or kids can simply visit homebound church members with other adults. Children should be included wherever possible to experience and understand the meaning of compassionate service. Youngsters need to see how God has personally gifted them and how he can use them to serve others. Again, these tasks align themselves with children's need for "belonging" and "identity" as they personally contribute within the faith community.

Personalize ministries for children to do themselves. Children also can be encouraged to have their own ministries in the church and community, such as reading stories and putting on puppet shows, singing in worship services, praying for church ministries, and visiting at nursing homes. As important as it is to include children in the general ministry efforts of the church, helping kids take responsibility for planning and carrying out their own ministries encourages growth of their leadership skills, a sense of responsibility, empowerment, and ownership of personal ministries. All this takes careful planning and coordination. At the same time, parents and church leaders must avoid the temptation to belittle these children's ministries because they are "less effective" than adult ministries.

Conclusion

Four models — ministry through parents, ministry with the whole church, church ministries to children, and children ministering to others — encourage our children to learn and mature in the body of Christ. Children are enabled to understand the Christian faith story, to see the reality of faith in the lives of those around them, to respond to the gospel, to participate in and contribute to the faith community, and to grow in their relationships with God. In short, our children become who they were created to be — fully restored into Christlikeness.

Each one of these four ministries, then, is prized as invaluable — a critical investment by parents and by congregations alike. We dare not neglect such a significant cause. May our children and our children's children grow to know and love God in part because we have deliberately and prayerfully engaged in a full and diverse range of effective ministries.

NOTES

1. Appendix 11.1 describes the unique blessings that Jesus gave to children.

2. See Ronald T. Habermas and David Olshine, *Tag-Team Youth Ministry: 50 Ways to Involve Parents and Other Caring Adults* (Lincoln, NE: iUniverse.com, 2000). Although the primary age focus of this book is teens, tag-team ministry to older children is also pertinent much of the time because the reading audience is parents — enabling them to be better serve the home.

3. See Ronald T. Habermas and David Olshine, *Down But Not Out Parenting: 50 Ways to Win With Your Teen* (Lincoln, NE: iUniverse.com, 2000). Although this guidebook primarily emphasizes teenagers, its major objective is to empower parents of teens and older children.

4. I am indebted to two resources for these five effective structures: Michael Anthony's *Perspectives on Children's Spiritual Formation: Four Views* (Nashville: Broadman and Holman, 2007) and Scottie May et al., *Children Matter: Celebrating Their Place in the Church, Family, and Community* (Grand Rapids: Eerdmans, 2005).

Chapter 12

RESTORING ADOLESCENTS: ESSENTIALS OF WORLDWIDE MINISTRY

Dave Rahn

*H*ow do adolescents — as a subgroup of God's creation masterpiece — mature into the "holy whole" persons desired by our heavenly Father? This foundational question, in some variation, is the cornerstone of the practice of every youth ministry. Whether a Bible talk is given with computer-aided graphics, or kids are asked to spin into small groups, or peers lead one another in passionate worship singing, or "fun and games" are included as part of the youth curriculum, we youth leaders always work under the assumption that our activities somehow help teens encounter Christ and grow in him. It's imperative to examine this assumption from time to time.

Youth ministry has distinguished itself from other ministries, in part, because we observe that young people have different developmental needs. Because of this observance, a rich harvest of ministry applications has been gathered from empirical insights about adolescent learning, growth, and maturity.

But in designing activities for young people, our opening foundational question is first of all a *theological* one, not a human *developmental* one.[1] Our answers must always be anchored in Scripture's transformational principles, which apply to everyone everywhere. Our commitment to those universal principles grounds us to an approach to youth ministry that is not limited to a particular culture or a certain period of history. Furthermore, the restorative changes we seek in young people must be the *supernatural* kind. Unless we cooperate with the Spirit of God, our best efforts to bring restoration of the soul, mind, and body will always fall short. In addition, when compared to these biblical principles, issues like creativity and innovation are not nearly so important as Truths that stand the test of time. These Truths are the sine qua non (literally, "without which not"). They are the essentials that *we cannot do without* in worldwide youth ministry.

There's a popular icebreaker that asks individuals to pretend that their houses are on fire. "Indicate what is most valuable to you," each person is instructed, "by identifying a handful of items you most want to remove from your burning house." Modifying that exercise, which sets personal priorities, we youth leaders must likewise ask ourselves, "What's most important in serving adolescents? What are the essentials?" Then we need to ask, "Why did I choose those particular items?"

Take a moment to write down *your* top five essentials of serving teens.

The five suggestions below are borrowed from Youth for Christ/USA. Each portrays a component universal to all youth ministries. And each indicates a prerequisite: any youth worker must be faithful, attentive, and responsive to the Holy Spirit's transforming power in the lives of young people.

Essential #1: *Prayer*

Prayer is a must for our lives and work in Christ.[2] This is such a familiar component that it can be overlooked easily. Consider, for starters, one ultimate goal of helping young people experience total restoration in every relationship for which they were created. At their core, teens need the *redemption* Christ offers. In addition, strained relationships with parents and friends testify to the range of alienation they frequently experience, which demands attention. Consequently, low self-esteem is quite common, and it is often expressed as identity confusion, one cry for teen *rejuvenation*. Together, teens need God's total package of *restoration*.

Sometimes their hurt is so deep that teens can't even articulate their pain. Our strategies for healing must match those deep hurts. If their problems were simply social, then perhaps our human-made environments of hope would be sufficient remedies. But time and again, we have witnessed that those designs are not adequate. We desperately need God to act supernaturally in the lives of young people *because the goals we seek can't be accomplished without his transformational power.*

Paul's ministry pattern reveals the transforming work of Christ in people (Gal. 4:19; Col. 1:24 – 2:8). And he makes it no secret that prayer is a significant component of that work. His prayers for the Ephesians seek breakthroughs in their understanding that can only be accomplished by God (Eph. 1:17 – 19; 3:14 – 19). Jesus similarly taught his disciples that they couldn't meet the needs of certain troubled people without prayer (Mark 9:28 – 29).

When you're working in youth ministry, you may also be misled to lean too heavily on useful principles from the field of management. Great planning skills from that discipline may allow you to prioritize your work, so you might embrace them as a master strategy. In doing so, your personal and profession life may even demonstrate a semblance of balance. But none of these standard management outcomes provide the guarantee that you are moving with the precision, pacing, and personal renewal that comes from God's directing. The need for such guidance was the reason that the apostles consistently coveted the believers' prayers (Acts 8:26 – 40; 10; 12:5 – 12; Rom. 15:30; 2 Cor. 1:8 – 11; Eph. 6:18 – 20; Col. 4:2 – 4; 1 Tim. 2:1; and James 1:5 – 6).

Another example dramatizes our need for prayer as an expression of faithfulness within our calling. It is common for youth ministers to be frustrated because there are not enough volunteers available to assist in the necessary work. Recruitment, screening, training, and supervision skills can be learned and applied with some success. But these skills must always be practiced against the backdrop of Jesus' own words — like how the challenge of an unharvested field will be met when we "ask the Lord of the harvest" to supply the necessary workers (Luke 10:2). His own example of choosing the Twelve to be deputized for ministry was bathed in prayer (Luke 6:12 – 19). And early church leaders at Antioch were right in the middle of their worship when the Holy Spirit called out Barnabas and Saul as the very first missionaries. After a time of fasting, prayer, and laying on of hands, this pair was sent off by that local church (Acts 13:1 – 3).

What if youth ministers followed the biblical wisdom (which Youth for Christ/USA is also following) of *deliberately engaging lots of Christians to intercede on behalf of their ministry sites?* By soliciting frequent and specific prayers from teams of committed people, the youth minister acknowledges their dependence on God to accomplish what is most important.

Essential #2: *Love*

Prayer requests quickly move from the general to the specific when you actually live among the teens you serve. That's because your obligation of love is always the "up close and personal" variety (Rom. 13:8; James 2:5 – 10; 1 John 3:11 – 18). Consequently, your generous love *of* young people must inform your specific prayers *for* them.

The love of God is a transformational powerhouse for all who encounter it. This fact particularly includes those — like teens — who hunger for meaningful relationships. Youth ministers are emissaries of a God whose love is both undeserved and inescapable (John 3:16; Rom. 5:8; 8:31 – 39). One of your chief roles is to initiate and maintain those loving relationships with young people. But the love of God is also a force to be reckoned with, and no amount of program creativity or innovative activities can match that supernatural impact in a teen's life. Youth ministry strategies must foster this type of radical love of God.

Youth for Christ's mission lies within the evangelism aspect of youth ministry. They implement this second essential by *consistently pursuing lost kids and engaging them in lifelong relationships with Jesus.* That application correctly recognizes that God's love always takes the initiative. In the same way, Jesus punctuated his encounter with Zacchaeus by reminding those who questioned his actions that he came to "seek and save" the lost (Luke 19:1 – 10). We are called to follow that same pursuing pattern of Christ (John 20:21).[3] Obedient youth ministers are propelled toward compassion for young people through the aggressive love of God (2 Cor. 5:14).

Restoring Adolescents: Essentials of Worldwide Ministry   163

Among other things, this essential of love means that youth ministry substantially takes place in the teen's world, not ours. It occurs where they live and hang out: schools, athletic events, coffee shops, fast food places, malls, social networks on the Web — the possibilities are endless. By meeting them in their world, showing genuine interest in what's important to them, and discovering their stories, God's love is engaged to break through to youth.

The ensuing challenge, then, is to build a community where God's love flourishes and provides a foundation for young people (Eph. 3:16 – 19; Phil. 1:9 – 11). As befitting the intent of the Great Commandment, extraordinary life change can be expected when caring adults, incarnating Jesus' love, surround a teen (Mark 12:28 – 34).

Essential #3: *God's Word*

Love for young people proves itself in any culture. That bond with teens has been especially resilient amid postmodern values. But the youth landscape is also characterized by pervasive beliefs that right and wrong as well as good and evil are relative concepts, subject to interpretation and culture; that absolute knowledge comes only from firsthand experience; and that one can't trust authoritative sources. This makes it tricky to navigate contemporary waters while holding fast to this third transformational absolute: *Our lives must be reconfigured by God's Truth.*

As Jesus concluded his famous sermon on the mountainside, he offered the crowd the accessible way of life he had just described by a narrow road and small gate. He warned of teachers who would lead people away from the ultimate goal of knowing and doing God's will. Finally, he used a parable to dramatize that people who build their lives around hearing and practicing Jesus' words are able to withstand any trouble (Matt. 7:13 – 27). The Bible must be taught — and learned — for total life obedience, not just for knowledge (Matt. 28:20; Mark 7:11 – 13; Luke 8:11 – 15; 11:28; John 5:36 – 40; 15:1 – 11; Phil. 3:15 – 17; 2 Tim. 3:14 – 17; Heb. 5:11 – 14; James 1:22 – 25; 1 Peter 1:22 – 25; and 2 Peter 1:3 – 4).

Many youth ministers fall into one of two traps. Entangled by their own formal schooling experiences, some think Bible teaching means *presentation*. This approach is often impersonal and content-centered. It tends to undercut the power of God's Word when it is practiced in a real life, at a real time, and in a real place. Others emphasize Bible teaching as *contribution*, based on the myth that having more resources with greater variety in a lesson is better than fewer. Consequently, some youth leaders teach lessons that use peer discussions, movie reviews, music reviews, and other types of advice-giving resources. Unwittingly, this second approach similarly forgets that the Bible itself is an irreplaceable force for shaping students into dedicated Christ-followers.

To avoid these errors, Youth for Christ asks their staff to accurately handle biblical truth, regularly coaching kids to apply it in their lives. They are asked to be diligent, not just in their study of the Bible, but also in their walk with young people, showing them how to make connections between their lives and the Bible.[4]

Real change requires a two-way street. Scripture becomes a powerful force for restoration when it can be lived out in a young person's experience. Sometimes this encounter with God *begins when the Bible is opened up*. At other times, teens may infuse their lives with the Word's directions, when they submit their experiences to Scripture for scrutiny. In these cases, supernatural encounter *begins when kids open up their lives*. Either way, this intense focus on the Word is affirmed every time teens increase the "traffic" back and forth between their experiences and God's Word.

Essential #4: *Unity*

Ironically, some youth ministers try to fabricate biblical unity. They fashion comfortable meetings, prepare activities that don't promote any serious personal challenge to grow, and never come close to stirring up any necessary controversies. Rather, every teen from those churches is invited to participate in these "nice" experiences, along with other youth who are "just like us." The most prized goal of these fabricated sessions is to hear a parent exclaim: "We have a good Christian youth group!"

In truth, this illustration teaches us three facts about *what biblical unity is not*.

First, biblical unity in youth groups is *not fabricated program unity*. It is not controlled, obsessive-compulsive. It is not like highway signs that push service station restrooms as nice, neat, and clean. And it is not relegated to Sunday evenings between 7 and 8:30 p.m. On the contrary, our initial picture of biblical unity in the early days of the church was nothing short of *God's unleashed power* — the same supernatural power that broke down barriers also harmonized broken relationships (Acts 1:12 – 14; 2:1 – 4, 42 – 47; 5:12 – 15). Biblical unity, then, means *power* — *the power to transform people*, to daily mature any willing teen to be individually — and collectively — more like their Lord.

Second, biblical unity in youth ministry is *not manufactured cultural unity*. A cultural definition of unity falls well short of radical biblical unity, which is the subject of admonishment in many of the inspired letters to the early church. Paul made it quite clear that the church was multicultural, so much so that all sect and party affiliations must be set aside, because a permanent indwelling of the Holy Spirit was occurring within diverse individuals from various races and ethnicities (1 Cor. 1:13 – 15; 3:16 – 17; Eph. 2:19 – 22; 4:1 – 6, 11 – 16). To the Colossians alone, this apostle describes the divine plan to establish the supremacy of Christ, subjecting all cultural and ethnic distinctions to him, so that each believer might weave together the smallest details of his or her personal life into a unified tapestry of other saints, honoring the name of God (Col. 1:15 – 20; 2:1 – 3; 3:11 – 17). On a much smaller scale — but one of considerable value — the apostle John wrote a personal letter to encourage a friend to hold together the coalition in his church, who were dedicated to hospitality and love in spite of the disruptive threat of one person's love for power (3 John).

Biblical unity means *the power to transcend* all cultures, replacing former disunities with union in the body of Christ. Ideally, every teen should get the opportunity to imagine, as Revelation 5:9b foretells, what a youth group "from every tribe and language and people and nation" looks like. By investing in biblical unity, adolescents have the best chance of literally experiencing a microcosm of the world.

Third, biblical unity in service to teens is *not narcissistic navel-gazing*. It does not settle for a "we-four-and-no-more" attitude, which conveniently values quality over quantity growth. The "leave us alone, we were fine till you came" mindset is antithetical to Scripture, for biblical unity is never an internal health plan that opposes all attempts to externally reach out to others. By contrast, biblical unity at this juncture means *the power to transport* — to transport people beyond themselves, for their own good and their own health. It means the power to practice oneness with all believers in their communities who also represent the body of Christ. Youth for Christ staff are similarly asked to *intentionally work together with local churches, agencies, and other partners to provide sustainable youth and family ministry in the community.*

This three-part vision of biblical unity, then, presents a diverse, exciting, compelling, and worthy-of-sacrifice design. It is far more alluring than any human-concocted attempts at unity. And it produces a more fruitful bounty than all lesser fabrications.

Essential #5: *Exemplars*

Total biblical restoration takes place largely through informal socialization. And very few socialization factors have as much impact on adolescents as human modeling. The *diagnostic* question (which analyzes youth culture) that we must ask when we work with young people is: *Who are the most influential exemplars that set the pace for our teens' behaviors and values?* The *intervention* question of ministry follows naturally: *Who are the exemplars that must be identified to establish an alternative and attractive pace for Christlike behaviors and values?*

Research in social science reveals that the most effective models are people who are similar to those they influence. Effective models are also those who are observed frequently and in a variety of situations and those who invite conversation that might explain their behaviors to others. Teens naturally gravitate toward other teens as exemplars, though accessible adults may also have a strong impact.[5]

But the bottom line is that kids, like all of us, need to be *shown* how to follow Christ. They need to be shown how to pray, to love, to conform their lives to biblical teachings, and to live together in unity with all believers. Jesus' investment in his disciples' lives and Paul's offers to serve as a daily human example testify to the timelessness of this restoration principle of godly models (Mark 3:14; Luke 11:1; 1 Cor. 11:1; Phil. 1:27 – 30; 2:5; 3:17; 4:9; 1 Thess. 1:4 – 9; 2:1 – 12; and 1 Peter 2:18 – 21).

Youth for Christ applies this fifth principle by *strategically developing leaders to reach young people from every people group.* Since young people are influenced by emulating worthy exemplars, those of us who serve youth must be deliberate in our very best modeling strategies.

Conclusion

Now that we have reached the end, let's return to our original questions:

- How do adolescents — as a subgroup of God's creation masterpiece — mature into the "holy whole" persons desired by the Father?
- What's most important in serving adolescents? What are the essentials?
- Why were those particular items chosen?

I hope you have been encouraged to consider the foundational theological directions *before* you look at helpful human development insights. I hope that prayer, love, God's Word, unity, and godly exemplars have taken on new significance for you as well. Together, may we cooperate with the Holy Spirit's work of growth and maturity in young people, so that each teen becomes more and more like his Savior and Lord.

NOTES

1. This statement is *not* a mutually exclusive one. Social science studies (in general) and developmental theories (in particular) certainly have their place in youth ministry. But they are *always* supplemental to biblical-theological foundations.
2. "Pray continually" (1 Thess. 5:17) is one of the rare commands that are to be done constantly. Two similar directives are also here in this context: to be joyful and to give thanks always (vv. 16 and 18). Furthermore, these three commands are directly linked to "God's will."
3. This verse, of course, is a post-resurrection passage. But Jesus portrays this pursuing pattern throughout his ministry, starting at the very beginning, as noted in John 1:35 – 39.
4. Among many Scriptures that accent both believing and doing, the book of James is the foremost, with its representative passage of James 2:14 – 17. Regarding how one's personal "talk and walk" matches up with helping others, there are frequent passages that use the two-letter word *as.* That is, we are to empower others just *as* God has empowered us (see John 13:14 – 15; 15:12; 20:21).
5. This paragraph illustrates how the social sciences can — and must — be used.

Chapter 13

RESTORING ADULTS:
A CALL FOR MULTICULTURAL
EDUCATION-FORMATION

Robert W. Pazmiño

It is critical that all students of the Bible — no matter what their ethnicity or culture — are educated equally. This should be self-evident, but it's important to affirm this principle when you are teaching or learning. In general, Christian life requires holistic restoration committed to justice, righteousness, and God's shalom as non-negotiable values to be made manifest. Educational equality is committed to similar values: impartial access to instructional resources, respect for differences, equal opportunity to be heard, appropriate role models, and shared power to make educational decisions. *Educational equality, then, is a complementary subset of biblical restoration.*

Beyond the basic insights shared by Dettoni on lifespan human development in chapter 5, Christian educators also should focus on the specific adult histories in their own cultures and who their learners are. To put it another way, developmental theories normally anticipate helpful transitions for *many* adults in the *general population*, but those ideas must always be verified by the *particular* ways that *individuals* from diverse cultures mature.

Jesus' own teaching as well as the models of the New Testament churches at Jerusalem and Antioch follow this intentional multicultural design.

Multicultural Adult Education in Scripture

As a Christian educator, you start with the biblical record. Jesus himself lived and ministered in Galilee's multicultural settings. Galilee, which literally means *a ring* or *circle*, referred to a region made up of Gentiles with diverse ethnic backgrounds. The population was in constant flux from infiltration and migration. In its history, Galilee was controlled by Babylon, Persia, Macedonia, Egypt, Syria, and Assyria. It was the center of diverse (and sometimes colliding) cultural currents. The primary language in Galilee in Jesus' time was Koine Greek, although Jews primarily spoke Aramaic in daily life and Hebrew in the synagogue.[1]

It was within this multicultural setting that God chose to be incarnated in the person of Jesus of Nazareth, and where our Lord's restorative ministry began. One striking example of ministry across cultural lines is found in John 4:1–42, where Jesus surprises three categories of people: a Samaritan woman with whom Jesus privately converses at the well, a subsequent crowd of Samaritans whom the Master Teacher instructs, and his astonished disciples. Multicultural communication wasn't difficult for Jesus. In fact, it was in place by design.

Unfortunately, that same successful multicultural communication is avoided today in Christian education of ethnic adults. But the church can no longer afford to dismiss her Lord's example. His instructional pattern was intentional, not optional.

The book of Acts describes critical facts about the Jerusalem and Antioch churches regarding their multicultural communities. Acts 6 features the Jerusalem church and a conflict between ethnic groups. The Grecian Jews (or Hellenists) complained against the Hebrews (or the Aramaic-speaking Palestinians) because their widows were being overlooked in the daily food distribution. Ethnic tensions over resource distribution existed in the New Testament just as they do now. This problem was resolved through the appointment of seven new leaders, who were likely Hellenistic Jews because of their Greek names. This precedent suggests a useful strategy for adult education with diverse ethnicities: *Equip and empower ethnic leadership to serve their own communities along with communities that cross cultural borders.*[2]

An even more diverse ethnicity is found among the Antioch church leadership in Acts 13:1. Simeon was Black. Lucius was Greek. Manaen was Jewish. An African, an Asian, and a Palestinian helped lead this congregation. In addition, Barnabas and Saul are named. Barnabas was a Levite and a native of the island of Cyprus (Acts 4:36). Like Saul of Tarsus, he was a Jew of the Diaspora and a Hellenist. Thus, Antioch provides one model for the inclusion of ethnic persons as well as the importance of ethnic leaders.

A couple of other pertinent facts should be highlighted: Acts 11:26 notes that the disciples were first called "Christians" at this Antioch church.[3] Also, Antioch's multicultural congregation became known for its missionary outreach. Starting with the commissioning of Saul and Barnabas, this divergent group of believers advanced the gospel across even wider cultural borders, eventually expanding into Europe.

An Overview of Multicultural Adult Education

Besides similar patterns of cultural diversity, contemporary Christian educators in the United States are further confronted by their own history of racism and discrimination, which still affects individuals whose ethnic heritage is not identified as Anglo. Furthermore, from my personal perspective and experience as a North American-Hispanic Christian educator, all ethnic groups express additional concern for adult education. The church must advocate and exhibit an alternative inclusive community that embraces the gospel's radical demand to love our neighbor as ourselves. Today that "neighbor" may not only be a member of an ethnic group but also a Christian sister or brother. Moreover, Christian educators often confront a host of supplementary issues that may not be apparent to them whenever Anglo conformity, assimilation, and segregated education are wrongly accepted as norms.

For these and other reasons, a biblical model of multicultural education deserves careful consideration. This relevant subject will be analyzed through four prominent factors: the learner's identity, the role of the learner's experience, the learner's readiness to learn, and the learner's concern for immediate application.

But first, consider this definition of the term "education." Education is described by three elements, each of which is italicized in the following definition: "Education is the process of sharing *content* with *persons* in the *context* of their community and society."

First, *content* is foundational. For instance, think about the influence that content has when it comes to effectively teaching the gospel of Jesus Christ and to challenging hearers with the demands of discipleship. As James Michael Lee suggests, content includes not just cognitive input, but also affective and lifestyle content so that a combined head, heart, and hand response to the gospel is fostered.[4]

Second, terms like "learning" and "the individual" are frequently found at the core of popular Christian education. But those two words may represent a cultural bias for ethnic groups who value the opposite, yet complementary, sides of those same two words: valuing teaching (vs. learning) transformative information and focusing on *persons* (vs. the individual) in community. Once again, cultural assumptions — like supposing that "learning" and "the individual" are highly rated in every culture — should be avoided. The worst assumption is that every adult learner is the same.

Third, *context* is also a significant concept. If teachers desire to transfer learning beyond each student, they must envision every adult within the web of their social relationships, where all of life is experienced. Context is primary for ethnic adults because it so closely relates to the learner's identity and to his or her expected participation in the Christian community. Within the Hispanic community, as an example, the Christian educator must realize that personal advancement is never a higher goal than familial and communal loyalty.

Within this framework of education, then, recall the four earlier-noted factors that encourage effective multicultural education.

Factor #1: The Learner's Identity within Multicultural Adult Education

Adult education, in general, assumes that the main source for the learner's identity emerges from individual life and roles. Moreover, the teaching emphasis is primarily oriented to the present and secondarily focused on the future. This standard does not recognize the number of ethnic adults whose identity, by contrast, is linked with their families and extended communities. This standard also misses those whose identities are tied more closely to the past — grounded by respect for ancestors, lands, and traditions. Furthermore, the constant challenge for persons from ethnic communities is balancing the expectations of their dual identities within conflicting combinations (like Hispanic and North American, or African and American, or Asian and American identities). This challenge is heightened when the historical understanding of what it means to become an "American" is analyzed — specifically to leave one's previous ethnic distinctions in a new society and to embrace an identity mainly derived from a Northern European Protestant heritage. This process is further complicated if one's skin color, accent, values, or commitments do not fit the dominant cultural norm.

Essential undertakings of adult Christian education, then, must not automatically view alternatives to the larger cultural agenda as deficient or inferior. Nor should it be assumed that when identity has been formed, the dominant culture's approach was automatically accepted. The strengths of each suggested alternative should be weighed. For instance, persons from ethnic groups may have much to offer regarding commitment to community, and that value is especially important in light of mounting contemporary cries against radical individualism. This affirmation of diverse ethnic heritages also advances a broader, more creative unity of all humanity — which is doctrinally bound by the image of God.

Factor #2: The Learner's Experience within Multicultural Adult Education

The contributions of learner experience can be best advanced by adhering to these guidelines of effective instruction:

+ Take care to see that shared learner experiences do not become a pooling of ignorance. Appropriate structuring of experiential content diminishes this potential for ignorance. For example, the educator should emphasize the need for learner experiences to be informed and examined, which often occurs when each learner takes personal responsibility for his or her own critical reflections.
+ Basic pertinent skills of discussion should be understood, valued, and achieved by all participants. This process starts with the willingness to hear different voices and is closely followed by genuine robust dialogue. These early phases of discussion often stimulate additional participant responses, which promote deeper levels of dialogue.
+ Esteem learner experiences — both personal and corporate. First establish the rudimentary context from the experience before it is critiqued and revised. Welcome the corporate voice in Christian settings. It upholds age-old wisdom from the faith community.

- Balance personal experiences by the broader scope of multicultural education. For example, by itself, curriculum content may become superficial if it is separated from life. Likewise, experience in and of itself may become mere activity. Strike a balance between curriculum content and learner experience as well as between the learner's personal faith and his or her corporate life.

Factor #3: The Learner's Readiness within Multicultural Adult Education

Standard educational practice usually establishes programs in relation to individually perceived needs. This practice, based on certain views of developmental psychology, assumes that adult learners participate best when their personal needs are met, enhancing their motivation to learn. But who are the ones that identify those needs? And do those same decision makers select the prominent needs of *each* learner? Members of ethnic communities, for instance, have unique needs for survival in a culturally alien and discriminatory society that often standardizes the framework for everybody's education. These needs may force ethnic learners initially to become dependent upon gaining essential resources before exploring alternatives and maintaining hope despite an ethnic history of exclusion. Divergent learner needs — like need for the basics of everyday living — are rarely identified by the influential persons who set the one-size-fits-all curriculum objectives *and* who have never personally faced the demands of survival needs.

At a more foundational level, the traditional emphasis on human needs may also be problematic when it comes to the learner's readiness. Abraham Heschel warned of the tyranny of needs that characterizes much of life. More significantly, this emphasis on "need" may fail to address the demands of God upon people and the place of human responsibility in relation to God.[5] Needs that go beyond survival are often determined by cultural norms and expectations, which must be evaluated in light of biblical values. When identifying any learner need, educators should exercise careful, prayerful, and deliberate discernment. They are to be receptive to essential demands of other ethnic learners, which initially may not have been considered in early curriculum planning.

One particular example of a need not readily named in most Christian education designs is the need for celebration and worship in life. People in an urbanized and highly technological society often do not reserve time for worship. Times set aside to gain a sense of wonder for God's multifaceted creation are rare. However, in Hispanic culture, for example, the place of fiesta reserves this space for celebration.

Factor #4: The Learner's Concern for Immediate Application within Multicultural Adult Education

Heschel reflected on the dominant American drive of educational pragmatism ("If something is useful, it is valued"), as he contrasted the goals of educational systems from Greek and Hebrew cultures. He pointed out that the average student in the United States learns in order to *use*. However, the Greeks learned in order to *comprehend* and the Hebrews learned in order to *revere*.[6] Obviously, those three purposes reflect vastly different values and objectives. Yes, the need for immediate application should be affirmed, but not at the expense of what the other two respected cultures model: learning for its inherent value and learning to gain wisdom in order to worship. Placing a high priority on pragmatic learning may blind participants to an array of other significant benefits. One benefit is that of forgotten values, which are often nourished in a subculture or alternative culture. A specific illustration of forgotten values is reaffirming the importance of interpersonal relationships. This forgotten value holds a lower priority in traditional education (vs. alternative forms of education), because of the competing, higher-rated value of time and its inherent restraints.

Summary and Conclusion

Serious attention directed at biblical, holistic restoration requires contemporary Christian educators to heed three challenges: multicultural awareness, analysis, and cooperation. First, we must understand the ethnic cultures we serve. The apostle Paul describes his own efforts of awareness when he attempts to live like a Jew in order to win the Jews and like a Gentile to win the Gentiles (1 Cor. 9:19 – 23). Clifford Geertz, a cultural anthropologist, describes a culture in terms of a unique worldview and an ethos. A worldview is the picture that a particular person or group holds of the way life is perceived. Ethos is the tone, character, and quality of life found within each ethnic group.[7] In order to understand reasonably both the worldview and ethos of ethnics, Christian instructors need to spend adequate time with representatives from the ethnic group with which they hope to partner in education. The goal of multicultural awareness is both a greater knowledge of and a stronger trust in the people we serve.

Christian educators also need to compare the worldview and ethos of specific ethnic groups with that of the historic Christian faith. This is what multicultural analysis means. This process assumes that educators have already critically analyzed their own culture in similar ways, which then allows them to determine which values from a particular ethnic culture confirm, complement, or contradict the Christian faith.[8] Areas that confirm Christianity should be identified before any criticisms are raised. This analysis requires extensive interaction with leaders who represent identified ethnic communities. When areas of confirmation and complement are found, those contributions are to be preserved and celebrated. In areas of contradiction or conflict, the grace of God is required to redeem and transform cultures. Discernment to know these differences is best done by those who are native to the culture analyzed. Implicitly, that requires the empowerment of ethnic leadership.

Finally, Christian educators must create working principles that meet the challenges of multicultural cooperation. These principles uniquely address the worldview and ethos of selected ethnic groups. They should be drawn from biblical, theological, and philosophical foundations as well as from tested insights emerging from the social sciences. The creation, articulation, and implementation of this total strategy need the complete cooperation of ethnic leaders to avoid the danger of cultural imposition.

In conclusion, this call for multicultural adult education has raised pertinent issues for ethnic communities and for the larger Christian community. Prudent Christian teachers should be able to recognize the distinct needs of ethnic persons while sidestepping the common yet perilous temptation to segregate adults into ethnically compartmentalized groups. The church's purpose should reclaim the vibrant multicultural mix that characterized Jesus' ministry and the maturing nature of the churches at Jerusalem and Antioch.

NOTES

1. K. W. Clark, "Galilee," in *The Interpreter's Dictionary of the Bible*, ed. George A. Buttrick (Nashville: Abingdon, 1962), 344–47.
2. Consider Acts 15 for additional strategies of resolution within multiethnic conflicts.
3. Thom Hopler, *World of Difference: Following Christ beyond Your Cultural Walls* (Downers Grove, IL: InterVarsity Press, 1981), 104–10.
4. James Michael Lee, *The Content of Religious Instruction: A Social Science Approach* (Birmingham: Religious Education Press, 1985).
5. Abraham J. Heschel, *Between God and Man* (New York: Free Press, 1959), 129–55.
6. Ibid., 35–54.
7. Clifford Geertz, *The Interpretation of Cultures* (New York: Basic Books, 1973), 126–27.
8. Lawrence A. Cremin, *Traditions of American Education* (New York: Basic Books, 1977), 128.

Applications of Global Tasks
for Every Church

Chapter 14

OUR GLOBAL TASK OF EVANGELISM-PROCLAMATION: RESTORING PEOPLE FROM THE INSIDE OUT

Jerry Root

Then Jesus came to them and said, "All authority in heaven and on earth has been given to me. Therefore go and make disciples of all nations, baptizing them in the name of the Father and of the Son and of the Holy Spirit, and teaching them to obey everything I have commanded you. And surely I am with you always, to the very end of the age." (Matthew 28:18 – 20)

Evangelism isn't confined to soap boxes, street corners, and television studios. It isn't the exclusive purview of a gifted few. No, it's for all disciples. Being shy or uncertain about what to say is no excuse. Sharing Christ's saving message is the duty of every Christian. God gave us the Great Commission, *not* the great suggestion.

I have framed my discussion on worldwide evangelism within the theoretical design created by William K. Frankena,[1] joining the handful of authors in the field of Christian education-formation who have amplified his model during the past couple of decades. Like others, I have modified Frankena's five-box model to meet my specific purposes. While Frankena's model has the liabilities inherent in any model (inflexibility, tempting us to limit our imaginations), it also gives us the ability to visualize a design from foundation to practice. We have a concise framework that, when used properly, can be easily communicated and is a complete structure that encourages assessment and planning.

Five subtopics or "boxes" organize Frankena's model: Box A deals with one's ultimate goal, which in this case is evangelism. Box B focuses on the nature of people. Box C combines the content of the first two boxes, expressing the intermediate objectives for the individuals being analyzed. Box D includes methodology or "tools" for evangelism. Box E combines Boxes C and D, describing pertinent applications for life — that is, how evangelism will "look" when it is practiced.

Box A: Ultimate Ends

We must start with the fact that a mature Christian is spiritually reproductive. Dawson Trotman, the founder of the Navigators, an organization designed to equip Christians to disciple other believers, saw evangelism through this particular indicator of spiritual growth. He emphasized that the ability to evangelize is essential to Christian maturity. Conversely, a person is considered spiritually immature until he or she can lead another person to Christ and nurture the new believer to reproduce as well. Box A, then, as it pertains to evangelism, represents Christians who pass the good news on to the lost.

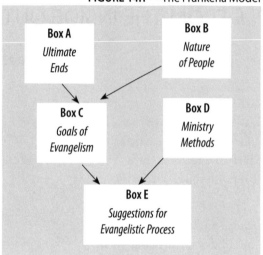

FIGURE 14.1 — The Frankena Model

In light of this overarching goal, it's important to dispel the myth that evangelism is only for those with a divine gift for witnessing. While it's true that some believers are especially gifted for this essential task, all saints are called to do this work. This same principle is found elsewhere in the body of Christ. For example, not all believers have the gift of giving, yet all are called to give. Not everyone has the gift of hospitality, but each Christian is to be hospitable. And so on.

Before Jesus ascended into heaven, he was clear, emphatic, and unequivocal about the task he left his followers. He told them to go into the world and make disciples, "teaching them *to obey everything* I have commanded you" (Matt. 28:19 – 20).

In order to make disciples — to grow people who have accepted Jesus as their Savior — the Christian first has to witness to those people who have not yet come to faith in Jesus Christ. Evangelism, at its essence, is the proclamation of these components of the good news:

- God loves fallen humanity, even though we are beset with sin and estranged from him.
- God himself has taken care of the problem of sin by sending his Son, Jesus Christ, to bear the burden of all sin and its consequences.
- Christ died the death that all others deserve and arose from the dead as proof that his death atones for sin and reconciles to God all who believe in him.
- God also provides all believers the hope of a purposeful life now and eternal life beyond the grave.[2]

To summarize Box A, the Creator-Savior-Lord wants our very best. *He desires our total restoration — to be completely healed — starting with God's redemption at* our core, saving us from the inside out. This is biblical evangelism. Discipleship, which can never be fully separated from evangelism, centers on *God's rejuvenation*, the continuous healing of all other aspects of who we believers are from physical to moral domains.

Box B: Nature of People

The Great Commission is rooted in the character and nature of God but is assigned to people. There are three realities pertaining to the nature of people that require careful attention when examining the mandate of evangelism.

The first of three realities is that *humans are relational*. The particular doctrine of the Trinity indicates that Christianity is a relational faith, where three persons of the Godhead fellowship together. The importance of relationship is illustrated by the fact that people are created to reflect God's image as both male and female.[3]

The second reality is that *humans sin*. Even though men and women are made for healthy relationship with God, our rebellion causes estrangement from him.[4] That means that our humanity is diminished, because sin shrinks and distorts people.

The third reality is that *humans are broken and need restoration*. In Ephesians 4:12, the apostle Paul tells church leaders to equip all believers for the work of Christian ministry. The Greek word used for "equip" (*katartismos*) had many meanings in the ancient world, but there is one meaning that provides some helpful parallels to evangelism. *Katartismos* was a medical term that emphasized the need to properly set a broken bone. Once healing occurred, the patient was physically restored to live for the purposes for which he or she was created. In a more figurative application of *katartismos*, disciples recall their own spiritual brokenness and woundedness as well as their healing, which helps them acquire the necessary empathy of and capacity to care for others.

In sum, Box B declares that all people need God's restoration — starting with nonbelievers who need redemption. Again, we saints who need continuous *rejuvenation* portray the complementary side of discipleship.

Box C: Ministry Goals of Evangelism

Box C combines the contents of Boxes A and B. When merged, both of these foundational categories affect the short-range objectives of evangelism that we set for the unsaved we have described. Box A specifically features the Trinity's ultimate desire for total human restoration, centering on redemption in Christ. Box B advances the complex reality of people, including our creation as perfect, relational beings who sinlessly reflect our Maker and our sinful rebellion that breaks and distorts all our relationship. We are also made to understand that in discipleship, believers need to be regularly "healed" in order to reach out to the spiritually lost. Thus, there are two groups of people, believers and nonbelievers respectively, who desperately require aspects of God's grace.

When these two foundational categories from Boxes A and B converge, one major outcome is the incarnation, "God with us." Jesus Christ bridges the Trinity's ultimate purpose of redemption (Box A) and the ultimate human need of all people (Box B) to be fully restored. The perfect God-Man is the *only* solution to the universal predicament of human sin and all that it took to satisfy the Father's requirement for a holy sacrifice. The Son is not just the perfect sacrifice for humankind; he is also the perfect exemplar for godly living of both evangelism and discipleship.[5]

As perfect exemplar, Jesus doesn't merely tell followers how to live; he shows them. So Jesus models evangelism — as the center of a holistic plan of restoration — before he sends his disciples out to replicate their Master's testimony. John 9 may be the best expression of our Lord's commitment to total restoration. Verses 1 to 5 focus on Jesus' deliberate *teaching* to restore thinking about "the work of God." Verses 6 and 7 note Jesus' purposeful *healing* to restore physical health to the blind man. And verses 35 to 41 stress Jesus' intentional *preaching* to restore the soul of the former "spiritually" blind man.

Box D: Ministry Methods

In Mark 3:14 – 15 Jesus "appointed twelve … that they might be *with him* and that he might *send them* out to preach and to have authority to drive out demons." Our Lord's commitment to relationships is predominant, as is his commitment to holistic ministry. Thus, the two methods of relational (or dialogical) instruction and hands-on experience provide the crucial processes by which Christianity was (and is) spread to the world.

Jesus daily demonstrated these methods to his disciples. He later provided the Twelve with the necessary authority and power to achieve their own ministry goals using those methods. In John 15:1 – 8 Jesus told his disciples that if they would abide in him, they would bear spiritual fruit. It was in this abiding that the disciples' earlier-noted personal wounds were also mended. And it was also where his followers began to discover the heart of God for the lost.

Contextually, it is within these two methods that Jesus promised his disciples the power of the Holy Spirit (Acts 1:8) to fully enable them to be his witnesses, telling others of the love and forgiveness of God. This abiding process causes Christ's passions to become our passions. And we want to bear even more fruit that imitates Jesus' ministry.

Jesus used some similar methods for both smaller and larger groups of disciples. In Luke 9:1 – 6 Christ's disciples were sent out to preach, teach, and heal. Luke 10:1 – 9 repeats these same three ministry methods for his seventy-two followers. The Great Physician put each of them in risky circumstances where they could either succeed or fail. When the seventy-two returned, Jesus added another method: he gathered them and had them report their experiences. With that feedback, Jesus publicly evaluated all that had happened so that his disciples could start maturing from that self-examination.

As a case in point, the most prominent correction Jesus made with this larger group centered on issues of ministry priorities and directly on evangelism. Luke 10:17 records the disciples' collective enthusiasm over their successful exorcisms, using Jesus' mighty name. Our Lord did not dismiss this healing ministry altogether, but he quickly contrasted those miracles with a much grander blessing: their personal salvation. "Do not rejoice that the spirits submit to you," Jesus instructs in Luke 10:20, "but rejoice that your names are written in heaven." He pointed out the extra value of evangelism.

Box E: Suggestions for Evangelistic Practice

Box E blends the contents of Boxes C and D. Since the task of evangelism can be complex, appropriate ministry skills need to be cultivated. Two basic skills are particularly important. First, believers need to *know the basic content of the gospel* and be able to present it clearly and concisely. Second, believers need to *listen to each non-Christian's perceived needs* that relate to the message of God's love and forgiveness.

Regarding this first skill, note five key points that the apostle Peter included in his evangelistic message to Cornelius, the first Gentile convert (Acts 10:34–43):

1. The gospel is for all people; God does not show favoritism toward individuals or nations (vv. 34–35).
2. God the Father sent his Son, Jesus, to proclaim the "good news of peace" (v. 36).
3. The Father anointed the Son with the power of the Holy Spirit, so that he "went around doing good and healing" (vv. 37–38).
4. Peter and others were eyewitnesses of Jesus' ministry, death, and resurrection (vv. 39–41).
5. Jesus' followers are commanded to preach that Jesus is now the judge of all people and that "all the prophets testify" of this fact: "Everyone who believes in him [Jesus] receives forgiveness of sins through his name" (vv. 42–43).

Regarding the second skill of evangelism, that of *listening*, disciples must be sensitive to the personal needs of the lost. Contemplate these five principles from Jesus' own evangelistic testimony, extracted from the gospel of John:

1. Start with the listener's personal understanding and then connect new, yet related spiritual truths to that knowledge. In John 3:5–8, Jesus introduced his listener to the Holy Spirit's role in evangelism by beginning with some

common understandings about the wind. Recall that in the Greek, the words "spirit" and "wind" come from only one term, *pneuma* (which Jesus deliberately selected). A natural link from "old" to "new" knowledge was forged.

2. Know and prudently address any primary controversies between Christianity's basic beliefs and those of other religions or ethnicities that may be presented by the listener. (Jesus modeled this principle in John 4:19 – 26.)

3. Acknowledge pertinent universal human needs, then springboard the conversation to related spiritual truths that pertain to the listener. Jesus followed this principle by emphasizing the universal needs of thirst (John 4:7 – 14) and hunger (John 6:35), as he then moved toward spiritual restoration.

4. Exercise patience and wisdom, waiting for the listener to express an uncoerced response of need. Both John 5:6 and John 6:39 – 41 identified Jesus' sensitivity to this principle through the respective cases of physical and spiritual impairment.

5. In addition to having patience for the listener's expression of *personal need*, show patience for the listener's voluntary expression of *personal faith*. Both John 2:11b and John 9:35 – 38 feature this essential evangelistic principle.

God bless you as you take seriously God's universal call of evangelism. God bless you in your daily obedience.

NOTES

1. William K. Frankena, *Philosophy of Education* (New York: Macmillan, 1965).
2. 1 Corinthians 15:1 – 5 states the keys to the gospel.
3. See Genesis 1:26 – 27 and 2:18, 21 – 25.
4. See Genesis 3:1 – 8.
5. See John 4:1 – 42 and John 9:35 – 41 regarding Jesus' model of evangelism.

Chapter 15

OUR GLOBAL TASK OF SERVICE: MINISTERING TO "THE LEAST OF THESE"

(with Cheryl Fawcett)

Did you smile at someone today? Did you hold the door? Did you listen attentively? Did you lend a helping hand? And did you do those things without thinking — without expecting any type of reward?

If so, congratulations! You acted like sheep! Now, don't get offended or roll your eyes to heaven. "Sheep" is a good thing. Sheep, according to Matthew 25:31 – 46, means "authentic Christ-follower." The alternative is a goat.

"But those things aren't so tough! And it also sounds like you're focusing on works," someone criticizes.

At that point, Jesus walks out of the shadows, joins our little circle, and repeats those deeply convicting words: "Haven't I been with you long enough? And you still don't get it?"

We all stare at the ground and gulp hard. Total silence. Shame.

"It's not about how 'big' your service is — it never has been! When will you stop your 'bigger-is-better' judgments? And 'works' don't have to play any part! *I'm after your heart.* I always am. If you don't serve me with your whole heart in the little things, what good is it when we need to talk about the bigger responsibilities?"

Again, we make no eye contact.

"Matthew 7:22 – 23 says it pretty well: 'In the last days, some people will submit some pretty impressive resumes. Some will have prophesied, exorcized demons, and done a lot of miracles.' Impressive indeed. But I'll look them right in the eye and say, 'Sorry, but you never gave me your heart. So I never knew you.' That's where it all must begin."

Analyzing Matthew 25

The huge difference between evangelical Christians and members of all other major religions is this: the individuals in the former group realize they are *never* going to heaven because of the good they've done, whereas the people in the latter group think their eternal reward *only* comes because their good works outweigh their bad. That's a massive distinction.

The sheep in Matthew 25 are totally shocked that Jesus — "the King" (v. 34) — rewards them with "the kingdom" *for serving needy people.*

"So, isn't *that* salvation by works?" the same earlier critic interrupts.

No — not by a long shot — for four reasons. First, the sheep's eternal reward is sovereignly "prepared … since the creation of the world" (v. 34b) — long before any person (or animal) has a chance to do any good works. Reasons two, three, and four also affirm this truth about predestined reward, since Matthew 25 points out three facts the sheep did *not* know:

- They didn't know anybody was watching their behavior.
- They didn't know that, when they served the needy, they were really serving Jesus.
- They didn't know they were going to receive any kind of reward.

"Salvation by works," in contrast, requires prior knowledge of those three facts. People with a "works" mindset proactively plan the moral behavior they will perform. Their hope is to get those "good behavior points" swapped for heaven — sort of like spiritual frequent-flyer miles.

"Sheep" help needy people because a genuine Christian, by God's grace, reaches out to assist others. That's not always the case, but for the mature Christ-follower this is the rule, not the exception. Inherently, sheep treat all people as they would treat the Creator. I call this reality the "Creation Equation" because it is based on the spectacular blessing of God's image in all people. God's image is so strong, so powerful, that there is a permanent bond between the Creator and all human creatures. So how we act toward any human creature — whether kindly or not — *equals* how we act toward the Creator.[1]

Notice that the "goats" are equally surprised in Matthew 25 — but for totally different reasons. Their response to Jesus, in verse 44, could just as well be paraphrased: "Lord, *had we known* someone was videotaping our lives — and *had we known* that serving those needy people really meant *serving you* — *you know* we would have served those needy folks, *so we could be rewarded!*"

You see, it's the goats — not the sheep — who adhere to the "salvation by works" philosophy, which lands them in hell. Using a contemporary illustration, sheep will act like sheep act, serving the needy — even when the YouTube camera is not on. But goats will *only* serve when they see the camera's red bulb lit.

More of "the Least" Needs

Almost ten years now into this new millennium, we see that a huge "army" of global Christian servants (who left the United States after World War II) are reaching the end of their "tour of duty." As they pass the baton on to the next generation of servants, the earth's population has exceeded six billion.[2] Globally, the center of spiritual revival and significant service has shifted from Western Europe and North America to its new epicenters in Central and South America, Africa, and the underground church in China. The evangelical church in Western Europe is currently on the world religions' endangered-species list, and their North American counterparts are (more often than not) too self-absorbed in meeting their own concerns. When pastors challenge these congregants to reach out to the cries of the "least of these" strangers, antagonists in the pews retort: "But, what about *our* unmet needs?"

The next generation of Christian servants is more globally aware, more widely traveled, more cyberspace connected, and more easily enlisted in short-term service safaris. However, they are reeling from their own personal hurts, including a range of destructive consequences from the fragmentation of their own families. These wounded warriors are thus wary of long-term commitments.

Sheep Sightings

Glimmers of hope exist for more much-needed, worldwide servants who want to serve Christ through the universal church. Dr. John Piper, pastor of Bethlehem Baptist Church in Minneapolis, trains servants who are motivated by strong biblical reasons for global service. Members are grounded in the biblical truths that say that God must be praised among all nations. Mobilizing children for global service is the identifying mark of Mechanicsville Christian Center of Mechanicsville, Virginia. Associate Pastor Pete Hohmann begins a missions library for children, integrates missions into aspects of the child's church experience, launches missions prayer meetings for kids, provides meaningful giving outlets, and forms a children's outreach team. Rick Warren, pastor of Saddleback Church, calls Christians to overcome five global giants: spiritual darkness, egocentric leadership, poverty, disease, and illiteracy. Warren's P.E.A.C.E. plan intends to slay these giants as churches: *Plant churches, Equip servant leaders, Assist the poor, Care for the sick, and Educate the next generation.

Established evangelical mission agencies engage in "least of these" outreaches alongside of their traditional church-planting initiatives. Various denominational and interdenominational mission agencies sponsor global service initiatives that focus on the special needs of the "least of these."[3] WEC International's subministry, Rainbows of Hope, trains collegians to work with street children, sexually exploited children, and children victimized by HIV/AIDS and war. Through short-term service, many people experience enough "ministry success" to commit for longer stints of service. Other agencies follow similar patterns.[4]

Micro-loans creatively relieve global poverty and are being used effectively in Bangladesh, India, and other poverty-stricken countries. World Vision (as well as other organizations) assist the poor, mostly women, to begin personal businesses by granting them loans from $50 to $5000. Groups work locally to police their own loan repayment plans so as to not require collateral. At the time of this writing, 97 percent of the loans were being repaid. The subsequent growth of businesses empowers women to care for themselves and their children as well as make contributions to their communities.

Conclusion

Matthew 25 "sheep" are fashioned from the inside out. Meaningful change in people always begins with changed hearts. Then adapted strategies and experimental approaches follow, as these servants grow more sensitive to God's heart for the hurting.

Every follower of Jesus (regardless of ethnicity, gender, or race) is characterized by service to "the least of these." Chinese believers demonstrate their genuine affection for Christ as they send one out of every ten believers to share their faith and their lives with followers of Buddha, Muhammad, and Confucius. Christ-followers from Brazil declare their love for Christ as they act in kind and helpful ways with Portuguese speakers in Mozambique and East Timor. Spanish-speaking believers from South and Central America reveal their allegiance to Christ when they serve migrant Hispanic farmers in the southern and northwestern regions of the United States and other national urban centers where Hispanics have emigrated.

For the Christian, global service is not something "nice" to dabble in now and again. It is not limited to times when the circumstances are right and sacrifice is kept to a minimum. Jesus describes service as fully integrated into his followers' everyday lives. Regardless of their own needs, Christians are called to reach out. Biblical service often comes at inconvenient times, when sheep are tired, and sometimes uses up resources earlier committed to their own needs. Sheep help those who cannot return any favors. Sheep serve in dangerous places, doing risky service. Sheep serve — like all sheep — without expectation of being acknowledged, applauded, or publicly rewarded.

So permit me to repeat a couple of earlier questions: Have you started to see "sheep signs" of maturity in your own life? Have you held the door open for someone today or lent a helping hand?

NOTES

1. Jeremiah 22:15 – 16 summarizes the testimony of one of Israel's kings:

> "Did not your father have food and drink?
> He did what was right and just,
> so all went well with him.

He defended the cause of the poor and needy,
and so all went well.
Is that not what it means to know me?"
declares the Lord.

2. There are more Christians on planet earth now than in all the past, but the number of those that have not once heard Jesus' love story grows exponentially.
3. For example, San Diego native Jason Russell recruits college classmates to assist his film documentation of the plight of Uganda's "invisible" children.
4. The I-TECH project (Indigenous People's Technology & Education Center), launched by Steve Saint, son of missionary Nate Saint, enables indigenous churches to overcome the technological and educational hurdles that impede independence. I-TECH equips nationals with technology requiring minimal outside support such as mobile dental labs, portable solar-powered radio transmitters, and computers.

Chapter 16

OUR GLOBAL TASK OF FELLOWSHIP-COMMUNITY: LIFE IN THE BODY OF CHRIST

Faye E. Chechowich

Education in the local church presumes communal teaching and learning, which matures disciples within that fellowship. Both the goal of educating the local church and the means of achieving it are expressed in the Greek word *koinonia*, which is translated into various English words, including fellowship, communion, contribution, offering, participation, sharing, taking part, having a part, partnership, help, and communication.

The word *koinonia* appears nineteen times in the New Testament. It first appears in Acts 2:42, where the activities of the early Christian church are described: "They devoted themselves to the apostles' teaching and to the fellowship (*koinonia*), to the breaking of bread and to prayer." This Greek word describes two key facets of the fellowship: a quality of horizontal relationship among believers, rooted in their vertical relationship with God (1 John 1:7).

Regardless of the chosen English word, *koinonia* is simply defined as *a group of Christ-followers who voluntarily participate in a shared community, offering themselves and their resources to one another for mutual benefit.*

Koinonia in the Gospels and Acts

Christ calls his disciples into a life of relationship with one another that is modeled after the relationship of the triune God. Just prior to his death, Jesus prayed that his disciples would particularly experience the unity of godly fellowship: "that they may be one as we are one" (John 17:11). In Acts 2:44 – 45 and 4:32 – 37, *koinonia* unity is further described as a direct answer to Jesus' prayer. Early Christians' lives were marked by a consistent concern for every person's needs. Thus, the early church is described as a gathering where people "had everything in common." Christians demonstrate *koinonia* fellowship when they provide for those with less — not because it is required but because it is a loving response from spiritual brothers and sisters to their family in Christ.

> Christianity means community through Jesus Christ and in Jesus Christ. No Christian community is more or less than this. Whether it be a brief, single encounter or the daily fellowship of years, Christian community is only this. We belong to one another only through and in Jesus Christ.
>
> — DIETRICH BONHOEFFER

Sincere *koinonia* prompts outstanding evidence of self-sacrifice and affection because biblical fellowship requires a radical reorientation within its participants. From the inception of the church, God's revolutionary *koinonia* transcends boundaries of ethnicity, gender, and social class (Gal. 3:28). The book of Acts portrays the expanding account of *koinonia* fellowship — from a first-generation group of Christ followers, who were all Jewish, to a post-Pentecost global movement that stretched across every distinguishing people marker.[1]

Pazmiño, in chapter 13 on adult multicultural education, states that the first major test for *koinonia* occurred in Jerusalem when Greek-speaking Jewish widows were overlooked in the daily distribution of food (Acts 6:1 – 7). The solution to this problem featured a model of inclusion, demonstrating the values of *koinonia* and kingdom. That conflict in Jerusalem, which initially disrupted fellowship, was corrected by appointing Greek-speaking Jews to be responsible for all food distribution. Ironically, from within the same group that was first excluded, seven new leaders emerged who significantly renovated this early fellowship.

Philip was one of the seven selected leaders. Beyond his duty to distribute food, Philip soon extended the church's *koinonia* boundaries through cross-cultural evangelism. First, many Samaritans (the northern geographic neighbors of Judea, whom the Jews hated for centuries) were responsive to his preaching and miracles (Acts 8:4 – 8). Next, Spirit-led Philip extends the boundaries of *koinonia* to Africa. He brings the God-fearing Ethiopian official to faith in Christ and then baptizes him after instructing him about the meaning of Isaiah's prophecy (Acts 8:26 – 40).

Peter experiences a different type of transformation — one that shakes the foundations of his thinking and his spirit regarding the nature of Christian *koinonia*. During his three-part afternoon vision, the apostle is instructed to eat everything he sees in a sheet dropped from heaven that contains unclean animals no Jew would ever touch. Peter is told to no longer think of food and people in the restricted categories of "clean or unclean" he previously held. His new understanding of the gospel's radical inclusivity is reinforced as he witnesses the conversion of the Gentile centurion Cornelius (Acts 10:44 – 48).

Koinonia Today

As in the days of the early church, a radical reorientation toward biblical *koinonia* is necessary if the contemporary church desires the vision and power of its forebears. And that change for us is not without its own version of "unclean" challenges. More than two decades ago Robert Bellah, in his classic study *Habits of the Heart*, described some harmful signs of individualism woven within the fabric of American religion.

That same individualistic bent, antithetical to any sense of healthy community, is confirmed in a recent report indicating a decline in interpersonal connectivity. Sociologists relayed two sobering trends in our population as a whole after a comparative analysis was made between the 1985 General Social Survey (GSS) and the 2004 GSS. First, in that span of twenty years, the number of adults claiming they have no other person with whom to discuss important matters tripled! Second, sociologists report that the average size of an individual's social network group has diminished by almost one-third, from 2.94 to 2.08 people.[2]

That report brings both good news and bad to the church, since these statistics include believers as well as nonbelievers. The good news is that the need for *koinonia* is greater than ever. The bad news is that we are not fully proclaiming God's good news. Besides the core issue of salvation, we are neither effectively teaching the truths of biblical fellowship, nor providing opportunities for genuine fellowship to flourish.

Some claim that technology offers the contemporary church increased potential for community, connection, and fellowship and so can provide an effective educational tool. Communication with a greater number of persons is possible in cyberspace, and some kinds of electronic communication are more efficient than face-to-face conversations. Many technologies further our educational ministry efforts, and Bible study via blogs and congregational conversations with blogger pastors are more and more common. There is also great benefit when local and global prayer needs are shared in real time through electronic communication. *Koinonia* fellowship is promoted by the opportunity to support the needy as we pray for them, even though we are separated by many miles. Youth ministers would be hard-pressed to imagine relating to teens without the tools that electronic communication offers. Without question, technology does provide many benefits for Christian fellowship — in the broadest meaning of that term.

Yet the theological implications of any medium must be evaluated. For instance, Ebersole and Woods caution that while virtual community can approximate certain dimensions of *koinonia* (and even enhance it), the gospel requires an incarnational touch, and a full, authentic Christian fellowship requires face-to-face relationships.[3]

In the early days of the church, obstacles like the cultural distance between Jews and Gentiles prohibited the full expression of *koinonia*. Impediments to unencumbered *koinonia* exist in our contemporary setting too. The growing generational segmentation in American churches decreases the potential for intergenerational interaction. The prevalent ministry model that promotes discrete, age-segregated subcongregations within the larger congregation (where youth and young adults are segregated in their church experiences) limits — if not cancels — any intergenerational interaction. Mark Driscoll, a church planter who focused his efforts on young adults, came to this conclusion:

The young urban arty types God had burdened me to build a church for generally came from jacked-up homes, which they wanted to overcome in hopes of one day having a decent future for themselves and their kids. But they had no idea what a decent Christian family looked like. So what they needed was a friendship with godly older families to learn about marriage and parenting. The last thing they needed was a mono-generational church.[4]

While homogenous educational programs may be popular, easier to organize, and more efficient, we still must ask the question: In what ways might biblical fellowship be compromised under these conditions?

One compromise is that global *koinonia* gets put on hold. The American church continues its perennial struggles to bridge racial and ethnic divisions within its own borders, so until we learn some valuable lessons in our own backyard, international fellowship (as far as the American church is concerned) can't make any substantive headway. Authors Michael O. Emerson and Christian Smith conclude that within the evangelical movement, the traditional emphasis on individualism exacerbates the inability of many Caucasian believers to see any systemic racial discrimination.[5] Their subsequent inability to empathize with the troubling experiences of sisters and brothers of color portrays a mammoth barrier to biblical *koinonia*.

Finally, in any conversation about global *koinonia*, the great disparity of wealth between Western Christians and those in developing nations must be highlighted. The definition of biblical *koinonia*, as earlier noted, requires that resources and relationships be offered in mutually beneficial ways for the greater Christian community. All fellowship from our shores that attempts to cross geographic, ethnic, and socioeconomic boundaries means Western believers must live responsibly in light of the physical and spiritual needs of our global family.

Conclusion

Here are five specific strategies to advance global *koinonia*:

+ Provide opportunities for prayer that focus on specific needs within both local churches and the worldwide church.
+ Create occasions to befriend saints locally or at a distance, especially those who are "not like us."
+ Design intergenerational and interracial learning experiences such as group projects to assist in community needs or emergencies.
+ Expose believers to the biblical values and examples of the diverse universal Christian community.
+ Establish at least one sister church relationship locally and one international relationship that could provide experiential opportunities for biblical *koinonia*.

Education *for* fellowship and *of* fellowship represent two dimensions of biblical *koinonia*. These dimensions encourage the church to overcome impediments to that fellowship. Instruction about the nature of fellowship, training associated with fellowship, and spiritual nurture within the context of fellowship lay the necessary foundation of knowledge, skills, and attitudes for *koinonia*. God's power is then released as believers obediently experience genuine Christian fellowship and are continually restored toward Christlikeness.

NOTES

1. Try this helpful exercise: Find a map of this early church period — one that includes Europe, the Middle East, and North Africa. Next read Acts 2:5 – 12. Then locate each of the cities or areas that are listed in this passage in order to comprehend the vast geographical influence the early church quickly experienced.
2. See M. McPherson, L. Smith-Lovin, and M. E. Brashears, "Social Isolation in America: Changes in Core Discussion Networks over Two Decades," *American Sociological Review* 71 (2006): 353 – 75.
3. Ebersole, S. E., and Woods, R., "Virtual Community: Koinonia or Compromise? Theological Implications of Community in Cyberspace," in *Christian Scholars Review* 31 no. 2 (2002).
4. See Mark Driscoll, *Confessions of a Reformission Rev.* (Grand Rapids: Zondervan, 2006), 65.
5. See Michael Emerson and Christian Smith, *Divided By Faith: Evangelical Religion and the Problem of Race in America* (New York: Oxford, 2000).

Chapter 17

OUR GLOBAL TASK OF KINGDOM-ADVOCACY: UNDERSTANDING AND INVESTING IN THE KINGDOM

Steve Kang

The kingdom of God, concisely stated, is *the realm where God rules, where his will is fully obeyed, and where evil is absent forever.* Controversies have always hovered around this alluring concept. This topic is further plagued by a paradox, because "kingdom of God" implies two seemingly opposite facts: theologians have long constructed this doctrine to mean that God's kingdom is present now, even though they also claim it's really not! Traditional words they have employed say the kingdom is both "now" *and* "not yet." So the kingdom is currently with us; however, it is not fully present until God finally ushers it in according to his plan.

We might comprehend this paradoxical "now-not yet" tension better if we analyze a parallel illustration from another familiar doctrine. The Bible describes salvation in terms of three phases of time: past, present, and future. Each phase plays an extremely important role; in fact, each phase completes the other two phases. Hebrews 10:14 identifies the first two salvific phases, stating that Jesus' one-time sacrifice "*has made perfect forever* those who *are being made holy.*" That is, his sacrifice provided our *past* righteousness for all eternity, while it continues to govern the ongoing *present* process of our holiness. Hebrews 10:36 adds the *future* phase, where saints are exhorted to persevere obediently to the end.

A Subsequent Challenge to Understanding the Kingdom

This kingdom paradox may tend to promote a certain "spiritual schizophrenia" among saints, because the two extremes of this continuum are labeled "now" and "not yet." An immature saint, for instance, may be pulled toward one pole on this continuum, while virtually excluding the opposite pole. Then he may be pulled back to the opposing side in an attempt to over-correct his first experience. To illustrate this — starting with the "not yet" pole on the continuum — think of someone so wrapped up in day-to-day ministry needs of this world that she has no time for worship or for any other important activities. Sadly, she may accept the falsehood: "It's better to *burn* out than to *rust* out" because, for all intents and purposes, this "not yet" saint has forgotten the joy of present Christian life and the hope of heaven. Conversely, an illustration of the believer who sits exclusively on the "kingdom now" side includes the well-known example of the man who is "so heavenly-minded that he is no earthly good."

Additional Directives Leading to a Balanced Kingdom View

A handful of guidelines face the contemporary disciple who wants a balanced picture of God's kingdom in his life. The four guidelines below are offered to saints who — like the aforementioned believers — choose one exclusive side of paradox over the other. In all four sets an attempt is made to shore up the traditionally weaker side, based on some of the imbalances often found within the Western church.

First, to gain a more evenhanded view of the kingdom, more attention should be directed to *general revelation sources of God's truth* (not just to special revelation sources). For example, most American evangelicals have understood the task of theology as mining truths out of "the ancient biblical text to the contemporary affirmation of doctrine" and labeling these truths as "self-evident."[1] One neglected area of general revelation features pertinent sociocultural studies. Among other contributions, this social science can provide valuable contextual and historical input — along with data on richly diverse Christian traditions — infusing the subject of God's kingdom with case-specific details that bring necessary breadth to the body of Christ.

Second, more focus should be placed on *our historical faith*, since the "kingdom now" view tends to be rootless. That "now" mindset prohibits kingdom depth. For instance, the generation immediately following Joshua tragically neglected both historical faith *and* personal faith. The entire book of Judges describes the outcome of such losses. Historical and personal faith always go hand in hand for the Christ-follower. Recall their self-destructive ending: "After that whole generation had been gathered to their fathers, another generation grew up, who knew neither the LORD nor what he had done for Israel" (Judg. 2:10).

Third, a necessary shift must be made from our overemphasis on individual faith to appreciating more of the contributions from *our corporate faith community*. The Apostles' Creed represents a concise statement of community faith, likely derived from a standard baptismal confession in the first century AD. The creed accents the believers' collective commitment. This document is no more than 110 words in length, yet its doctrinal list pinpoints key truths about each member of the Trinity, especially the person and work of Jesus Christ. The final sentence features a half-dozen additional doctrines, two of which particularly stress the value of corporate faith (identified here in italics): "I believe in the Holy Spirit, the *holy catholic Church*, the *communion of saints*, the forgiveness of sins, the resurrection of the body, and

The Apostles' Creed

I believe in God the Father Almighty; Maker of Heaven and Earth; and in Jesus Christ his only (begotten) Son our Lord; who was conceived by the Holy Ghost, born of the Virgin Mary; suffered under Pontius Pilate, was crucified, dead, and buried; he descended into hell; the third day he rose from the dead; he ascended into heaven; and sitteth at the right hand of God the Father Almighty; from thence he shall come to judge the quick and the dead. I believe in the Holy Ghost; the holy catholic Church; the communion of saints; the forgiveness of sins; the resurrection of the body; and the life everlasting. Amen.

---

life everlasting. Amen." The term "catholic," of course, means "universal" because it represents believers from international tribes, cultures, and nations.

Fourth, in order to ascertain a fuller, more balanced view of the kingdom, we Christians need to concentrate on the *global church*, not just the local church. Two specific Scriptures emphasize God's intention to value the global scope of his people. The first account is the Tower of Babel. In Genesis 1:28, God blesses Adam and Eve and then commands them to "be fruitful and increase in number; fill the earth and subdue it." Instead of obeying God's mandate, humankind congregates in the land of Shinar, intending to settle there rather than disperse to obediently subdue the earth. Consequently, "the LORD scattered them from there over all the earth, and they stopped building the city" (Gen. 11:8). This divine action is commonly understood and taught as a curse to human beings, and it is the source of much present-day strife among people of different backgrounds. Yet in light of the Creation Mandate,[2] the record actually reads as a divine intervention in order to fulfill God's original decree to reinstill a vision of his broader kingdom. Thus, Christian advocacy sides with our Maker's very first command.

The second account highlighting God's global intentions for his people is the day of Pentecost as recorded in Acts 2, when God powerfully demonstrates his desire to bring together his people from myriad languages across the world. This is a full reversal of humanity's sedentary disobedience at the Tower of Babel. Within this incredible diversity of humanity on that Pentecost, God sanctifies cultures and redeems his people.

However, it doesn't take long for the Babel pattern of rebellion to repeat itself. Christians began to settle in Jerusalem instead of expanding their witness from Jerusalem to all Judea and Samaria and to the ends of the earth, as God explicitly commanded in Acts 1:8. But after Stephen's death in Acts 7, "great persecution broke out against the church at Jerusalem, and all except the apostles were scattered throughout Judea and Samaria" (Acts 8:1).[3]

Reminiscent of the Tower of Babel incident, in his sovereign will, *God disperses his people throughout the world in order that they live both as kingdom-dwellers and as aliens and strangers in this world.* Contemporary Christians who learn from these two accounts will embody a global perspective of the church, acknowledging the triune God of all creation and all culture.

Kingdom Applications for Christian Education-Formation

True kingdom learning and teaching involves a holistic process that serves as an opportunity for the Holy Spirit's transformational work within every person involved. This instruction often takes place in and through the faith community. Teachers start by making it clear that they, too, are fellow sojourners on their Christian pilgrimage, and they are expecting to learn from students just as students are expected to learn from one another and from the teacher. That approach proposes another advocacy position — this time for full participatory learning and teaching, dependent upon the Holy Spirit's guidance. This environment requires constant adjustments in order to maintain necessary levels of humility and openness from every participant.

One important lesson that needs to be conveyed is that culture is not automatically antithetical to the goodness of creation; rather, culture is the result of God's intention for human beings to "fill" the earth through the processes, patterns, and products of human formation and restoration. To this end, teachers are to exhibit three important attitudes: (1) to love and to admire God's splendor as manifested in cultures near and far; (2) to express deep respect for all people, implementing the idea that any person can learn from any other person, regardless of race, ethnicity, class, gender, or age; (3) and to acknowledge that people don't know everything about their own sociocultural setting, even if they attain commendable expertise in that subject.

True knowing, or transformation in Christ, involves not only thoughts or assent to a set of beliefs but also attitudes, actions, and lifestyles. Therefore, both teachers and students are to model how Christians are to live as aliens and strangers — to be "in" but not "of" the world. Teachers and students need to exhibit continual transformation so that their life commitments are ultimately based on treasures that stand the test of time, like their eternal communion with saints in God's kingdom. If the teacher does not take the lead by seriously valuing the sociocultural dimension of Christian formation — authentically living out kingdom norms *outside* the learning community — students will probably not take her seriously *inside* the learning community.

Conclusion

The following eight suggestions offer extremely practical ways that teachers and students alike may promote Kingdom-Advocacy. Each biblical context explicitly addresses the kingdom.

1. Evaluate your personal priorities, putting God's kingdom first (Matt. 6:28 – 34).
2. Circulate the good news where you live (John 3:3 – 5; Luke 4:43; Acts 1:3).
3. Daily consecrate yourself to do God's will (Matt. 7:21).
4. Differentiate between serving God and everything else, especially money and materialism. Consistently assess your heart to determine where your treasure really lies (Matt. 6:19 – 24, 33).
5. Regularly ask the Father to bring his kingdom to earth (Matt. 6:9 – 10).
6. Faithfully teach all of God's Word, being sure to also apply its truth to your own life (Matt. 5:17 – 19).
7. Anticipate the soon coming of the "not yet" side of the kingdom every time you participate in the Lord's Supper (Luke 22:14 – 20).
8. Celebrate the "now" side of the kingdom by recognizing that every saint's name is already written down in heaven (John 5:24; Luke 10:17 – 20; 17:20 – 21).

What additional suggestions can you make to promote the cause of Kingdom-Advocacy?

NOTES

1. Stanley Grenz and John Franke, *Beyond Foundationalism: Shaping Theology in a Postmodern Context* (Louisville: Westminster John Knox, 2001), 13.
2. The Creation Mandate was God's first direction to Adam and Eve. They were to rule over and care for all creation (Gen. 1:26 – 28; 2:15). That direction was never cancelled or modified by our Maker.
3. Acts 1:8 and 8:1, as inverse numbers of each other, make it easier to remember two important early church events.

Chapter 18

OUR GLOBAL TASK OF WORSHIP: ENGAGING UNIVERSAL PRAISE

(with Gary A. Parrett)

After this I looked and there before me was a great multitude that no one could count, from every nation, tribe, people and language, standing before the throne and in front of the Lamb.... And they cried out in a loud voice: "Salvation belongs to our God, who sits on the throne, and to the Lamb." (Rev. 7:9 – 10)

Three underlying aspects of worship are featured in this chapter:

+ What Worship *Means*
+ What Worship *Yields*
+ What Worship *Involves*

What Worship Means

In simplest terms, Christian worship may be described as *the believer's faithful response to God's gracious revelation*.[1] Worship begins when God reveals something of himself to us — his person, his work, his will. As worshipers, we subsequently respond in trustworthy fashion to what God has revealed: to revere his person, to continue his work, and to submit to his will. God's *general* revelation comes to us in many ways — through the beauty of creation, the unfolding drama of human history, and our conscience, for instance.[2] Christians further affirm that God chiefly makes himself known in *special* revelations, specifically in the Scriptures and in his Son, Jesus Christ.[3] In fact, our incarnate Lord unveils the full heart of God — his self-revelation — through his life, teachings, death, resurrection, and ongoing ministry of transforming lives today (e.g., John 1:14, 18; Col. 1:15; 2:9; Heb. 1:1 – 3).

And we must respond. All revelation requires a response.

To repeat, worship is defined as the believer's faithful response to what God has revealed. It is a revelation-response paradigm.

What Worship Yields

One of the lesser-known attributes of God's image is that *all people are created to worship*. Worship may be directed at a person, a thing (like a possession), or a concept (like the ideal of freedom or more selfish "gods" like wealth and fame). In Eden, Adam and Eve initially worshiped their Maker through obedience. They did as they were commanded: they ruled over and cared for creation (Gen. 1:26 – 28; 2:15, 19 – 20a). They also refrained from doing that which they were commanded *not* to do: they did not eat the forbidden fruit (Gen. 2:17). When they subsequently disobeyed, they shifted their worship to another "god" — greed, self, curiosity, power (Gen. 3:1 – 8).

Worship yields *life change for each participant*. Regardless of the type of worship, *people are always changed*. Change may be good or bad. It may produce health or illness, *c*onformity toward Christlikeness or *d*eformity. When Paul illustratively notes that Corinth's worship gatherings were doing "more harm than good" (1 Cor. 11:17), he assessed the practices of those saints participating in the Lord's Supper as being sinful. If we are honest, we may conclude that the same negative assessment might be made of our own worship times. But it need not be so.

Scripture supplies two noteworthy facts regarding worship. First, *we eventually become what we worship*. Note the sobering affirmations from Psalms 115:4 – 8 and 135:15 – 18. Jesus similarly reminded us that a fully trained "student" (literally a "disciple") will become like his teacher (Matt. 10:24 – 25). For Christians, this includes the consequence of being hated by the same type of people that hated Jesus (John 15:18). So our life goal of Christlikeness is really tied to one outcome of faithful worship.

Second, *we choose what we worship*. Joshua sets up the classic question and challenge of choice that leads to worship when he confronts Israel: "But if serving the LORD seems undesirable to you, then choose for yourselves this day whom you will serve" (Josh. 24:15a).

The worship offered by God's people on the Lord's Day is vitally important then, for there are few practices in the life of the church that are as powerfully formative as congregational worship. Through the gathered church experiences of the worshiping community, God can be honored and glorified, and the transformative power of the Spirit can wonderfully work in our fellowship (1 Cor. 14:25; 2 Cor. 3:17 – 18; Eph. 5:18 – 21; Col. 3:16). In sum, the faithful worship of God's people does nothing less than confirm our collective choice to revere God, which inches us closer to the restorative Christlikeness that we desire.

What Worship Involves

We have looked at the five tasks of Christian education-formation: evangelism-proclamation, service, fellowship-community, kingdom-advocacy, and worship. Worship was described as a synthesis of the previous four *horizontal* tasks. Beyond that, it was described as the one *vertical* dimension of praise to our Creator. Worship can be described, then, as "four and more." Acts 2:42 – 47 locates these "four and more" tasks of Christian education-formation from the early church's testimony:

> They devoted themselves to the apostles' teaching and to the fellowship, to the breaking of bread and to prayer. Everyone was filled with awe, and many wonders and miraculous signs were done by the apostles. All the believers were together and had everything in common. Selling their possessions and goods, they gave to anyone as he had need. Every day they continued to meet together in the temple courts. They broke bread in their homes and ate together with glad and sincere hearts, praising God and enjoying the favor of all the people. And the Lord added to their number daily those who were being saved.

Did you find evidence for all five tasks? In reverse, notice that the last sentence documents the noble task of *evangelism-proclamation*. Also, *service* to the areas surrounding Jerusalem reflects the fact that these believers voluntarily sold their possessions and gave "to anyone as he had need" (v. 45b), which led to the church's "enjoying the favor of all the people" (v. 47a). *Fellowship-community* is explicitly cited in verse 42, evidenced through their daily gatherings and common meals (v. 46). *Kingdom-advocacy*, portrayed whenever any eternal virtue is valued, finds plenty of support in this passage: kindness, self-sacrifice, gladness, sincerity, generosity, enjoyment, perseverance, favorable reputation, and celebration. Again, *worship* is the culmination of these four "horizontal" tasks. Moreover, worship is specifically demonstrated by these "vertical" evidences in Acts 2: "prayer" (v. 42), "wonders and miraculous signs" (v. 43b), and "praising God" (v. 47b).

Notice how the Trinity is glorified through these four tasks: salvation of the lost, gifts to the needy, godly fellowship, and the affirmation of eternal values.

Two Examples of Global Worship

It is difficult to synopsize the relevance of comprehensive subjects such as worship, especially when it's framed by global focus. So I* will delegate part of this responsibility of determining application to you! I conclude with two international worship experiences I was privileged to encounter recently. I share these occasions so that you might gain new understanding of the struggles and joys of fellow members in Christ's body and so that this knowledge might inflame your passion for these spiritual brothers and sisters. I also tell these personal stories in order to provide you with one more opportunity to identify all five ("four and more") tasks of the church.

One Sunday morning in Cambodia, believers gathered in a small rented space for worship. They were led in songs of praise by a team of young girls, ages eleven to

---

*All references to "I" in this chapter come from Gary A. Parrett.

fifteen, who sang and danced reverently as young musicians played nearby. The songs told of God's holiness and offered heartfelt thanks to God for his saving work in Jesus Christ. These teen girls had been "redeemed by the blood of the Lamb," and they loved to proclaim it. They had been rescued from the sex trafficking industry that plagues so much of today's world. Thus, the worship service manifested the earlier-noted "revelation-response paradigm" on multiple levels. For example, these believers gathered to engage and to respond to God's revelation by fighting for the freedom of these young girls, part of a daily battle for justice and mercy. This is the very worship that pleases God most, since these expressions are "better than sacrifice" in his sight (1 Sam. 15:22; Ps. 51:16 – 17; Prov. 21:3; Hos. 6:6; Mic. 6:8; Matt. 9:9 – 13).

As the preacher at this early morning service, my heart was strangely warmed by the Holy Spirit. I was supernaturally moved and affected as I heard these young girls' stories. I also marveled when I heard about another little girl, seated a few rows away, who had been delivered from demonic attacks the day before. It was also paramount for me to hear that *every* person in the room had lost someone — a brother, sister, father, uncle, grandparent, child — during the holocaust that brought death to more than two million Cambodians under the Pol Pot regime.

Some time later, I was invited to teach a group of Sri Lankan church leaders on the subject of worship. It didn't take me long to ask myself, "Who is teaching whom here?" These leaders had lived with civil war for more than twenty years. Sitting over on the side was a pastor whose church had been burned down by local thugs. Closer to the front sat a woman who now pastors because her husband, the former pastor, had been murdered. Each of these Christian leaders lived daily in deep poverty — a poverty recently complicated by the ravages of a devastating tsunami.

As I readied myself for the evening instruction, this "teacher" listened as the group sang heartfelt praise to God. Some of the songs I recognized as translated from English to Singhalese. Other songs I did not recognize at all, even though they resonated with my soul. One song in particular, because of both its powerful melody and the passion with which the worshipers sang, tugged at my heart and would not let go! When I inquired, I was told that the song was based on Isaiah 6 and the refrain declared the *holy, holy, holiness* of the Lord.[4] This was one praise I promised to learn, translate, and teach when I returned home to America.

Conclusion

As God continues to glorify himself throughout the world today (Ps. 46:10; John 12:32), what a beautiful opportunity presents itself to us! We have much to learn from the manifold depths of God's self-revelation and from the worship practices of one another. We also need to continue maturing in our faithful response to God's self-revelation. It is true that only "together with all the saints" do we begin to grasp how wide, long, high, and deep is the love of Christ (Eph. 3:14 – 21). As we learn and grow through the wonders of global worship, Christ is being more fully formed in us (Gal. 4:19), his body — the one holy apostolic church of the living God.

NOTES

1. What are the pros and cons of this simple definition that Christian worship is "the believer's faithful response to God's gracious revelation"?

2. These two fundamental areas of God's *general* revelation, creation and conscience, are often cited in Paul's opening argument of Romans 1:20 – 32 and 2:14 – 16 respectively. Also see Psalm 19:1 – 4a for a familiar reference to *natural* revelation, one subset of general revelation.

3. *Special* revelation through the Scriptures is frequently supported from 2 Peter 1:21 and 2 Timothy 3:16 – 17. *Special* revelation through Jesus Christ is often associated with John 1:1 – 14 and Colossians 1:15 – 20.

4. Isaiah 6:3 testifies of Isaiah's eyewitness account of the heavenly seraphs who praise the Lord by calling to each other, "Holy, holy, holy is the LORD Almighty; the whole earth is full of his glory." Subsequently, the doorposts and thresholds shake and smoke fills the temple where the Lord is seated. The prophet cries out his confession of uncleanness, he is cleansed, and he volunteers to serve the Lord.

Applications in Daily Life for Every Believer

Chapter 19

CONCLUSION: EXPERIENCING PART OF HEAVEN NOW

For Christians, *heaven has arrived!* At least a slice of eternity is here — and it brings a generous portion of God's restoration to all creation.

On the day of Pentecost, as related in Acts 2, a bit of eternity came to earth when the Holy Spirit came to indwell all believers. Heaven in its fullness, of course, is still to come when all restoration is complete.

The traditional notion of the kingdom of God that is both "now" and "not yet" is a paradox supported in Scripture as a way to conceptualize the limitless continuum of eternity. But what if we challenge the paradox of the kingdom being both "now" and "not yet"? What if we consider another biblical idea altogether? What if we join other thinkers, such as C. S. Lewis, who suggests that earth is in fact a part of heaven itself? Instead of taking a "now — not yet" polarizing view, perhaps we can blend the two factors of time.

From that angle, there are two final signposts for us to contemplate as we continue our pilgrimage on God's holy way. Both signs are powerful illustrations of grace.

- *God's second-to-last sign originates in heaven,* then it points toward earth. It's our Maker's kind reminder of eternity's presence in this temporal life. This first marker demonstrates the "now" of the eternal kingdom.
- *God's last supernatural sign starts on earth,* and then it aims at our Home, identifying the "not yet" of eternity.

God's Next-to-Last Sign: The *Now* of Heavenly Earth

Most people grasp the still-to-come feature of eternity pretty easily. The commencement of heaven's final arrival promises to be terrifyingly spectacular: "But the day of the Lord will come like a thief. The heavens will disappear with a roar; the elements will be destroyed by fire, and the earth and everything in it will be laid bare.... That day will bring about the destruction of the heavens by fire, and the elements will melt in the heat. But in keeping with his promise we are looking forward to a new heaven and a new earth, the home of righteousness" (2 Peter 3:10 – 13). God's thorough purification sets the stage for his final restoration.

It's easy to consider heaven from an "either-or" perspective — either it's here or it's not. These words of promise are so familiar to students of Scripture that most of us conclude that heaven is "not yet." And because it is not, we live almost as if heaven doesn't exist at all!

Yet Scripture is clear that a bit of heaven is here now.

Peter Kreeft writes, "We are in Heaven already, whether we know it or not, just as a fetus is already in the world, though the womb masks it from his eyes. How do we know this is true? Simply because God has repeatedly told us so. We know it by faith — faith means simply believing what God says."[1] This is the "now" of heaven.

Heaven is completely real — and present now — even if we can't see it, even if we can't touch it, and even if we don't believe it.

Jesus verifies this remarkable heaven-now fact in John 5:24: "I tell you the truth, whoever hears my word and believes him who sent me *has* eternal life and will not be condemned; *he has crossed over from death to life*." Did you get that? Jesus twice claims that, when we trust him, we immediately change zip codes! We're citizens of heaven *now* — and forever. We figuratively have one foot on earth and one foot in heaven. We are eternal beings on a temporal planet, so if we often feel we *don't* really belong, it's because we don't! The Bible calls us "strangers" and "aliens" in this world (Heb. 11:13b; 1 Peter 2:11). And those "alien" experiences are part of God's design to keep us heaven-focused. Being Home-sick is a good thing!

Good-Better-Best

In my book *The Complete Disciple*, this wholeness of eternity is explained in some detail. Here it is again, in the nutshell version: Whatever we experience in this present life that is *good* was even *better* in Eden (before sin), and it will be *best* in heaven![2] Every kindness, beauty, and satisfying encounter now — say, helping a needy person, having an abiding love, and doing a hard day's work — originated in the kindness, beauty, and satisfaction that God first fashioned for people in Eden (our past). It represents a fraction of the perfect pleasures that have always awaited us in heaven (our future).

How can a past tense word in that last sentence ("awaited") be matched with the phrase "our future?" Matthew 25:34 contends that the eternal kingdom and all its rewards were actually established "since the creation of the world." So yes, the kingdom represents our future, but in part it's also linked with creation. We could say *eternity past* is tied to *eternity future*.

Arguably, the most significant event of all time is God's redemption of his people through Christ. The Passover from Exodus 12 prefigures that glorious victory in the

PART 3: Applications of Restoration—*Applications in Daily Life for Every Believer*

Old Testament. And it was not coincidental that the cross and the resurrection occur on that precise weekend of Passover celebration hundreds of years after the inaugural account. It is then, during that holy week, that Jesus instituted the Lord's Supper (Eucharist). In Luke 22:14–20, the Messiah proposes a marvelous connect-the-dots teaching, tying together all three eras of past, present, and future. In something like glorified time travel: (1) Jesus cites God's *past* restorative work, explicitly referring to "Passover" in verse 15b; (2) Jesus proclaims God's *present* restorative work, acknowledging how eager he is to eat this last meal with his disciples before he suffers. He subsequently assigns new meanings for the wine and the bread, which predict his own impending sacrifice (vv. 15a and 17–19); and (3) Jesus announces his anticipation of God's *future* and completed restorative work, stating that he "will not eat it [the Passover meal] again *until it finds fulfillment in the kingdom* of God" (v. 16).

Notice how this passage in Luke 22 parallels the earlier "good-better-best" scenario:

+ *Present:* Jesus is very eager to eat this last Passover with the Twelve, which was a "good" celebration — but clouded by the forecast of suffering from Jesus' own words.
+ *Past:* The annual recollection of Israel's deliverance (Exodus 12) is historically and spiritually monumental — yet the Passover's link to Christ's predicted sacrifice makes this yearly occasion even "better," the *eternity past.*
+ *Future:* Jesus promises not to eat the Passover meal again until heaven, because that's when all restorative efforts reach fulfillment — clearly the "best" of God's marvelous plan.

Connecting the Dots

Of course, Jesus personifies the past, present, and future through his well-known descriptor as the one "who was, and is, and is to come" (Rev. 4:8; 1:4). The Creator sculpts his human creatures within that same triad of time, for we yearn for all good things — we can't do otherwise — and that yearning eventually ties us to his very best. We all long for security, purpose, satisfying relationships, safety, rest, fulfillment, nurture, pleasure, justice, and beauty. Whenever we encounter just a portion of those good things, we experience part of what heaven will be like.

The Bible promises that one day we will enter "the new heaven and earth." Both are "new" because God will radically purify everything with fire. He will "restore everything," as Peter preached in Acts 3:21. He will transform all creation. But that future reality is still called "heaven and earth"[3] because in eternity, we find ourselves living in somewhat familiar territory.

As on earth today, heaven's perfect relationships include godly care and community — as they always have. That won't change in eternity. Also, work in heaven still requires diligence and responsibility — as they always have. And so on. This good-better-best connection, which we experience daily, should stir as much excitement in us as if we were young children who have caught a glimpse of the Christmas presents we have been dying to open.

From these practical heaven-now truths, *God consciously shows us how to connect the dots between eternity and earth.* By starting in heaven, then pointing to earth, our Father explains how to live with a practical heaven-now attitude by giving us the ability to experience something of heaven's joys today. Who would not want those daily pleasures?

But, somebody might ask, isn't that a guaranteed formula for frustration? Why would God put desire in our hearts for a state of perfection that we can't fully attain in this world? When we know heaven's perfection is entirely beyond our reach, don't our present struggles become magnified?

No. Though perfection is out of our reach for now, all of heaven's pleasures are not. The delightful surprise of heaven — the heart of kingdom *now* — is that eternity is not only about the future.

Heaven touches us every day in ways most of us haven't fully understood.

Paul wrote to Timothy: "Command those who are rich in this present world not to be arrogant nor to put their hope in wealth, which is so uncertain, but to put their hope in God, who richly provides us [now!] with everything for our enjoyment. Command them to do good, to be rich in good deeds, and to be generous and willing to share. In this way they will lay up treasure for themselves as a firm foundation for the coming age, so that they may take hold of the life that is truly life" (1 Tim. 6:17 – 19).

Here's a paraphrase: "Command anyone who is rich now not to trust in their uncertain wealth. When we trust God, he *richly gives us everything to enjoy right now!* Whoever wants lasting riches should be 'rich' in good deeds by sharing what they have with the needy. That generous lifestyle provides a solid foundation of heavenly treasure one day — and *it also allows you to grab hold of life now, which is the richest and fullest you will ever know.*" That sure sounds like heaven is touching us daily!

But there's more: How we live now is directly related to how we will experience eternity. There is no disconnect. A pastor friend recently stumbled onto this idea when he challenged his congregation to stop putting so much worldly effort into trying not to die and instead to start figuring out how to really live.

Within the context of the command to immediately invest in heavenly currencies (Matt. 6:19 – 21), Jesus says something similar to what my friend says. Four verses following the claim that our hearts will naturally follow our heavenly investments, Jesus singles out an example of one particular earthly reward tied to heaven. That's evidence of restoration to be sure.

He selects an enticing reward that most people would pay anything to have: worry-free living. He makes this heaven-to-earth connect-the-dots link for us: "Therefore I tell you, do not worry about your life, what you will eat or drink; or about your body, what you will wear" (v. 25). Jesus later proposes, "But seek first his kingdom and his righteousness, and all these things will be given to you as well" (v. 33). Worry-free living is just one of several huge dividends that originate in heaven *but then are directed toward earth for us to experience today* — whenever we transfer our earthly treasures (along with our related anxieties about materialism) into celestial currency.

An Unexpected Blessing of Heavenly Earth

Here's another practical heaven-now example: Isaiah 65:21 – 22 exclaims that we will "long enjoy the work of our hands," specifically identifying the tasks of building and gardening. If you currently find pleasure in either of these tasks — or you think you might — then by contemplating heavenly building and gardening plans that honor God, you link heaven to earth and experience part of heaven's joy and thanksgiving. Such contemplation should also prompt us to bring these two tasks under the lordship of Christ, as we anticipate current ways to become more Christ-like as builders and gardeners.

As I was recently contemplating these truths for my own life, God blessed me in an unexpected and delightful manner. Among other things I hope to do on earth or in heaven is to glorify our Creator through music. The Bible cites several references to glorifying the Trinity through music in both settings.

Other than learning to play the guitar in my teen years, I've had no musical training. But I specifically long to play the piano and to write praise music. If that opportunity does not open up here on earth, there is plenty of time to pursue that desire in eternity.

As I was feverishly writing this textbook for weeks on end, the Lord jolted me awake one morning — on May 15, 2007 — with a simple chorus and tune.

I was overwhelmed with gratitude and anxious to jot down everything I could remember. Because I'm not a morning person and I've never had a good memory, I kept thinking, "You know, Lord, this is quite a challenge you've given me!" Furthermore, being without much musical background, I had to wait for my wife, Mary, to remind me where "middle C" was on our piano.

I proceeded to scribble the tune and words the Lord gave me the best I could. Mary made some necessary alterations, added appropriate chords, and the result was "Maranatha! On My Mind."

I share this personal illustration to encourage you to pursue *your* heavenly dreams too — and to pursue them *now*. God wants to bless us — through this heaven-to-earth tie — more than we can ever imagine.

FIGURE 19.1—"Maranatha! On My Mind'

God's Last Sign: *Not Yet* Indicators That Point beyond Earth to Heaven

The truth is, we can't *not* think about heaven. We are hardwired by our Creator to perpetually think of and feel eternity. Figuratively speaking, it is as though God is playing something of the father's part in the story of the prodigal son, telling us he waits for us to come Home. In fact, he is far more excited for the day we go Home than we are.

Even though we are created to contemplate heaven (and we can't completely shut off those thoughts), most of the time most of us *don't* think consciously about heaven. So our Maker fashioned one last sign that starts here on earth and points directly Home as a reminder.

The Creator has made us so that our present life is intricately woven into our future. Our current perceptions of "what is" represent a reality that is (in God's mind) just as vital as and united to our hope for "what shall be." But perception is where most of us get tripped up, especially when our perception is drawn primarily from emotions that come and go. Most days it's hard to see the connections between earth and heaven — especially through all the daily "fog" of work, the kids' soccer practices, paying bills, and dental checkups. Even the fog of positive activities, like worship and Christian fellowship, is still fog.

Fog of any sort makes it tough to see a connecting kite string, even though the high-flying kite is visible enough. When you find yourself fogged in — overwhelmed with the craving to "see" more of heaven, yet earthbound — consciously start where you are, then connect the dots to your eternal Home. Study the Word of God as it pertains to the pricelessness of heaven.[4] And ask the Father to help you to remember that it is Truth, not feelings, that provides the very best navigation for our lives — and that goes double when the fog is thickest.

Besides those foundational habits, there is something more we can do to align ourselves with God's last sign.

Start Packing Your Suitcase for Heaven

Ben and Jerry (no, not the ice cream guys) were best friends. From elementary school through their later years, Ben pitched and Jerry caught. No other pitcher-catcher combo was ever closer. Their unflagging love for baseball cemented their friendship. They played on every ball team you could imagine, and they shared fantasies about several more teams. During any time of year, when you saw one, the other was close behind. Ben and Jerry were always in baseball attire, whether at church or on the beach!

But one day, after many years, everything changed. In his late fifties, the doctors told Jerry he didn't have much longer to live — perhaps just a few more baseball seasons. Refusing to dwell on that sad news, Ben and Jerry started wondering if there would be any baseball in heaven. Then, months later when Jerry was on his deathbed, their passionate baseball discussions reached new heights — literally. Half-jokingly, Ben began, "So you think you can ask St. Peter that baseball question?"

"What question?" Jerry asked.

Ben turned unusually quiet, somewhat embarrassed. He never wanted Jerry to think his one-track mind showed irreverence for Jerry's condition or for their Maker. After several moments of awkward silence, Jerry turned to Ben and softly whispered, "Sure."

Jerry's single word was well-timed — and his last. The catcher passed on before the seventh inning stretch of a game the two men were watching.

Not long afterward, Jerry appeared to Ben in a dream. "Ben, I've got *good* news, *better* news, and *best* news — sort of like in that Habermas guy's discipleship book we read in our small group men's meeting."

"Let's hear it!"

"The *good* news is 'Yes! There *is* baseball in heaven.' And you would not believe how spectacular everything looks, every game — right down to the immaculate ball diamond, chalk stripes, and perfectly manicured grass!"

"The *better* news resolves your concern of irreverence. Gabriel told me that you should think of baseball like this: On earth, when someone totally loves what he does for a living — with everything he's got — people say, 'I can't believe they're paying me to do this!' Well, in heaven, when we totally love what we do, with everything we've got — we say, 'We're doing exactly what the Creator shaped us to do. So we're worshiping God when we play ball.'"

"Wow!" Ben responded. "Thanks for easing my mind."

"Then there's the *best* news. I took a peek at the line-up schedule for my baseball team next week — we're called the Triple A's ("*A little Above the Angels*"). And … ah … well … I don't exactly know how to put this."

"Just say it, Jerry! Tell me!"

"Okay, Ben. Don't make any plans after Wednesday. And be sure to keep your glove with you at all times!"

Whether it's baseball, understanding how to manage money better, gardening, learning to play a new instrument, or helping a neighbor build a fence, the best practical advice for *any* believer to help him connect today with heaven is to *anticipate what one of his favorite earthly experiences might look like in eternity.* Undoubtedly, such activities in heaven also glorify our Maker.

There are a couple of exceptions to this advice, but more often than not, when Christ-followers project one favorite activity on earth into eternity, we receive "the best of both worlds." Heaven becomes far more real — and more available to our senses. Earth instantly takes on grander meaning and relevance through this connection. The Bible refers to this link as earthly "shadows" and heavenly fulfillment.[5]

When you think of it like this, heaven is just around the corner.

Maranatha! Even so Lord, come!

NOTES

1. Peter Kreeft, *Everything You Ever Wanted to Know about Heaven … But Never Dreamed of Asking* (San Francisco: Ignatius Press, 1990), 198.
2. See Ronald T. Habermas, *The Complete Disciple: A Model for Cultivating God's Image in Us* (Colorado Springs: Chariot Victor, 2003), 44ff.
3. See Isaiah 65:17ff; 66:22ff; 2 Peter 3:13; and Revelation 12:1ff.
4. See John 14:1 – 4; 2 Corinthians 4:16 – 5:9; and Philippians 1:20 – 26.
5. When one does a Bible study of the word "shadow" or "shadows," helpful implications of these truths will supply meaning for faith-in-life now.

I value your thoughts about what you've just read.
Please share them with me. You'll find contact information
in the back of this book.

Faye E. Chechowich

Professor of Christian educational ministries, dean of faculty development, and director of the Center for Teaching and Learning Excellence at Taylor University. BA, Taylor University; MRE, Trinity Evangelical Divinity School; PhD, Indiana University. Thirteen years of youth ministry experience in the US and Africa; travel and living experiences on every continent except Antarctica; diverse ministry experiences with children and adults of all ages. Research focus on spiritual development in older adults. Currently working on a project that explores factors which precipitate late-life conversion.

John Matthew Dettoni

President and cofounder with wife, Carol, of Chrysalis Ministries, Inc., an international Christian organization for leader-teacher development. Serves as pastor, professor, author, and peripatetic professor without portfolio with Chrysalis Ministries. Travels throughout the world teaching, mentoring, consulting with Christian organizations, to develop effective biblical leaders and teachers worldwide. BA, Wheaton College; BD (MDiv), Fuller Theological Seminary; MA, Wheaton Graduate School. PhD, Michigan State University.

Cheryl Fawcett

Youth ministry educator missionary with ABWE. PhD, Trinity International University. Twenty-three years' experience as college professor in Pennsylvania, Ohio, and California. Speaker for youth camps, local church training volunteers, ladies' events. Taught youth ministry in Peru, United Kingdom, South Africa, Kazakhstan, Portugal, Romania, and Mexico. College-age minister-educator, local church youth ministry volunteer for thirty years, freelance writer, kayaker, and rose gardener. Contributor to several journal articles in the *Christian Education Journal* and elsewhere. Author of several books, including *Know & Grow*, Vols. I and II; *I Have a Question about God: Doctrine for Children and Their Parents*; and *Understanding*

People. Contributor to several books, including the *Baker Evangelical Dictionary of Christian Education.*

Jennifer L. Jezek

Adjunct instructor in the department of Christian formation and ministry at Wheaton College. BA, Wheaton College; MSEd in curriculum and instruction, Northern Illinois University. Has served in parachurch ministries, first as curriculum development director for Evangelical Training Association and currently as senior writer of curriculum for Awana Clubs International. Active in her local church as a small-group leader for girls and second-grade Sunday school teacher.

Steve Kang

Associate professor of educational ministries at Gordon-Conwell Theological Seminary. PhD in religion in society and personality, Northwestern University. Research and teaching interests: cultural analysis and engagement, educational and formation processes, and the psycho-social-theological formation of self. Author of *Unveiling the Socio-culturally Constructed Multi-voiced Self* and coauthor of *A Many Colored Kingdom: Multicultural Dynamics for Spiritual Formation.* Coeditor of *Growing Healthy Asian American Churches* and contributor to *This Side of Heaven: Race, Ethnicity, and Christian Faith.* Articles published in the *Journal of Organic Chemistry, Ex Auditu, Christian Education Journal,* and *Religious Education.* Has served on executive board of the Association of Professors and Researchers in Religious Education and the North American Professors of Christian Education and currently on the editorial board of *Religious Education* and *Teaching Theology and Religion.*

Kevin E. Lawson

Professor of Christian education and director of PhD and EdD programs in educational studies at Talbot School of Theology, Biola University. EdD, University of Maine. Served as a Minister of Christian Education in churches for eleven years. Interested in the spiritual life and nurture of children, historical and theological foundations for Christian education, and ministry leadership.

Gary A. Parrett

Associate professor of educational ministries and worship and chair of the division of the ministry of the church at Gordon-Conwell Theological Seminary. BA, Faith Evangelical Lutheran Seminary; MDiv, Regent College; EdD, Columbia University. Taught youth ministries and biblical studies at Gordon College for two years. Twenty years of pastoral ministry, serving churches in Boston, New York City, New Jersey, Seattle, and Seoul, Korea. Regular speaker at conferences, retreats, and Christian education workshops. Articles on Christian education and worship published in

Christianity Today and other publications. Coauthor of *A Many Colored Kingdom*. Has composed hymns and choruses for congregational worship. Former vice president of the North American Professors of Christian Education.

Robert W. Pazmiño

Valeria Stone Professor of Christian Education at Andover Newton Theological School, where he has taught since 1986. EdD, Teachers' College, Columbia University in cooperation with Union Seminary. Taught at Gordon-Conwell Theological Seminary five years. A missionary from Brooklyn, New York, to New England for the past twenty-nine years. Academic work centers on educational foundations, drawing upon theological wells for the renewal of Christian education.

Dave Rahn

Vice-president, chief ministry officer of Youth for Christ/USA, and professor of youth ministries, Huntington University. MA, Wheaton Graduate School; PhD, Purdue University. Veteran youth minister, strategist, researcher, and author.

Jerry Root

Assistant professor of evangelism and spiritual formation at Wheaton College, and associate director of strategic evangelism at the Billy Graham Center. BA, Whittier College; MDiv, Talbot Seminary; PhD, Open University at Oxford Center for Mission Studies in Oxford, England. Visiting faculty at Biola University, Talbot Graduate School of Theology, and Trinity International University. Published widely and lectures internationally on C. S. Lewis and his work, including coeditor of *The Quotable C. S. Lewis*.

SELECT BIBLIOGRAPHY

(A more complete bibliography is in the online Appendix Folder at www.zondervan. com/icef.)

Alford, Deann. "Free at Last: How Christians Worldwide Are Sabotaging the Modern Slave Trade." *Christianity Today* 51, no. 3 (March 2007): 30–37.

Anthony, M. *Perspectives on Children's Spiritual Formation: Four Views.* Nashville: Broadman and Holman, 2007.

Bandura, Albert. *Social Foundations of Thought and Action: A Social Cognitive Theory.* Englewood Cliffs, NJ: Prentice-Hall, 1986.

———. *Social Learning Theory.* Englewood Cliffs, NJ: Prentice-Hall, 1977.

Banks, James A. *Multiethnic Education: Theory and Practice.* 2nd ed. Boston: Allyn and Bacon, 1988.

Belenky, Mary Field, Blythe McVicker Clinchy, Nancy Rule Goldberger, and Jill Mattuck Tarule. *Women's Ways of Knowing: The Development of Self, Voice, and Mind.* New York: Basic, 1986.

Bellah, R. N., R. Madsen, M. S. Sullivan, A. Swidler, and S. M. Tipton. *Habits of the Heart: Individualism and Commitment in American Life.* New York: Harper and Row, 1985.

Bloom, Benjamin, et al. *Taxonomy of Educational Objectives. Handbook 1: Cognitive Domain.* New York: David McKay, 1956.

Bonhoeffer, Dietrich. *The Cost of Discipleship.* Rev. ed. New York: Macmillan, 1963.

———. *Life Together.* New York: Harper and Row, 1954.

Borthwick, Paul. *How to Be a World Class Christian: You Can Be Part of God's Global Action.* Waynesboro, GA: Operation Mobilization, 2000.

Bowman, Locke E., Jr. *Teaching for Christian Hearts, Souls, and Minds: A Constructive, Holistic Approach to Christian Education.* San Francisco: Harper and Row, 1990.

Breckenridge, James, and Lillian Breckenridge. *What Color Is Your God? Multicultural Education in the Church.* Wheaton, IL: Victor Books, 1995.

Bright, Bill. *How You Can Be Filled with the Holy Spirit.* Orlando: New Life Publications, 1971.

Brookfield, Stephen D. "Grounded Teaching in Learning." In *Facilitating Adult Learning,* edited by W. Galbraith. Malabar, FL: Krieger, 1991.

———. *Developing Critical Thinkers: Challenging Adults to Explore Alternative Ways of Thinking and Acting.* San Francisco: Jossey-Bass, 1987.

Bruce, F. F. *The Defence of the Gospel in the New Testament.* Grand Rapids: Eerdmans, 1959.

Bushnell, Horace. *Christian Nurture.* New Haven, CT: Yale University Press, 1916.

Bussau, David, and Russell Mask. *Christian Microenterprise Development: An Introduction.* Costa Mesa, CA: Regnum Books, 2003.

Buzzard, Lynn R., and Laurence Eck. *Tell It to the Church: Reconciling out of Court.* Elgin, IL: David C. Cook, 1982.

Carroll, Joyce A., and Ron Habermas. *Jesus Didn't Use Worksheets, a 200 Year Old Model for Good Teaching.* Houston: Absey & Co., 1996.

Clapp, Rodney. *A Peculiar People: The Church as Culture in a Post-Christian Society.* Downers Grove, IL: InterVarsity Press, 1996.

Clark, Chap. *Hurt: Inside the World of Today's Teenager.* Grand Rapids: Baker Academic Youth Ministry, 2004.

Clark, K. W. "Galilee." In *The Interpreter's Dictionary of the Bible,* edited by George A. Buttrick. Nashville: Abingdon Press, 1962.

Coleman, Robert Emerson. *The Master Plan of Evangelism.* Westwood, NJ: Revell, 1964.

Conde-Frazier, Elizabeth, S. Steve Kang, and Gary A. Parrett. *A Many Colored Kingdom: Multicultural Dynamics for Spiritual Formation.* Grand Rapids: Baker Academic, 2004.

Cooper, John W. *Body, Soul, and Life Everlasting: Biblical Anthropology and the Monism-Dualism Debate.* Grand Rapids: Eerdmans, 1989.

Corbitt, J. Nathan. *The Sound of the Harvest: Music's Mission in Church and Culture.* Grand Rapids: Baker, 1998.

Crabb, Lawrence J. *Understanding People.* Grand Rapids: Zondervan, 1987.

Cremin, Lawrence A. *Traditions of American Education.* New York: Basic Books, 1977.

Dean, Kenda Creasy, Chap Clark, and Dave Rahn, eds. *Starting Right: Thinking Theologically About Youth Ministry.* Grand Rapids: Zondervan/Youth Specialties Academic, 2001.

Delnay, Robert G. *Teach as He Taught.* Chicago: Moody, 1987.

Dewey, John. *Experience and Education.* New York: Collier Books, 1938.

DeYoung, Curtis P., Michael O. Emerson, George Yancey, and Karen Chai Kim. *United By Faith: The Multicultural Congregation as an Answer to the Problem of Race.* Oxford: Oxford University Press, 2003.

Dieter, Melvin, et al. *Five Views on Sanctification.* Grand Rapids: Eerdmans, 1987.

Dillon, J. T. *Jesus as a Teacher: A Multidisciplinary Case Study.* Bethesda, MD: International Scholars Publications, 1995.

Downs, Perry. "Child Evangelization." *Christian Education Journal* 3, no. 2 (1983): 5–13.

Driscoll, Mark. *Confessions of a Reformission Rev.: Hard Lessons from an Emerging, Missional Church.* Grand Rapids: Zondervan, 2006.

Dueck, Gerry. *Kids for the World: A Guidebook for Children's Mission Resources.* Pasadena: William Carey Library, 1990.

Duska, Ronald, and Mariellen Whelan. *Moral Development: A Guide to Piaget and Kohlberg.* New York: Paulist Press, 1975.

Dworetzky, John. *Introduction to Child Development.* St. Paul: West, 1981.

Dykstra, Craig. "Learning Theory." In *Harper's Encyclopedia of Religious Education,* edited by Iris V. Cully and Kendig B. Cully. San Francisco: Harper and Row, 1990.

Dykstra, Craig, and Sharon Parks, eds. *Faith Development and Fowler.* Birmingham: Religious Education, 1986.

Ebersole, S. E., and R. Woods. "Virtual Community: Koinonia or Compromise? Theological Implications of Community in Cyberspace." *Christian Scholars Review* 31, no. 2 (2002): 185–216.

Eisner, Elliot. *The Educational Imagination.* 2nd ed. New York: Macmillan, 1985.

Elias, John. *Foundations and Practice of Adult Religious Education.* Malabar, FL: Krieger, 1986.

Elkind, David. *All Grown Up and No Place to Go: Teenagers in Crisis.* Reading, MA: Addison Wesley Publishing Company, 1984.

———. *The Hurried Child.* New York: Addison-Wesley, 1981.

Elwell, Walter A., and Robert W. Yarborough. *Encountering the New Testament: A Historical and Theological Survey.* Grand Rapids: Baker, 1998.

Emerson, Michael, and Christian Smith. *Divided by Faith: Evangelical Religion and the Problem of Race in America.* New York: Oxford, 2000.

Erikson, Erik. *Childhood and Society.* 2nd ed. New York: Norton, 1963.

———. *Identity: Youth and Crisis.* New York: Norton, 1968.

———. *The Life Cycle Completed: A Review.* New York: Norton, 1982.

Fackre, Dorothy and Gabriel. *Christian Basics: A Primer for Pilgrims.* Grand Rapids: Eerdmans, 1991.

Ferris, Robert W. *Renewal in Theological Education: Strategies for Change.* Wheaton, IL: Billy Graham Center, Wheaton College, 1990.

Festinger, Leon. *A Theory of Cognitive Dissonance.* Stanford, CA: Stanford University Press, 1957.

Fields, Doug. *Purpose-Driven® Youth Ministry.* Grand Rapids: Zondervan/Youth Specialties, 1998.

Folmsbee, Chris. *A New Kind of Youth Ministry.* Grand Rapids: Zondervan/Youth Specialties, 2006.

Foster, Richard J. *Celebration of Discipline: The Path to Spiritual Growth.* Rev. ed. San Francisco: HarperCollins Publishers, 1988.

Fowler, James W. "Faith and the Structure of Meaning." In *Faith Development and Fowler,* edited by Craig Dykstra and Sharon Parks. Birmingham: Religious Education, 1986.

———. *Becoming Adult, Becoming Christian: Adult Development and Christian Faith.* San Francisco: Harper and Row, 2000.

———. *Faith Development and Pastoral Care.* Philadelphia: Fortress, 1987.

———. *Stages of Faith: The Psychology of Human Development and the Quest for Meaning.* San Francisco: Harper and Row, 1981.

Frankena, William K. *Philosophy of Education.* New York: Macmillan, 1965.

Fredriksen, K., J. Rhodes, R. Reddy, and N. Way. "Sleepless in Chicago: Tracking the Effects of Adolescent Sleep Loss During the Middle School Years." *Child Development* 75 (2004): 84–95.

Friedeman, Matt. *The Master Plan Teaching.* Wheaton, IL: Victor, 1990.

Gaebelein, Frank. *The Christian, the Arts, and Truth.* Portland, OR: Multnomah, 1985.

———. *Patterns of God's Truth.* Chicago: Moody, 1954.

Gangel, Kenneth O., and Howard G. Hendricks. *The Christian Educator's Handbook on Teaching*. Wheaton, IL: Victor, 1988.

Gangel, Kenneth O., and James C. Wilhoit, eds. *The Christian Educator's Handbook on Adult Education*. Grand Rapids: Baker, 1997.

Gangel, Kenneth O., and Warren Benson. *Christian Education: Its History and Philosophy*. Chicago: Moody, 1983.

Gannon, Martin. *Understanding Global Cultures: Metaphorical Journeys Through 28 Nations, Clusters of Nations, and Continents*. Thousand Oaks, CA: Sage, 2003.

Garcia, Ricardo L. *Teaching in a Pluralistic Society: Concepts, Models, and Strategies*. New York: Harper and Row, 1982.

Geertz, Clifford. "Religion as a Cultural System." In *Reader in Comparative Religion*, edited by W. A. Lessa and E. A. Vogt. 3rd ed. New York: Harper and Row, 1972.

———. *The Interpretation of Cultures*. New York: Basic Books, 1973.

George, Carl F. *Prepare Your Church for the Future*. Tarrytown, NY: Revell, 1991.

Getz, Gene. *Sharpening the Focus of the Church*. Chicago: Moody, 1974.

Gilligan, Carol. *In a Different Voice: Psychological Theory and Women's Development*. Cambridge, MA: Harvard University Press, 1982.

Glatthorn, Allan. *Curriculum Leadership*. Glenview: Scott Foresman, 1987.

Glickman, Carl. *Supervision of Instruction: A Developmental Approach*. Boston: Allyn and Bacon, 1985.

Goldsmith, H. H. "Generic Influences on Personality from Infancy to Adulthood." *Child Development* 54 (1983): 331–55.

———. "Roundtable: What Is Temperament? Four Approaches." *Child Development* 58 (1987): 505–29.

Goleman, Daniel. *Emotional Intelligence*. New York: Bantam Books, 1995.

———. "Major Personality Study Finds That Traits Are Mostly Inherited." *New York Times*, 2 December 1986, 17–18.

Gonzalez, Justo. *Mañana: Christian Theology from a Hispanic Perspective*. Nashville: Abingdon, 1990.

Goodwin, Bennie. *Designing Curriculum for Urban and Multiracial Christian Education*. Grand Rapids: CSI Publications, 1981.

Gorman, Julie. *Community That Is Christian: A Handbook on Small Groups*. 2nd ed. Grand Rapids: Baker, 2002.

Grenz, Stanley, and John Franke. *Beyond Foundationalism: Shaping Theology in a Postmodern Context*. Louisville: Westminster John Knox, 2001.

Grigg, Viv. *Cry of the Urban Poor: Reaching the Slums of Today's Mega-cities*. Monrovia, CA: World Vision, 2004.

Groome, Thomas H. *Sharing Faith: A Comprehensive Approach to Religious Education and Pastoral Ministry*. San Francisco: Harper and Row, 1991.

Habermas, Ronald T. "Boldly Teaching Like the Master Teacher." *Vision* 44, no. 1 (Fall 1998): 6–7; 14–15.

———. "Does Peter Pan Corrupt Our Children?" *Christianity Today*, 8 March 1993.

———. "Gray Matters." *Christianity Today*, 7 August 1987, 23–25.

———. *Teaching for Reconciliation.* Eugene, OR: Wipf and Stock, 2001.

———. *The Complete Disciple: A Model for Cultivating God's Image in Us.* Colorado Springs: Chariot Victor, 2003.

Habermas, Ronald T., and David Olshine. *Down But Not Out Parenting: 50 Ways to Win with Your Teen.* Lincoln, NE: iUniverse.com, Inc., 2000.

———. *Tag-Team Youth Ministry: 50 Ways to Involve Parents and Other Caring Adults.* Lincoln, NE: iUniverse.com, Inc., 2000.

Hadidian, Alan, et. al. *Creative Family Times: Practical Activities for Building Character in Your Preschooler.* Chicago: Moody, 1989.

Hall, Christopher. *Reading Scripture with the Church Fathers.* Downers Grove, IL: InterVarsity Press, 1998.

Harper, Norman E. *Making Disciples: The Challenge of Christian Education at the End of the 20th Century.* Memphis: Christian Studies Center, 1981.

Harrow, A. *A Taxonomy of the Psychomotor Domain: A Guide for Developing Behavioral Objectives.* New York: David McKay, 1969.

Hauerwas, Stanley. "The Family as a School for Character." *Religious Education* 80 (Spring 1985): 272–85.

Hawn, C. Michael. *Gather into One: Praying and Singing Globally.* Calvin Institute of Christian Worship Liturgical Studies Series. Grand Rapids: Eerdmans, 2002.

Hegeman, David Bruce. *Plowing in Hope.* Moscow, ID: Canon Press, 1999.

Hendricks, Howard G. *Teaching to Change Lives.* Portland, OR: Multnomah, 1987.

Heschel, Abraham J. *Between God and Man.* New York: Free Press, 1959.

Hess, Carol Lakey. *Caretakers of Our Common House: Women's Development in Communities of Faith.* Nashville: Abingdon, 1997.

Hesse, Petra, and Dante Ciccheti. "Perspectives on an Integrated Theory of Emotional Development." In *Emotional Development,* edited by D. Ciccheti and P. Hesse. *New Directions for Child Development* 16. San Francisco: Jossey-Bass, 1982.

Hesselgrave, David J. *Communicating Christ Cross-culturally.* 2nd ed. Grand Rapids: Zondervan, 1991.

Hestenes, Roberta. *Using the Bible in Groups.* Philadelphia: Westminster, 1985.

Hiebert, Paul G. *Anthropological Insights for Missionaries.* Grand Rapids: Eerdmans, 1985.

———. *Cultural Anthropology.* 2nd ed. Grand Rapids: Baker, 1976, 1983.

Hill, Edward V. "A Congregation's Response." Lecture given at Gordon-Conwell Theological Seminary, 21 January 1976.

Hoekema, Anthony. *Created in God's Image.* Grand Rapids: Eerdmans, 1986.

Hohmann, Pete. *Mobilizing Kids for Outreach.* Springfield, IL: Gospel Publishing House, 1998.

Hopler, Thom. *World of Difference: Following Christ beyond Your Cultural Walls.* Downers Grove, IL: InterVarsity Press, 1981.

Horne, Herman H. *Teaching Techniques of Jesus: How Jesus Taught.* Reprint. Grand Rapids: Kregel, 1982.

Houston, James. *The Transforming Friendship: A Guide to Prayer.* Oxford: Lion, 1989.

Hybels, Bill, and Mark Mittelberg. *Becoming a Contagious Christian.* Grand Rapids: Zondervan, 1994.

Ingle, Clifford, ed. *Children and Conversion.* Nashville: Broadman, 1970.

Issler, Klaus. "Conscience: Moral Sensitivity and Moral Reasoning." In *Christian Perspectives on Being Human: A Multidisciplinary Approach,* edited by J. P. Moreland and David Ciocchi. Grand Rapids: Baker, 1993.

———. "The Spiritual Formation of Jesus: The Significance of the Holy Spirit in the Life of Jesus." *Christian Education Journal* 4, no. 2 (2000): 5–24.

———. *Wasting Time with God: A Christian Spirituality of Friendship with God.* Downers Grove, IL: InterVarsity Press, 2001.

Issler, Klaus, and Ted W. Ward. "Moral Development as a Curriculum Emphasis in American Protestant Theological Education." *Journal of Moral Education* 18, no. 2 (1989): 131–43.

Jenkins, Philip. *The Next Christendom: The Coming of Global Christianity.* Oxford: Oxford University Press, 2002.

Jeschke, Marlin. *Believers Baptism for Children of the Church.* Scottdale, PA: Herald Press, 1983.

Jewell, Dawn Herzog. "Red-Light Rescue: The 'Business' of Helping Sexually Exploited Help Themselves." *Christianity Today* 51, no. 1 (January 2007): 28–37.

Johnson, S. E. "Son of Man." In *Interpreter's Dictionary of the Bible,* edited by George A. Buttrick. Nashville: Abingdon, 1962: 414–15.

Joyce, Bruce, Marsha Weil, and Beverly Shower. *Models of Teaching.* 4th ed. Englewood Cliffs, NJ: Prentice-Hall, 1992.

Jutila, C., et al. *Children's Ministry That Works: The Basics and Beyond.* Loveland, CO: Group Publishing, 2002.

Kang, S. Steve. "The Church, Spiritual Formation, and the Kingdom of God." *Ex Auditu* 18 (2003): 137–51.

Keesing, R. M., and F. M. Keesing. *New Perspectives in Cultural Anthropology.* New York: Holt, Rinehart and Winston, 1971.

Kegan, Robert. *The Evolving Self: Problem and Process in Human Development.* Cambridge, MA: Harvard University Press, 1982.

Kilbourn, Phyllis, ed. *Children Affected by HIV/AIDS: Compassionate Care.* Monrovia, CA: MARC Publications, 2002.

———, ed. *Children in Crisis: A New Commitment.* Monrovia, CA: MARC Publications, 1996.

———, ed. *Healing Children of War: A Handbook for Ministry to Children Who Have Suffered Deep Traumas.* Monrovia, CA: MARC Publications, 1995.

———, ed. *Street Children: A Guide to Effective Ministry.* Monrovia, CA: MARC Publications, 1997.

Kilbourn, Phyllis, and J. McDermid, eds. *Sexually Exploited Children: Working to Protect & Heal.* Monrovia, CA: MARC Publications, 1998.

Knight, George R. *Philosophy of Education: An Introduction in Christian Perspective.* Berrien Springs, MI: Andrews University Press, 1980.

Knowles, Malcolm S. *The Adult Learner: A Neglected Species.* Houston: Gulf, 1990.

———. *The Making of an Adult Educator.* San Francisco: Jossey-Bass, 1989.

———. *The Modern Practice of Adult Education: From Pedagogy.* Rev. ed. Englewood Cliffs, NJ: Prentice-Hall, 1980.

———. *Self-directed Learning: A Guide for Learners and Teachers.* New York: Cambridge, 1975.

———. *Using Learning Contracts*. San Francisco: Jossey-Bass, 1986.

Kohlberg, Lawrence. *Essays on Moral Development*, vol. 2: *The Psychology of Moral Development*. San Francisco: Harper and Row, 1984.

———. *The Philosophy of Moral Development*. San Francisco: Harper and Row, 1981.

Kohlberg, Lawrence, Charles Levine, and Alexandra Hewer. *Moral Stages: A Current Formulation and a Response to Critics*. Basel, Switzerland: Karger, 1983.

Kraft, Charles H. *Christianity in Culture*. Maryknoll, NY: Orbis Press, 1979.

Krathwohl, David, Benjamin Bloom, and Bertram Masia. *Taxonomy of Educational Objectives: The Classification of Educational Goals. Handbook II: Affective Domain*. New York: David McKay, 1964.

Kreeft, Peter. *Everything You Ever Wanted to Know about Heaven ... but Never Dreamed of Asking*. San Francisco: Ignatius Press, 1990.

———. *Three Philosophies of Life*. San Francisco: Ignatius Press, 1989.

Kuhmerker, Lisa, et al. *The Kohlberg Legacy for the Helping Profession*. Birmingham: R. E. P. Booser, 1991.

Lee, James Michael. *The Content of Religious Instruction: A Social Science Approach*. Birmingham: Religious Education Press, 1985.

Lee, James Michael, ed. *Handbook of Faith*. Birmingham: Religious Education Press, 1990.

LeFever, Marlene. *Creative Teaching Methods*. Elgin, IL: David C. Cook, 1985.

Lewis, C. S. *The Great Divorce*. New York: Simon & Schuster, 1946.

———. *The Last Battle*. New York: Macmillan, 1956.

———. *The Lion, the Witch and the Wardrobe*. New York: Macmillan, 1950.

———. *Mere Christianity*. New York: Macmillan, 1979.

———. *The Problem of Pain*. New York: Macmillan, 1978.

———. *The Screwtape Letters*. San Francisco: HarperSanFrancisco, 1942.

———. *Surprised by Joy*. London: Fontana, 1959.

———. *The Weight of Glory and Other Addresses*. San Francisco: HarperSanFrancisco, 1949.

Lickona, Thomas. *Raising Good Children: Helping Your Child Through the Stages of Moral Development*. New York: Bantam, 1983.

Lifton, Robert Jay. *History and Human Survival*. New York: Vintage, 1971.

Lingenfelter, Sherwood. *Transforming Culture: A Challenge for Christian Mission*. Grand Rapids: Baker, 1992.

Loder, James E. *The Logic of the Spirit: Human Development in Theological Perspective*. San Francisco: Jossey-Bass, 1998.

Lowman, Joseph. *Mastering the Techniques of Teaching*. San Francisco: Jossey-Bass, 1984.

MacArthur, John, Jr. *Found: God's Will*. Rev. ed. Wheaton, IL: Victor Books, 1977.

Macaulay, Susan Schaeffer. *How to Be Your Own Selfish Pig*. Colorado Springs, CO: Chariot Books, 1982.

Mager, Robert. *Preparing Instructional Objectives*. Rev. ed. Belmont, CA: David S. Lake, 1984.

Maloney, H. Newton. "The Concept of Faith in Psychology." In *Handbook of Faith*, edited by James Michael Lee. Birmingham: Religious Education, 1990.

Marcia, James E. "Development and Validation of Ego Identity Status." *Journal of Personality and Social Psychology* 3 (1966): 551–58.

———. "Identity in Adolescence." In *Handbook of Adolescent Psychology*, edited by Joseph Adelson. New York: Wiley, 1980.

Marty, Martin. "Did Baby Jesus Have Diaper Rash?" *Christian Century*, 22 December 1976, 1159.

Maslow, Abraham H. *Motivation and Personality*. 2nd ed. New York: Harper and Row, 1954, 1970.

———. *Toward a Psychology of Being*. Princeton, NJ: Nostrand, 1962.

Matlock, Mark. *Don't Buy the Lie*. Grand Rapids: Zondervan/Youth Specialties, 2004.

May, S., B. Posterski, C. Stonehouse, and L. Cannell. *Children Matter: Celebrating Their Place in the Church, Family, and Community*. Grand Rapids: Eerdmans, 2005.

McDonald, H. D. "Man, doctrine of." In *Evangelical Dictionary of Theology*, edited by W. A. Elwell. Grand Rapids: Baker, 1984.

McDonald, P., and E. Garrow. *Children at Risk: Networking in Action*. Monrovia, CA: MARC Publications, 2000.

McGrath, Allister E. *Spirituality in an Age of Change*. Grand Rapids: Zondervan, 1994.

McPherson, M., L. Smith-Lovin, and M. E. Brashears. "Social Isolation in America: Changes in Core Discussion Networks over Two Decades." *American Sociological Review* 71 (2006): 353–75.

Moore, Mary Elizabeth Mullino. *Teaching from the Heart: Theology and Educational Method*. Minneapolis, MN: Fortress, 1991.

Moreland, J. P. *Scaling the Secular City: A Defense of Christianity*. Grand Rapids: Baker, 1987.

Moreland, J. P., and Norman Geisler. *The Life and Death Debate: Moral Issues of Our Time*. New York: Praeger, 1990.

Mueller, Walt. *Engaging the Soul of Youth Culture: Bridging Teen Worldviews and Christian Truth*. Downers Grove, IL: InterVarsity Press, 2006.

Muggeridge, Malcolm. *Jesus Rediscovered*. New York: Doubleday, 1979.

Muller, Roland. *Missions: The Next Generation*. Xlibris Corporation, 2003.

Murdock, George Peter. "The Common Denominator of Cultures." In *The Science of Man in the World Crisis*, edited by Ralph Linton. New York: Columbia University Press, 1945.

Myers, Bryant, ed. *Working with the Poor: New Insights and Learnings from Development Practitioners*. Dubuque, IA: World Vision International, 1999.

Niebuhr, Richard. *Christ and Culture*. New York: Harper and Row, 1951.

Osmer, Richard Robert. *A Teachable Spirit: Recovering the Teaching Office in the Church*. Louisville: Westminster John Knox, 1990.

Packer, J. I. *Knowing God*. Downers Grove, IL: InterVarsity Press, 1973.

Patton, Michael Quinn. *Utilization-Focused Evaluation*. Beverly Hills, CA: Sage, 1978.

Pazmiño, Robert W. "Adult Education with Persons from Ethnic Minority Communities." In *The Christian Educator's Handbook on Adult Education*, edited by Kenneth O. Gangel and James C. Wilhoit. Grand Rapids: Baker, 1997.

———. "Double Dutch: Reflections of an Hispanic-North American on Multicultural Religious Education." *Apuntes* 8 (1988): 27–37.

———. *Foundational Issues in Christian Education: An Introduction in Evangelical Perspective*. Grand Rapids: Baker, 1988.

———. *Latin American Journey: Insights for Christian Education in North America*. Eugene, OR: Wipf and Stock, 2002.

———. *Principles and Practices of Christian Education: An Evangelical Perspective*. Grand Rapids: Baker, 1992.

Perry, William G. *Forms of Intellectual and Ethical Development in the College Years: A Scheme*. New York: Holt, Rinehart and Winston, 1968.

Peterson, David. *Engaging with God: A Biblical Theology of Worship*. Downers Grove, IL: InterVarsity Press, 2002.

Peterson, Eugene H. *The Message: The Bible in Contemporary Language*. Colorado Springs, CO: NavPress, 2003.

Piaget, Jean. *Science of Education and the Psychology of the Child*. Reprint. New York: Viking Press, 1969.

Piaget, Jean, and Barbel Inhelder. *The Psychology of the Child*. New York: Basic Books, 1969, 2000.

Plantinga, Cornelius, Jr. *Not the Way It's Supposed to Be*. Grand Rapids: Eerdmans, 1995.

Postman, Neil. *Amusing Ourselves to Death*. New York: Viking, 1985.

———. *Teaching as a Conserving Activity*. New York: Dell Publishing, 1987.

Postman, Neil, and Charles Weingartner. *Teaching as a Subversive Activity*. New York: Delacorte, 1969.

Power, F. Clark, Ann Higgins, and Lawrence Kohlberg. *Lawrence Kohlberg's Approach to Moral Education*. New York: Columbia University Press, 1989.

Priest, Robert, and Alvaro Nieves, eds. *This Side of Heaven: Race, Ethnicity, and Christian Faith*. New York: Oxford University Press, 2007.

Radcliffe, Robert. "Jesus — The Teacher Revisited." *Christian Education Journal* 16, no. 1 (Fall 1995): 85 – 97.

Rahn, Dave, and Youth for Christ. *3Story: Preparing Teenagers for a Lifestyle of Evangelism*. Grand Rapids: Zondervan/Youth Specialties, 2007.

Redfield, Robert. *The Primitive World and Its Transformations*. Ithaca, NY: Great Seal, 1953.

Richards, Lawrence O. *Church Leadership*. Grand Rapids: Zondervan, 1988.

———. *Creative Bible Teaching*. Grand Rapids: Zondervan, 1970.

———. *A Practical Theology of Spirituality*. Grand Rapids: Zondervan, 1987.

———. *Teaching Youth*. Kansas City, MO: Beacon Hill Press, 1982.

Richards, Lawrence O., and Gib Martin. *A Theology of Personal Ministry*. Grand Rapids: Zondervan, 1981.

Richardson, Rick. *Evangelism Outside the Box: New Ways to Help People Experience the Good News*. Downers Grove, IL: InterVarsity Press, 2000.

Robbins, Duffy. *The Ministry of Nurture*. Grand Rapids: Zondervan/Youth Specialties Academic, 1990.

———. *This Way to Youth Ministry: An Introduction to the Adventure*. Grand Rapids: Zondervan/Youth Specialties Academic, 2004.

Sanneh, Lamin. *Whose Religion Is Christianity? The Gospel Beyond the West*. Grand Rapids: Eerdmans, 2003.

Schaeffer, Francis A. *The God Who Is There*. Downers Grove, IL: InterVarsity Press, 1968.

————. *Pollution and the Death of Man*. Wheaton, IL: Tyndale, 1970.

Schaeffer, Francis A., and C. Everett Keep. *Whatever Happened to the Human Race?* Old Tappan, NJ: Fleming H. Revell, 1979.

Schaller, Lyle. *Survival Tactics in the Parish*. Nashville: Abingdon, 1977.

Schattenmann, J. "Fellowship." In *The New International Dictionary of New Testament Theology*, edited by Colin Brown, 1:639 – 44. Grand Rapids: Zondervan, 1975.

Sell, Charles M. *Transitions through Adult Life*. Grand Rapids: Zondervan, 1991.

Simpson, Elizabeth. *Taxonomy of Objectives: Psychomotor Domain*. N.p.: 1966.

Sire, James W. *Discipleship of the Mind, Learning to Love God in the Ways We Think*. Downers Grove, IL: InterVarsity Press, 1990.

Smart, James D. *The Teaching Ministry of the Church*. Philadelphia: Westminster, 1954.

Smedes, Lewis B. *Choices: Making Right Decisions in a Complex World*. San Francisco: Harper and Row, 1986.

————. *Shame and Grace: Healing the Shame We Don't Deserve*. San Francisco: HarperCollins, 1993.

Smith, Christian, and Melinda Denton. *Soul Searching: The Religious and Spiritual Lives of American Teenagers*. Oxford: Oxford University Press, 2005.

Stedman, Ray. "The True Man," Sermon based on Hebrews 2:5 – 18, preached March 14, 1965 (see Hebrews Series 1, Message No. 2, Catalog No. 85). Discovery Publishing, a ministry of Peninsula Bible Church, Palo Alto, California, ©1995.

Stigler, James W., Richard A. Schweder, and Gilbert Herdt, eds. *Cultural Psychology: Essays on Comparative Human Development*. Cambridge: Cambridge University Press, 1990.

Stonehouse, Catherine M. "Learning from Gender Differences." In *The Christian Educator's Handbook on Adult Education*, edited by Kenneth O. Gangel and James C. Wilhoit. Grand Rapids: Baker, 1997.

Strommen, Merton, Karen Jones, and Dave Rahn, eds. *Youth Ministry That Transforms: A Comprehensive Analysis of the Hopes, Frustrations, and Effectiveness of Today's Youth Workers*. Grand Rapids: Zondervan/Youth Specialties, 2001.

Strong, Augustus H. *Systematic Theology*. Valley Forge, PA: Judson, 1907.

Telford, Tom. *Today's All-Star Missions Churches: Strategies to Help Your Church Get into the Game*. Grand Rapids: Baker Books, 2001.

Thompson, M. *Family, the Forming Center*. Nashville: Upper Room Books, 1989.

Trotman, Dawson. *Born to Reproduce* (booklet available online as PDF: www-rohan.sdsu.edu/~sdsunavs/resources/BornToReproduce.pdf).

Trueblood, D. Elton. *The Teacher*. Nashville: Broadman, 1980.

Vanhoozer, Kevin. "But That's Your Interpretation: Realism, Reading, and Reformation." *Modern Reformation* (July/August 1999): 21 – 27.

Wadsworth, Barry J. *Piaget's Theory of Cognitive and Affective Development: Foundations of Constructivism*. 5th ed. Boston: Allyn and Bacon, 2003.

Wainwright, Geoffrey. *Types of Spirituality*. New York: Oxford University Press, 1986.

Walls, Andrew. *The Cross-Cultural Process in Christian History*. Maryknoll, NY: Orbis Press, 2002.

———. *The Missionary Movement in Christian History: Studies in the Transmission of Faith*. Maryknoll, NY: Orbis Press, 1996.

Ward, Ted. "Development Levels of the Teacher." Unpublished manuscript, n.d.

———. "Non-formal Education." Unpublished manuscript, n.d.

———. *Values Begin at Home*. 2nd ed. Wheaton, IL: Victor, 1989.

Webber, Robert E. *Worship Old and New*. Grand Rapids: Zondervan, 1994.

Wilhoit, Jim. *Christian Education and the Search for Meaning*. Rev. ed. Grand Rapids: Baker, 1991.

Wilken, Robert. *Remembering the Christian Past*. Grand Rapids: Eerdmans, 1995.

Wilkerson, Barbara, ed. *Multicultural Religious Education*. Birmingham: Religious Education Press, 1997.

Willard, Dallas. *The Spirit of the Disciplines*. San Francisco: HarperSanFrancisco, 1988.

Williams, D. H. *Retrieving the Tradition and Renewing Evangelicalism: A Primer for Suspicious Protestants*. Grand Rapids: Eerdmans, 1999.

Yoder, Gideon. *The Nurture and Evangelism of Children*. Scottdale, PA.: Herald, 1959.

Youth for Christ. *Conversations with Jesus*. Grand Rapids: Zondervan/Youth Specialties, 2006.

Yust, K. M. *Real Kids, Real Faith: Practices for Nurturing Children's Spiritual Lives*. San Francisco: Jossey-Bass, 2004.

SCRIPTURE INDEX

SUBJECT INDEX

A

Ability, 90–91, 154
Accommodation, 66
Adolescents, 80, 161–67
Adult education, multicultural
   learner's roles, 171–74
   overview, 170–71
   in Scripture, 169–70
Agape, 77, 116
Anthropology, 47–49
Apostles' Creed, 199 (box)
Autonomy vs. shame and doubt stage, 79

B

Balance, 67, 93–94, 121n15
Barnabas, 34–35, 69, 114, 120n9, 170
Basic trust vs. basic mistrust stage, 79
Basileia, 14
Beauty of nature, 27, 212
Bellah, Robert, 192
Bethlehem Baptist Church, 187
Bonhoeffer, Dietrich, 14–15, 17, 192
   (box)
Boundary, 92–93
Brown, Donald E., 48, 57n2
Bunyan, John, 107

C

Centering, 74
Chariots of Fire (film), 55
Children
   cognitive development, 74–75
   media manipulation of, 153
   ministry by the church to, 156–57
   ministry challenges for those who
     serve, 152–53
   ministry models for those who serve,
     154–58

ministry motivations for those who
   serve, 151–52
ministry objectives for those who
   serve, 153–54
ministry together with, 155–56
ministry to others by, 158
ministry to parents for, 154–55
parental disempowerment and, 153
professional disinterest in, 153
societal devaluation of, 152
transition from elementary to middle
   school, 73
Choice, human, 140, 145n13
Christian education-formation. *See*
   also Evangelism-Proclamation;
   Learning
ability and, 90–91
for adolescents, 161–67
for adults, 169–75
boundary and, 92–93
change in, 16–17
for children, 151–59
development theories and, 81–82
fellowship-community in, 14,
   191–95, 204–5
godly self-love, 115–18
human deformity traits and, 93–94
identity and, 97–98
inclusivity and, 95
kingdom-advocacy in, 197–201,
   204–5
mis-education in, 59–60
multicultural, 169–75
objective of, 60–64
perceptions in, 17
personality and, 91–92
rationality and, 95–96
sensitivity and, 94–95

service in, 185–89, 204–5
teachability and, 96–97
worship in, 203–7
Cognitive development, 74–75
Columbus, Christopher, 24
Complete Disciple, The (Habermas), 212
Concrete Operational stage, 75
Conjunctive stage, 79
Conklin, Carli, 51–52
Conventional Morality, 76
Creation, 24–25, 51–52
   God's ultimate purpose for, 33–34
   Jesus' references to Eden and, 88–89
   restoring image traits from, 90–99
Cultural Mandate, 37, 54–55
Culture and history, human, 52–53

D

David, King, 38
Deformity, 93–94
Denton, Melinda Lundquist, 54
Descriptive understanding, 101
Destiny, 55–57
Development, 73–79. *See also* Maturity
   Christian ministry and theories
   on, 81–82
   cognitive, 74–75
   faith, 77–79
   moral, 75–77
   psychosocial, 79–80
Dewey, John, 30 (box), 59, 60, 70, 81
Diakonia, 14
Dialogue and learning, 105
Disciplines, Christian, 62–64
Disequilibrium, 66
Disinterest in children, professional,
   153
Dissonance, 66–67

Doubt and maturity, 66–68
Driscoll, Mark, 193–94

E

Eden, 24–25, 88–90, 98n2, 142 (chart)
Egocentrism, 74
Ego integrity vs. despair stage, 80
Emerson, Michael O., 194
Equilibrium, 66
Erikson, Erik H., 79–80
Evangelism-Proclamation. *See also*
    Christian education-formation
  listening in, 183–84
  ministry goals of, 181–82
  ministry methods, 182–83
  model of, 179–84
  nature of people and, 181
  practice, 183–84
  ultimate ends in, 180–81
  worship and, 204–5
Exemplars, 166–67

F

Faith development, 77–79, 198
  in children, 154
  ownership and, 141–42, 145n14
  worship and, 203–7
Faithful Learner, Jesus as, 102–8
Fall, the, 25–26
Fear, 138–39, 144n8
Fellowship-community, 14, 191–95,
  204–5
Formal Operational stage, 75
Formal Operations, 76–77
Foster, Richard, 62
Foundational Issues in Christian Educa-
  tion (Pazmiño), 13, 14
Fowler, James, 77–79
Fox, Robin, 48
Frankena, William K., 179

G

Garden of Eden. *See* Eden
Generativity vs. stagnation stage, 80
Goals of evangelism, 181–82
God
  commitment to total restoration,
    36–38, 131–32
  creation intentions, 33–34, 51–52
  Cultural Mandate by, 37, 54–55
  Eden legacies as partnerships with,
    24–25

image traits reflected in humans,
  49–50 (chart), 90–98
interruptions by, 14–16
kingdom of, 197–201
love of, 113–18, 145n10, 154
natural world and, 27–28
present-day signs, 26–29
restoration goals of, 41–42 (chart)
sovereignty of, 137–42, 143n2
three purposes of, 33–35
will of, 38–39, 55–57, 60–62, 64–65
worship to, 203–7
Gospel Mandate, 37
Government authority, 129
Grace of God, 28, 209
Great Commission, 125–27, 130, 181
Great Physician, Jesus as, 123–32

H

Habits of the Heart (Bellah), 192
Happiness and joy, 51–52. *See also*
  Pleasure
  maturity and, 68–70
Heaven, 28, 211–18
Hedging, symbolic, 52
Heschel, Abraham, 173–74
Hill, Edward V., 13, 14
History and culture, human, 52–53
Hockett, Charles F., 48, 58n7
Hohmann, Pete, 187
Holiness, 40–41
Holistic maturity, 61–62
Holocaust, the, 15
Holy Spirit, the, 39–41, 65, 68–70,
  106–7, 182
Home, 129, 155
Hopes and hungers, human, 29
Humanity of Jesus, 111
Humans. *See also* Life plan
  ability, 90–91, 101–2, 154
  anthropological study of, 47–49
  boundaries, 92–93
  called by Jesus, 42n5, 126–28, 132n7
  choice, 29–30
  common qualities of, 47–49,
    57–58n7
  creation of, 24–25, 33–34, 51–52
  deformity and, 93–94
  destiny, 55–57
  doubt and, 66–68
  fear in, 138–39, 144n8
  God's image traits reflected in,
    49–50 (chart), 90–98

God's purpose and, 33–35
happiness and, 51–52
history and culture, 52–53
holiness of, 40–41
identity, 53–54
interrupted by God, 14–16
Jesus' beliefs about, 111–13
learning by, 101–2
lifework, 54–55
ownership of beliefs, 141–42, 145n14
personalities, 91–92
pleasure and, 52–57
rationality, 95–96
seasons of life, 62–64
self-care, 118–19
shared structures in, 46–47
sin, 25, 27–28, 112–13
submission to God, 60–61
suffering by, 64–65
teachability, 96–97
theological findings on, 49–51
universalizing faith stage and, 79
universal questions, 48–49, 57
universal themes, 48, 57–58n7
will and choice, 140, 145n13
worry by, 139–40
yearning for restoration, 35–36

I

Identity, 53–54
  Jesus on, 97–98
  vs. role confusion stage, 80
Idolatry and television, 30–31
Inclusivity, 95, 154
Individualism, 192–93
Individuative-Reflective stage, 78
Industry vs. inferiority stage, 80, 82n4
Initiative vs. guilt stage, 79–80
Intergenerational learning, 156
Interruptions by God, 14–16
Intimacy vs. isolation stage, 80
Intuitive-Projective stage, 78
Irreversibility, 74
I-TECH project, 189n4

J

Jesus Christ
  beliefs about people, 111–13
  call to believers, 42n5, 126–28,
    132n7
  commitment to total restoration,
    38–39, 182–83

current experiences and learning, 104–5
doubts from, 67–68
evangelism by, 181–82
example for adolescents, 166–67
as Faithful Learner, 102–8
on fear, 138–39
fellowship and community in, 191–95
final hours on earth, 60–61, 67–68, 135–36, 144n7
global tasks of, 13–14
godly self-love and, 115–18
on God's will, 164
as Great Physician, 123–32
on heaven, 212–15
holistic maturity and, 61–62
Holy Spirit and, 69–70, 106–7
humanity of, 111
on identity, 97–98
life roles of, 87–88
on making disciples, 180
as Master Teacher, 88–99
miracles of, 136–37
modeling of the disciplines, 62–64
natural sources of learning, 103–5
New Eden Standard, 90, 98n2
past knowledge and learning, 104
on personality, 91–92
on rationality, 95–96
restoration by, 34, 124–32
sacrifice of, 25–26, 40
salvation through, 25–26, 31
seasons of life and, 62–64
on sentimentality, 94–95
as servant to God's plans, 38, 60–61
as Son of Man, 13, 109–21
as Submissive Servant, 133–45
suffering of, 64–65, 71n9, 72n12
supernatural sources of learning, 105–7
on teachability, 96–97
as the ultimate demonstration of agapic level of moral judgment, 77
unity in, 165–66
vocational calling, 127–28
who is, 110–11
John the Baptist, 39
Joseph, 137–39
Joshua, 204
Joy. See Happiness and joy
Joyful Christian, The (Lewis), 51

K

Kerygama, 13
Kingdom-advocacy, 197–201
worship and, 204–5
Kohlberg, Lawrence, 75–77
Koinonia, 14, 191–95
Kreeft, Peter, 51, 212

L

Learning. *See also* Christian education-formation
by adolescents, 161–67
by adults, 169–75
broader culture and, 105
by children, 151–58
current experiences and, 104–5
in diverse settings, 103
Holy Spirit and, 106–7
human ability for, 101–2
intergenerational, 156
by Jesus, 102–8
multicultural adult education, 169–75
natural sources of Jesus', 103–5
Pilgrim's Progress, 107–8
supernatural sources of Jesus', 105–7
Word of God and, 107
Leitourgia, 14
Lewis, C. S., 28, 29, 51, 53, 55, 70, 143, 209
Liddell, Eric, 55
Life plan
God's three purposes in, 33–35
Jesus as center of, 13, 30
seasons of life and, 62–64
Lifework, 54–55
Listening in evangelism practice, 183–84
Love, God's, 113–18, 145n10, 154, 163–64
Luke, 127

M

Maps, 23, 24, 26–30
Marriage, 41, 129
Master-Teacher, Jesus as, 88–99
Maturity. *See also* Development
of adolescents, 80, 161–62
doubt and, 66–68
Holy Spirit and, 68–70
obeying God's will for, 64–65
ownership of one's beliefs in, 141–42
parental, 154

spiritual, 60–62
Mechanicsville Christian Center, 187
Media, manipulation by, 153
Miracles of Jesus, 136–37
Mis-education, 59–60
Moral development, 75–77
Moralistic therapeutic deism, 54
Multicultural adult education
learner and, 171–74
overview, 170–71
in Scripture, 169–70
Murdock, George Peter, 47–48
Mythic-Literal stage, 78

N

Nature, beauty of, 27, 212
New Eden Standard, 90, 98n2
Non-transformations, 74–75

O

Objective of Christian education-formation, 60–64
Ownership of beliefs, 141–42, 145n14

P

Parents, 153–55
Passover meal, 213
Paul, apostle, 34–35, 69, 114, 166, 174, 204, 214
Pazmiño, Robert W., 13, 14, 192
Persistence, 141
Personality, 91–92
Peter, apostle, 192
Philip, 192
Piaget, Jean, 66, 67
cognitive development theory, 74–75
Pilgrim's Progress (Bunyan), 107–8
Piper, John, 187
Plantinga, Neal, 25
Pleasure, 53–57. *See also* Happiness and joy
Prayer, 45–46, 162–63
Preconventional Morality, 76
Pre-operational stage, 74
Prescriptive understanding, 101
Psychosocial development, 79–80
Purpose of restoration, 124–25

R

Radcliffe, Robert, 91
Rainbows of Hope ministry, 187
Rationality, 95–96
Redemption, 125–27

Share Your Thoughts

With the Author: Your comments will be forwarded to the author when you send them to *zauthor@zondervan.com*.

With Zondervan: Submit your review of this book by writing to *zreview@zondervan.com*.

Free Online Resources at
www.zondervan.com/hello

 Zondervan AuthorTracker: Be notified whenever your favorite authors publish new books, go on tour, or post an update about what's happening in their lives.

 Daily Bible Verses and Devotions: Enrich your life with daily Bible verses or devotions that help you start every morning focused on God.

 Free Email Publications: Sign up for newsletters on fiction, Christian living, church ministry, parenting, and more.

 Zondervan Bible Search: Find and compare Bible passages in a variety of translations at www.zondervanbiblesearch.com.

 Other Benefits: Register yourself to receive online benefits like coupons and special offers, or to participate in research.